STAR TREK MEMORIES

William Shatner

WITH CHRIS KRESKI

HarperCollins*Publishers*

HarperCollins*Publishers*
77–85 Fulham Palace Road,
Hammersmith, London W6 8JB

A Paperback Original 1993
9 8 7 6 5 4 3 2 1

First published in the USA by
HarperCollins*Publishers* US 1993

A catalogue record for this book is
available from the British Library

I S B N 0 00 637970 2

Printed in Great Britain by
Scotprint Ltd, Musselburgh

This book is dedicated to all the people who worked on *Star Trek*.
They are the phenomena who made the phenomenon.
W. S.

For Philip Oliveri . . .
my teacher, my pal, my poker partner, my grandfather.
He's the man I want to be when I grow up.
C. K.

CONTENTS

A C K N O W L E D G M E N T S

I went on an interesting voyage of discovery with this book. I must have been blind twenty-five years ago. Blind with personal problems, with fatigue and with the necessity of spending those incredibly hard hours shooting *Star Trek*, the series. I was fairly oblivious to the drama going on around me, oblivious to the people who composed the family of *Star Trek*, and like some beast of burden, eyes fixed to the furrow, I plowed on—despite any distraction. And so it was illuminating, twenty-five years later, to wend my way back along the path of an experience that I had almost forgotten. It was a joyful passage, and also a sad one.

Death had visited some, and deep bitterness others. But mostly I've come away from this journey with my memory refreshed, and a heart filled with love.

Helping me organize these thoughts is a man whose insight and perception are profound—Chris Kreski is my new hero.

Craig Nelson is a new hero also—urbane, sophisticated, knowledgeable.

Carmen LaVia is no hero; on the other hand, he's no villain either . . . he's my agent. Love covers many faults.

The authors would also like to thank the following people for their support, encouragement, assistance and tolerance in the writing of this book: Kevin McShane of the Fifi Oscard Agency, Mary Jo Fernandez, Dawn Kreski, Amelia Kreski, Judy McGrath, Abby Terkuhle, Laurie Ulster, Tracy Grandstaff, Lauren Marino, Michael O'Laughlin, John Muccigrosso, Felicia Standel, Larry Standel, Joe Davola, Michael Dugan, Geoff Whelan, Jackie Coon-Fernandez, Joe D'Agosta, Eddie Milkis, Jerry Finnerman, John Meredyth Lucas, Nicholas Meyer, Bob Justman, Bjo Trimble, Fred Freiberger, Ralph Winter, Harve Bennett, Bill Campbell, Matt Jefferies, Richard Arnold (whose photo work and unparalleled historical insight are tremendously appreciated), and of course Grace Lee Whitney, Majel Barrett, Walter Koenig, George Takei, Nichelle Nichols, DeForest Kelley and Leonard Nimoy.

Heartfelt thanks go out to all of you for your honesty, generosity and friendship.

CAPTAIN
L

Snoring, smiling broadly, I am secure in the warmth and comfort of a carefree, dreamless sleep, and then it hits.

Instantly, my peace is shattered by the brain-piercing electronic screeching that blares and buzzes from my evil digital alarm clock. Quickly I spring into action, tossing about heroically and finally employing the desperate maneuver known as "the old pillow over the ears trick." Nothing works, and I come to realize that this is truly a no-win situation . . . in Trekker, an early-morning *Kobayashi Maru*. Slowly, painfully, my eyelids begin to slide upward, and my semiconscious senses begin to contemplate the orangy-red block-style numbers that glare and blink at me, just out of reach, mocking my early-morning helplessness. Their blurry taunts immediately tell me that my eyesight isn't what it used to be, and, upon squinting, that it's also 5:15 A.M. I'm late.

Now, as a pronounced series of bodily cracks and pops serenades me from deep within most of my moving parts, I make a supreme effort to overcome my blissful inertia. I rise from bed and start walking. "Left foot . . . right foot, left foot, right." I repeatedly give this order to my brain, and after a short struggle, the gray matter grudgingly obeys. Still not quite conscious, I begin shuffling through the darkness, grunting and scratching in a sort of slumped-over posture. Basically, at this point I'm a Cro-Magnon in light blue pajamas.

Now I boldly go . . . into the bathroom, stumbling to the sink, where a sting of cold tile and a splash of cold water shock me at both extremities. The cobwebs finally begin to dissipate. I find my toothbrush, and in my nearly awakened state, I even manage to load it up. I now pause to admire my neatly symmetrical blob of tartar-control goo, lean in over the sink, look up into the mirror and come face to face with my own image, which scares me.

Here, by the dawn's early and uncompromising light, my face provides ample documentation of my own mortality. I look tired. I look old. This starts me thinking, but surprisingly, I'm not conjuring up any morose thoughts about the aging process. Instead, I'm almost immediately flooded with fond reminiscences of what got me here. My wrinkles, I muse, have been well earned, and they provide visual evidence of a career crammed with wonderful memories, and a life that's been extraordinarily rewarding, both personally and professionally.

To be perfectly honest, I've been unavoidably nostalgic of late, and this may account for my early-morning reminiscing. You see, today will mark the end of shooting on *Star Trek VI: The Undiscovered Country*. It's a film that's been promoted as "the final voyage of the Starship *Enterprise*," and even though I've heard that said about all five of the previous big-screen adventures, I think this time the rumors may bear some credibility. Consequently, I've been savoring every long and hectic day on the set, reveling in the company of my castmates and marveling at the skills of our writers, producers and technical crew.

Strangely enough, the idea that this might actually be the "last voyage" has allowed me to broaden my perspective, and I've found myself looking at the whole *Star Trek* phenomenon in a new light. Somehow, only as it's begun to slip away am I able to view it in the all-encompassing and appreciative light that it deserves. I mean, I must admit, I've never actually considered myself a "Trekker," nor have I ever fully understood the enormous enthusiasm that the show has always seemed to generate among its most rabid fans. For me it has always been first and foremost a job, and somehow only now, when it may be ending, am I able to see past the work, past the day-to-day machinations and into the very reasoning behind what made it so great.

Forty-five minutes later, I'm at Paramount Studios, where I'm made up and dressed as Captain James Tiberius Kirk, perhaps for the last time. Our last day of shooting is quite simple, really; just a couple of brief scenes. However, sentimentality begins to slow us down, as all of us, the entire cast and a large portion of the crew, have come to realize that every moment of this production, and especially of this day, is to be cherished.

By the time midafternoon has arrived, we've wrapped. Champagne bottles are popping, cast and crew are hugging, kissing and smiling broadly.

However, underneath the joy of having successfully completed our project, there is, really for the first time, a tangible undercurrent of sadness. I think it's weighing heavily on all of us that this time our good-byes may really mean "good-bye."

Flash forward four months. We're closing in on Christmas and *Star Trek* VI has opened to critical acclaim and even greater box-office success. Paramount is pushing the film tremendously and in the middle of all this activity, we original cast members have been asked to gather once more, to place our hand- and footprints in the fabled wet cement outside of Mann's Chinese Theater.

As I arrive, Nichelle and Walter are already working the crowd, smiling, waving and standing next to countless tourists as Instamatic flashbulbs glare. George Takei is there, too, and I swear to you this man thinks he's a Vulcan. I mean, it's either that or he's had some sort of operation on his hands, because wherever he goes, he's wearing an enormous smile, and displaying ambidextrous Vulcan hand signals for "Live long and prosper." Jimmy Doohan, as usual, is toying with reporters, answering their every question with his standard three-word answer: "Jimmy, do you think the studio means it this time when they say it's the last movie?" "It's a PLOY!" yells Jimmy. "Jimmy, they say the next film may star the *Next Generation* cast. Is that true?" "It's a PLOY!" "Jimmy, what's the weather forecast for tomorrow?" "It's a PLOY!!" And of course my good friend Leonard is there, too, smiling, playing it cool, and underneath it all, I'm sure he's just as excited as I am.

I mean this is Mann's Chinese Theater. This is something really special, and as I watch the masons preparing our wet-cement squares, I notice that all around our section are names like Wallace Beery, Norma Shearer and Buster Keaton. And it strikes me that these are *legends*, great stars of the silent screen. So of course I'm really impressed with myself.

But here's how our squares ended up being divided: Squeezed up in the top left was my name, squeezed up in the top right was Leonard's. And this was because smack in the middle of the squares, and taking up a good-sized chunk of all four, was the name DeForest Kelley. And nobody said anything resentful about it. We were all too well-mannered. But I'm sure I'm not the *only* one who looked askance and wondered, "Why does

DeForest Kelley get four whole squares?" In fact, DeForest was so excited, and so impressed with himself, that if you look closely at the square, you'll notice that he actually wrote D-E-F-O-R-O-T . . . in CEMENT! I swear the man forgot how to spell his own name! I mean in the past he'd certainly gone through that whole "I'm a doctor, not a bricklayer" schtick, but now he'd really proven it!

And so of course I got to spend the rest of the afternoon kidding him about losing his faculties and being too old to do any more movies. It was great.

Still, as I looked at my friends of the past quarter-century, I couldn't begin to hold back all of the memories that burst forward. I couldn't help thinking about the bigger picture and about the people whose lives have been changed and even shaped by Star Trek. Not just the cast, but our creators, our crew members, and above all else our fans. You're the ones who made it all possible, and the ones who celebrated and fought for every bit of Star Trek's existence. You're the reason it's endured, you're the reason it was able to become so great.

Later, after we'd all made our speeches, posed for our publicity stills and squashed our extremities into the cold, clammy immortality that Mann's had to offer, I got a chance

**Hmmm, D-E-F-O-R-O-uh-oh.
(© 1993 Paramount Pictures)**

to talk with my castmates. We shared laughs, hugs and lots of Star Trek stories that were known only among ourselves. Stories of good times and not-so-good times. Memories that even throughout the unparalleled documentation of the Star Trek universe have never before been told. It really struck me as odd, even unfair, that Star Trek supporters, who are indeed the world's most knowledgeable fans, have never really been told the whole story. There are truckloads of information that you've never been allowed to see, warehouses full of stories you've never been told, and with all that in mind, it struck me that somebody should write a definitive Star Trek book.

So in true Jim Kirk style, I immediately mapped out a plan and put it into action. Now that it's finished, I think that you'll find throughout the ensuing inches of paper that this book about Star Trek is very different from those that have preceded it. It's not going to run through detailed synopses of every episode (because quite frankly, you people already know them all by heart). It's not going to provide exacting blueprints of the Enterprise or speculate on adventures that might have been or delve into things like "the advanced tenets of the Vulcan philosophical mind-set." All of that's been done, and to be brutally honest, I don't know that I could write any of those books.

What I can tell you about, having spent more than a quarter-century mixed up in the middle of all this, is how Star Trek the series actually worked. I can tell you the tales of how Star Trek was created, produced, written, filmed, edited and polished by an army of technical wizards. I can also let you in on all of the onstage, sidestage and backstage goings-on that came together and became Star Trek. Above and beyond everything else, I'd like to tell you about the people who made Star Trek so great. They are the real story. They are the real heroes, and they deserve to be given their due.

With all that in mind, I'll have to ask you to proceed, warp factor two . . . Sorry, sometimes I can't help myself.

ORIGINS

The *real* story of *Star Trek* doesn't start at a television network, or in a film studio. In fact, it doesn't even start in Hollywood. It starts in a box. An ordinary cardboard box, 24" × 36" × 36". At one point a soap carton, this large corrugated rectangle, ragged and dusty, now sits in the sun-baked dirt backyard of a modest home, in the middle of El Paso, Texas, in the middle of the nineteen twenties. There is nothing at all special about the box *itself*; in fact, it's a rather beaten-up grocery store castoff. However, if you were to look *inside* this box, you would find something rather unexpected . . . a small, sickly, rather handicapped little boy.

The kid's got all kinds of problems. He has trouble breathing, and suffers frequent unexplained seizures. He squints because his eyes can't adjust properly to sunlight. His legs are weak, spindly, uncoordinated and unsteady. As a result, and as you might expect, he is *extremely* self-conscious, embarrassed about his physical stature and withdrawn.

Here, however, within the comfortable confines of his own backyard, he can escape the limitations of a less than perfect body by diving into his beloved collection of books, becoming a part of the dream world they hold captive within their pages. It is a world far preferable to the one that lurks ominously outside the picket fence, a world in which he can, with the turn of a page, perform any task imaginable, and become any great character he wants to be.

With a book in his hand, he can instantly become a Zane Grey cowboy, or Robinson Crusoe, D'Artagnan, Hawkeye, Ishmael, Huck Finn, literally anyone he can imagine. *Astounding Stories*, a science fiction magazine of the era, is an absolute favorite and a revered complement to his stacks of more formal literature. Its pulp pages are filled each week with fascinating and exciting stories of incredible, impossible stuff such as space travel, visits to the moon and the like. The cheap nickel magazine holds tremendous value for this particular kid, and that brings us back to the box.

This box, you see, is not *just* a box. It's a spaceship, at least as far as this boy is concerned. Its flimsy paperboard walls suggest the frame of a great and powerful vessel, and its tiny interior houses an entire crew of imaginary intergalactic heroes. At the helm, a bold and strong captain travels fearlessly about the universe discovering new worlds, societies and life forms, as well as routinely saving the cosmos from the ravaging advances of unfriendly space-traveling bad guys. The box, by now mis-shapen and rather tattered, serves an incredibly important purpose, in that it provides, on a regular basis, an outlet wherein this one sick child can completely forget about his physical shortcomings, his illnesses and the frightening impositions and realities of the real world. Inside the box, he's healthy, he's happy, he's safe.

Flash forward across twenty years and this sickly kid has grown up and completely out of his illnesses. In fact, this undersized boy has grown up to become an "extra-large" man. Still, despite the sweeping physical changes, he's retained his intrinsic shyness, his introspective nature and his raging fascination with literature. As a result, he exists now as a rather burly, gentle bear of a man, whose formidable exterior masks a quiet, rather delicate and extremely creative soul.

Today, however, this creative soul is sweating like a pig, as would any normal human being trapped in the middle of a Calcutta summer. The city is truly hellish, oppressively hot, extremely impoverished and teeming with sickness. The "kid" sits amid the nearly unbearable surroundings, alone in the shade of a grimy café umbrella. He's fanning himself with one hand while shooing flies and writing with the other, jotting notes into a dog-eared notebook. He's once again escaping into a literary dream world, only now he's the master of his own fate, penciling his way through short stories, nonfiction pieces and the occasional science fiction theme. Mostly, however, he's killing time.

He works as an airline pilot now, having recently signed on with Pan Am after completing a tour of duty as an army pilot during World War II. As low man on the Pan Am totem pole, he's of course been assigned the airline's least desirable route, drawing the godawful duty of piloting the company's New York–Calcutta run. Once in Calcutta, his flight plans regu-larly entail a twenty-two-hour layover, which without diversion in this steaming, unpleasant environment would prove virtually intolerable. As a result, he writes profusely, honing his literary skills, and effectively shutting out the unpleasantness that his Calcutta layovers entail. In time, he manages to get some spot work writing technical articles for an aeronautical magazine, and a frequent pastime is to draw upon his memories of *Astounding Stories*, and toy with some rough ideas for science fiction. He finds that he thoroughly enjoys writing, especially within the science fiction genre, and that he seems to have a real ability to tell stories that are both intelligent and compelling. He continues to pursue his aeronautical career, but he also allows himself to begin dreaming. Hoping that someday he might see his stories told in print, or on television or even in the movies.

By now, you've probably realized that the child, the pilot and the aspiring writer all grew up to one day become the "Great Bird of the Galaxy" himself, Gene Roddenberry. However, as you'll find out in the following pages, Gene took what could euphemistically be described as "the scenic route to success," struggling through a good number of lean years before *Star Trek* even entered his life.

By the time 1949 has arrived, Gene's taken his first leap of faith, quitting his job with Pan Am and moving, with his wife and children in tow, to Los Angeles, where he hopes to find work as a writer in the embryonic but exploding industry of television. He is extremely talented, diligent in his job-hunting, but like almost all young and inexperienced writers, he is entirely unsuccessful in his efforts.

It's a tough situation. Married, with kids to feed and bills to pay, Gene realizes the obvious, and decides that he's going to have to find a steady job . . . *any* steady job, fast. He peruses the local want ads, pounds the pavement and eventually decides to become a police officer with the LAPD.

Gene is trained, tested, sworn in and assigned to motorcycle duty. In time he rises to the rank of sergeant, and begins writing speeches for Los Angeles police chief William Parker. He enjoys writing for Parker, who seems genuinely interested in bettering the police department, but at the same time, Gene's determined to stop writing someone else's speeches and start writing his own scripts. However, at this point in time, he's had no luck at all in selling *any* of his own material, nor has he been able to secure an agent who'll agree to represent him.

This is an important point, because without an agent, Gene's scripts stand almost no chance of *ever* being read by *anyone* with the authority to hire him. It's part of a real Catch-22 situation that every young writer must deal with, even today. Quite simply, if you're a budding writer without much professional writing experience, most agents will refuse to represent you, due to their own perception that you're an amateur, not likely to be very good, and not likely to get hired very often—it's simply too much work for too little commission. With all that in mind, it becomes conceivable that even if Shakespeare himself were to rise from the dead, dig himself out of his grave and hop a transatlantic Concorde to L.A., showing up in the William Morris offices with TV spec script in hand, he'd most likely be turned away at the lobby. "Babe," the agents would say, "how can I sell you when you've never even written a sitcom?" In short, when it comes to finding representation, agents are more interested in your résumé than in your writing ability.

Compounding every young writer's frustration is the fact that actually *getting* any professional experience as a writer on any large-scale production is almost impossible *without* the assistance of a competent and rather crafty agent. With all that in mind, Gene Roddenberry knew he'd have to resort to some incredibly unusual guerrilla tactics in securing professional representation. And that's exactly what he did.

You see, during the period of time when Gene was serving in the Los Angeles Police Department as a motorcycle cop, he discovered that almost all of the *most* well-known, sought-after and respected agents in town hung out quite frequently at a gathering place . . . okay, bar . . . called the Cock and Bull. They'd spend their happy hours there, chatting and gossiping with one another, exchanging news of the trade, scarfing down platefuls of hors d'oeuvres from the complimentary buffet and of course guzzling down tumblerfuls of whatever was poured in front of them. First and foremost among these Hollywood agents was the fabled Irving "Swifty" Lazar.

Now what you've also got to understand before we can go any further is that most successful agents, and especially well-known players like Swifty, will run screaming for the hills at the first sight of a struggling young writer. It's not because they're insensitive or uncaring; it's simply because they are pounced upon all day every day by a virtual parade of aspiring wordsmiths. Given half a chance, these guys will invariably corner said agents bearing scripts in hand, chatting them up and hoping to make an impression so . . . impress*ive* that they'll be signed on as a client.

It almost never works, because quite obviously these very successful Hollywood ten-percenters can't *possibly* read all the scripts that are foisted upon them. There just isn't time in the day. Due to the same time constraints, no single agent can possibly represent *anything* but the *tiniest* fraction of Hollywood's most talented writers.

With that in mind, Gene formulates a plan, and as legend has it, Step One involves attiring himself in his full motorcycle cop's uniform. Step Two finds Gene placing a freshly mimeographed copy of a sample Roddenberry script into a plain manila envelope. He then tucks the package inside his black leather policeman's jacket, straps on his helmet and straddles his Hog. Then, with a mighty kickstart and some mechanical thunder, he smiles and roars off through the streets of L.A.

Step Three: With red lights flashing and sirens blaring, Gene pulls up in the doorway of the Cock and Bull, literally parking his huge policeman's cycle in the restaurant foyer. The cycle's lights are blinding, the sirens deafening, and with the restaurant doors thrown open and the setting sun lodged directly behind his helmet, Gene's hulking silhouette looms ominously, almost Schwarzenegger-like, over the room.

And now great gaggles of Hollywood agents, who tend as a group to be especially *wary* of police, scurry about trying their best to blend into the wallpaper and at least *look* innocent. Roddenberry now flicks aside the diminutive maitre d' and strides purposefully into the room.

At which point this hulking, helmeted, reflector-sunglassed policeman-from-hell yells out "Irving Lazar, which one of you is Mr. Irving Lazar!"

"Oh, SHIT!" whispers the now quaking, completely agitated Lazar, who sheepishly comes forward, prepared, I'm sure, to be hauled off to jail for some unknown indiscretion. Instead, Roddenberry just puts one large, leather-gloved hand upon Lazar's comparatively puny shoulder, leans forward, pulls the script out from under his arm, holds it under Lazar's nose and says, "This is for you! I suggest you read it." He then lays the script on the bar, turns on his size-twelve boots and strides out the door.

And now, of course, even as Gene's roaring back out into the night, Swifty's tearing open this envelope with the unbridled gusto of a two-year-old on Christmas morning. The contents spill onto the bar, and Swifty realizes he's been given a sample script to read, and that the cop was probably just another member of Hollywood's aspiring-writer glut.

Swifty's fellow agents now come scrambling back out of the woodwork to find out what all the commotion was about. They clamor around Lazar, asking, "What the hell was that?" and "Who was that guy?" To which Swifty replies, "I don't know, but whoever that son of a bitch is, he deserves to be read. I'll kill the bastard, but he deserves to be read."

Swifty goes home, reads Roddenberry's material and is so thoroughly impressed that within twenty-four hours, he's signed him to a contract.

With Lazar now pulling the strings, Gene actually begins to make some limited progress in his writing career, selling an occasional script pseudonymously in order to beat the police department's "no moonlighting" edict. Still, the economics of the situation dictate that Gene remain first and foremost a cop. However, as time passes, Gene's talents begin to gain recognition. He finds himself in demand, writing steadily, and as his reputation for tight, solid and substantive teleplays begins to grow, he becomes extremely busy, churning out scripts for many of the era's most popular shows. Within two years' time, he's earning far more as a writer than he is as a cop. Finally, when he simply becomes too busy to keep juggling both jobs, he says good-bye to the police force.

In the years that follow, Gene works very steadily, penning episodes for some of the best (*Naked City, Highway Patrol, Dr. Kildare*) and worst (*The Kaiser Aluminum Hour, Jane Wyman Theater, Boots and Saddles*) programs on TV. In his now extremely limited spare time, he begins constantly squirreling away handwritten notes to himself. They're full of creative ideas, roughed-out dramatic story lines and thoughts that might be helpful in writing future television shows. Among these random thoughts, Gene's also begun to scribble some ideas that he hopes will someday prove useful in the writing of a science fiction series.

Gene continues to work very steadily as a writer throughout the next half-dozen years, most frequently on the show *Have Gun Will Travel*, where he becomes head writer. Still, as busy as Gene has become, he begins to grow professionally dissatisfied, disillusioned with the formulaic westerns and cop shows he's most often hired to write.

Also, though Gene is earning a terrific amount of money throughout these years, he finds himself growing increasingly unhappy with the week-to-week uncertainty of life as a television writer, with the lack of creative control he is allowed over his work and with the puritanical mind-set of the network censors of the day.

At the same time, Gene is also growing dissatisfied on a personal level. He and his wife, Eileen, have become increasingly distant throughout the latter half of their almost twenty years of marriage, and by the early part of the sixties, they remain married, lovelessly, basically for the sake of their children. It is a difficult situation that becomes even *more* problematic when Gene meets and begins a relationship with the woman who will ultimately, after suffering through years of "other woman" status, become his second wife. Her name is Majel Lee Hudec, but she is far more recognizable to *Star Trek* fans by her stage name, Majel Barrett.

Having absolutely no idea about how the early Barrett/Roddenberry relationship was formed, and not wanting to simply speculate on such a personal matter, I thought it might be best to let Majel tell the story.

We weren't lovers at the very beginning, that sort of developed after we'd become friends, but I had known Gene since 1961. He had two kids at the time, and of course he was married, but even though he told me about how unhappy he was, I knew that he wasn't ready to leave them. You know, there's the tired old story about how the married man will say, "Ohhhh, my wife treats me terribly, she doesn't understand me, okay, let's have sex," but that wasn't the way Gene was at all. He didn't do that, and in the beginning he never gave me any real reason to think that he was interested in divorce.

Gene was not happy at home, but in his mind he had made a commitment, and this was a man who took commitment very seriously. When he made a promise, he kept it. It was very frustrating, though, in that up until Gene actually left his wife, I really couldn't anticipate spending the rest of my life with him. I felt I would spend the rest of my life loving him, but not necessarily *with* him.

By 1962, Gene's familial commitment, coupled with his own growing dissatisfaction in regard to a writer's career instability and frustrating lack of creative control, has prompted him to begin actively working toward attaining more job security. Toward that end, he begins writing original pilots, having them produced and hoping to sell them as series. One of the first was called 333 *Montgomery*, and it starred a man whose own career as an actor would, over the course of the next thirty years, become inseparably paired with Roddenberry's career as a writer and producer.

The star was DeForest Kelley.

Kelley would be playing the role of Jake Ehrlich, San Francisco's most famous real-life criminal lawyer, and I asked De to tell me about his first meeting with Roddenberry and how he managed to get the role.

I was testing for the role of Jake, but first I had to meet with the producer, who in this case turned out to be Gene Roddenberry. Now at this time Gene was working out of this absolutely tiny office in Westwood, which was about the size of a large . . . make that medium-sized closet. So I walked up the steps into the office, and I shook hands with a huge man who was sitting behind a tiny, tiny little desk. That was Roddenberry.

Gene had seen some of De's previous work, and as they discussed the project, they seemed to hit it off pretty well. Gene asked De if he'd screen-test for the role of Jake Ehrlich, and when De agreed, Gene informed him that in an unusual twist of circumstances, the *real-life* Jake Ehrlich had complete control over the casting of his role. In effect, Gene's hands were tied, and Ehrlich alone would pick the actor who'd play him.

And then Gene leaned over the little desk, saying, "And I have to tell you, this Ehrlich's a tough little son of a bitch."

Now it comes time to shoot the screen tests. There were about four or five of us up for this role, and we each played the same scene. In it, Ehrlich has to grill an uncooperative prisoner for some information. My turn came up, and because Gene had told me about how tough Ehrlich was, when I grilled this prisoner I really let him have it. I really leaned on him. And I can remember actually slapping this poor guy who was playing the prisoner around a little bit. I remember he tried to look away from me in the middle of the scene and I smacked him . . . hard, and said something like, "Listen, con, when I speak, you pay attention to ME!! Got it?"

Anyway, this must have appealed to Ehrlich, because when he saw my footage he apparently started jumping up and down yelling, "That's him! That's the guy I want!" A couple of weeks later we went up and shot the whole thing in San Francisco, and Gene and I and the rest of the crew just had a ball. Just a great time.

However, in what would become a recurring scenario in Roddenberry's life, when the network screened his pilot, they thought it was terrific. They absolutely loved it, but still they rejected it as a potential series. De Kelley explains:

> The problem we had was with the story, because in this pilot, Ehrlich defends this obviously guilty man against a murder charge and gets him off. And at the end of the story, the guy comes over to shake Jake's hand and I say to him, "Don't you dare shake my hand, I have no use for you." Well, they got scared by that and they thought the whole show was unacceptable. But it was an excellent pilot for that time.

Roddenberry also wrote two other pilots: *Defiance Country*, which was basically a sort of rewritten, recast and revamped version of 333 *Montgomery*; and APO-923, which was a sprawling action-adventure shoot-'em-up set during the then-recent history of World War II. Neither sold, but the experience of creating but not producing those three pilots led Gene toward taking complete control of his own material. He had been quite unhappy with the pilots, as the end result never quite measured up to his own original concept. Gene's inventive and creative programming ideas tended to get lost in the status quo of the limiting but accepted television production practices of the early sixties.

In short, Gene became absolutely convinced that in order for his own ideas to be accurately portrayed on screen, he'd have to produce his own properties, taking upon himself the responsibility for each and every aspect of production. As a writer, he was powerless in regard to the actual filming of his scripts. However, as a writer and *producer*, he could do it all. He could extract the germ of an idea out of his head, run it through his own typewriter, shoot it and have it beamed onto TV sets all over the country without ever diluting or distorting his original vision.

Gene wanted to do it all, to be in charge, to personally supervise and oversee every detail that went into creating his television programs. Casting, lighting, editing, pace, sets, costumes—all of these very important variables are off-limits to a writer. Not so the producer. On an even more basic level, should any of Gene's shows become a hit, as producer he'd stand to reap the lion's share of the financial reward. As a writer, he'd get in line just after the vultures.

Within a year, Gene's gotten his wish, and he's begun producing a series called *The Lieutenant*, which stars Gary Lockwood as Lieutenant William Rice, a young idealistic Marine officer thrown each week into dramatic and moralistic dilemmas involving the United States military. The show lasts only twenty-nine episodes, but it allows Roddenberry to develop working relationships with a series of people who will show up time and again later in his career. Actors Leonard Nimoy, Nichelle Nichols, Walter Koenig, Majel Barrett and Gary Lockwood all work with Gene for the first time while making *The Lieutenant*, as do future *Trek* directors Marc Daniels and Robert Butler. Last but certainly not least, when Gene's regular secretary comes in one morning, sits down and proceeds to burst her appendix, a young secretarial temp is called in. This temp, as it turns out, is also an aspiring writer, a *good* one. Her name is Dorothy (D. C.) Fontana, and thanks to that simple ruptured appendix, she unknowingly begins a long and fruitful relationship with Roddenberry that will, in time and with Gene's help, allow her to fulfill her dream of becoming a writer. She'll pen many of our very best *Star Trek* episodes, and Gene will ultimately show enough faith in her abilities to promote her into the supervisory position of script consultant. For now, though, she's Gene's secretary, and *The Lieutenant* is in full production.

However, even before *The Lieutenant* has premiered, Gene's becoming increasingly frustrated with the network's staunch refusal to allow him to say anything of substance in the series. The situation grows increasingly troublesome and comes to a head near the midseason mark, when NBC actually refuses to air an episode that deals with racism within the military. Not only do they refuse to *air* the episode, they refuse to *pay* for it as well. As a result, Metro-Goldwyn-Mayer, the studio that owns *The Lieutenant*, has to eat production costs totaling $117,000.

Gene is thoroughly disgusted, and as a result he comes to the conclusion that perhaps the only way he'll *ever* be able to say *anything* substantive within the confines of television will be to mimic *Gulliver's Travels* and do exactly as author Jonathan Swift had done. Like Swift, Roddenberry realizes that if he were to write a thinly veiled and substantive societal commentary within a less obvious and somehow more acceptable framework like fantasy or science fiction, he might be able to actually speak out on some fairly important, even controversial topics. Just as Swift's fantastic tales and Lilliputian settings allowed him to effectively mask his barbed satire of the times, so too would the outer reaches of the universe allow Roddenberry a chance to flex his own atrophied satirical muscles.

Still, at this point in time *The Lieutenant* is Gene's first priority. The show has garnered better-than-average reviews and below-average ratings and has begun spinning rapidly toward almost certain cancellation. Now, with the Grim Reaper moving ever closer to *The Lieutenant's* barracks, MGM comes to Gene asking if he might have any new series ideas that they could develop when and if *The Lieutenant* takes a bullet.

Gene, as would any good producer in this situation, says, "Oh, sure! Of course I do!" It doesn't particularly matter if that's true or not, but when presented with this kind of opportunity, producers will generally just smile broadly and say, "Of course I do!" At that point, they run home and rack their brains trying to think of something . . . anything . . . that they might be able to sell to the studio.

In Gene's case, however, he really *did* have an idea. In fact, the ultimate execution of *The Lieutenant* allowed him a perfect opportunity to draw upon his lifelong affection for science fiction. He dug through his tattered, yellowed personal notes in regard to producing a television series of the genre, and he went to work.

Gene found himself doubly enthused about the project, in that he might finally be able to work on his science fiction series while at the same time using the fantastic elements of the genre as the disguise that would actually allow him to avoid the blandness of standard television fare and infuse the series with some worthwhile social and political commentary.

As a result of Gene's enthusiasm, he went to work on the project with a driven, almost manic intensity. Dorothy Fontana, who was inescapably tossed into the middle of all this, explains:

> I'm not at all sure how long Gene had kept this idea cooking in the back of his mind, but I know that toward the end of *The Lieutenant's* first year, when we knew that there would not be a second season, he was working on it full-time.

I mean, here I was worrying about my own employment, thinking to myself, "better have something else that we can do. Gene can do. I can do." And by now Gene knew that I had been writing and that I had an empathy for writing scripts, and so he asked me one day to read something he'd worked up. It was about ten pages of format and presentation and it was called *Star Trek*. This was just as *The Lieutenant* was coming to the end.

So now Gene hands me these pages and says, "Tell me what you think of that. How do you feel about it?" And it was obviously still very loose, but his ideas were basically about a starship called the U.S.S. *Yorktown* which went out into space on its way toward an infinite series of journeys to incredible places and exciting adventures. The captain was named Captain Robert April, and Mr. Spock was a character too, although he was half-Martian then and very satanic, a very dark kind of character actually. Captain April was less defined, but not dissimilar to the early days of Captain Kirk. He never changed too much from that first presentation. He was a very intelligent man, a strong man, courageous with that spirit of adventure in him. That was always the beginning of that character.

And then Gene posed certain adventures, and different stories that were possible, and talked a little bit about the *Yorktown*. He hadn't yet formed a clear vision of what the ship would be like, but he knew it would be big with a crew of about two hundred. I thought it was neat. I really liked it, and of course there was nothing like it on television at that time. I thought it had lots of possibilities and you could see the stories. They'd begin to pop into your mind automatically.

As the weeks wore on and *The Lieutenant* died a lingering death, Gene was already at work, pulling all-nighters while he'd hack away at his typewriter, revising and reshaping the rough ideas that he'd shown Dorothy into his full-blown proposal for the series. Even in this early gestation period, Gene knew that he wanted *his* science fiction show to be different from the genre's standard, and tired, run-of-the-mill mix of self-important good-guy astronauts, evil mad scientists, cute kids, scary monsters, rocket ships and robots.

Gene always felt that the *best* science fiction was really about *people*, and not gadgetry, explosions or the solely scientific mysteries of space.

Toward that end he grounded his series ideas in reality, humanity and the interactions and adventures of the *Yorktown*'s crew. He stayed away from fantastic devices and scenarios that didn't at least conform to *some* thread of the known and accepted laws of physics. He also avoided superhuman characters with whom the audience could not possibly identify.

As you can see, Gene was not about to build *his* show around the prevailing clichés of TV science fiction. Instead, he based his ideas around believable stories, solid dramatic principles of human conflict and easily identifiable, uniquely "human" characters. He felt that as a writer it made no difference at all what genre of story he was telling, as long as it conformed to the most basic rules of drama. Science fiction, he felt, was no exception. If his *characters* were believable, if the *action* built to an exciting climax and if the *story line* held up throughout, Gene felt that the audience was certain to empathize and identify with his familiar, recognizable characters, even if they *were* seventy-two million miles from home.

With that in mind, Gene also struggled to make sure that the recurring characters on board the *Yorktown* would interact believably, behaving as a sort of extended intergalactic family. He hoped viewers might actually *care* if a crewman got sick, or lost a loved one, or was tormented by some inner turmoil. This in and of itself represented a vast leap forward from television's standard cookie-cutter characters.

Another concern sprang from Gene's insistence that viewers should, for the most part, forget about *Star Trek*'s novelty of outer-space travel and feel at home within the confines of the show's main setting, the *Yorktown*. Toward this end, he stayed away from standard rocket ship imagery and created *his* starship in such a way that viewers might actually grow familiar, even comfortable, within its confines. From the very beginning, Gene was convinced that the interiors of the *Yorktown* should be spacious, comfortable, airy and never seem too high-tech or intimidating. Instead, he felt they could best serve the series by becoming as intimate, inviting and easily recognizable as the Kramdens' kitchen, Andy Taylor's living room, or the Cartwrights' Ponderosa. There was no mistaking the fact that the *Yorktown*'s bridge was in fact going to serve as a sort of well-traveled living room.

For weeks, cigarette smoke puffed mightily out of Gene's office, accompanied by the furious tapping of typewriter keys. Crumpled, self-rejected eight-and-a-half-by-eleven ideas multiplied like Tribbles, flying through the air, littering the floors and providing unmistakable evidence of Gene's own perfectionist nature. Finally, when the nicotine cloud lifted and a polished, final draft was ready to see the light of day, Roddenberry crossed his fingers for luck and submitted his proposal to MGM.

On March 11, 1964, Roddenberry's self-proclaimed "outer-space baby" officially came into the world. This newborn proposal for a series downplayed the intergalactic aspects of the show by describing it (as all Trekkers worth their pointed polyvinyl ears know) as *Wagon Train* to the stars. And while Gene's *Wagon Train* was nowhere near hitched up, watered or ready to move out, he was able to describe its most powerful selling points in great detail. In fact, within the first few lines of Gene's proposal, he goes out of his way to explain that "*Star Trek* will be a television first!" . . . A one-hour science fiction series with *continuing characters*.

Gene was also wise enough to blatantly appeal to the penny-pinching fervor of most network executive types. In setting the scene for *Star Trek*, he begins with the declaration that *Star Trek* is uniquely constructed, "combining the most varied in drama-action-adventure with complete production practicality. And with almost limitless story potential." He goes on to explain that most of *Star Trek's* action will occur within the parameters of one "basic and amortized standing set," that any special effects created for the show can be reused time and again, making them more practical and cost-effective than ever before, and that the *Yorktown* will "confine its landings and contacts to Class M planets, approximating Earth–Mars conditions."

The Class M planet theory is quite simply brilliant, especially in the context of Gene's sales pitch. Termed the "similar worlds concept" in Gene's proposal, it read:

THE SIMILAR WORLDS CONCEPT. Just as the laws of matter and energy make probable other planets of Earth's composition and atmosphere, certain chemical and organic laws make equally probable wide evolution into humanlike creatures and civilizations with points of similarity to our own.

All of which gives extraordinary story latitude—ranging from worlds which parallel our own yesterday, our present, and our breathtaking distant future.

There, in two brief paragraphs, Gene's laid the groundwork that will become the main selling point of his series idea. Let's face it, the creative impetus behind the basic *Star Trek* idea is brilliant, absolutely incontrovertibly brilliant. However, in this particular instance and in this particular application, Gene's business acumen is as impressive as his creative genius.

You see, through the invention of the similar worlds concept, Gene has wiped out almost all of the enormously expensive aspects of most science fiction filmmaking. Because the *Yorktown* will only visit "similar worlds," *Gene's* space travelers usually won't need space suits, nor will they have to remain attached to air-supplying lifelines, or float about aimlessly without the benefit of that cost-effective production element known as "gravity."

At the same time, Gene's concept will allow the series to avoid having to constantly create enormously expensive sets. Class M planets, simply because they *are* Class M Planets, *must* simulate, at least vaguely, Earth–Mars conditions. This, stated Gene, "permits a wide use of studio sets, backlots and local locations, plus unusually good use of in-stock costumes, contemporary and historical."

As a final note, Gene's original proposal goes so far as to infer that even *Star Trek*'s alien life forms will remain cost-effective, thanks to his similar worlds concept. "To give continual variety," he states, "use will be made of wigs, skin coloration, changes in noses, hands, ears, and even the occasional addition of tails and such."

I can picture the standard reaction now. "Wow," say the programming executives who are reading Gene's proposal, "wigs, skin makeup, phony noses . . . that stuff's cheap. We can afford that. I like this concept."

In short, the opening of Gene's proposal, and more specifically his explanation of *Star Trek*'s cost feasibility, was simple, eloquent and exactly the kind of thing that programming executives love to hear. Now, with the opening broad strokes already appealing to the network's sensibilities (and pocketbooks), Gene goes into the finer details. He describes how the massive (and cheaply built) U.S.S. *Yorktown* (which of course will soon be renamed the U.S.S. *Enterprise*) will house a crew of 203 space explorers as they go about their business, poking their noses into all sorts of adventures each and every week in the outer reaches of a universe that, Gene clearly shows, could be constructed quickly and cheaply on any studio back lot.

The *Yorktown* was to be captained by the "unusually strong," "colorful," incredibly brilliant, handsome, capable and charismatic Captain Robert M. April (y'know, I can't help but think Gene had *me* in mind for the role all along). April would be assisted at all times by the intelligent, expressionless and always cool "Number One."

Number One was strong, competent, "efficient," "glacierlike" . . . and beautiful. It's incredible to think that in 1964, when the television world was telling the public that Lucy Ricardo and Laura Petrie were accurately portrayed modern women, Gene Roddenberry was sending one into space in a position of utmost authority. Even today, a female character of Number One's intelligence, competence and power would meet with uneasy stares at any pitch meeting.

The character of Number One was developed by Gene from the start with the intention that the role would be filled by Majel Barrett. In fact, she was cast in the role even before Jeff Hunter or Leonard Nimoy had come aboard. Certainly this presented a conflict of interest, but in a town wherein producers *routinely* cast mistresses in their series, it wasn't all that unusual. In fact, even though Gene's motivations were less than noble, he certainly could have done a lot worse. Majel has always been a fairly solid actress, and her eventual performance as Number One in the series pilot was rather good.

But back to Gene's proposal. Drop a half-level down the *Yorktown*'s pecking order and you'd find the ship's navigator, Jose Luis Ortegas, a handsome twenty-five-year-old boy wonder who manipulates the ship's controls with far greater ease than he does his own personal life.

Over in the sick bay, you'd find Dr. Philip Boyce, who bears a bit of resemblance to his descendant Dr. Bones McCoy, although he's described as a bit older, "well into his fifties." Described as cynical and usually annoyed about something, Boyce is also cited as "engaged in a perpetual battle of ideas and ideals with Jose" (foreshadowing the later Spock/Bones relationship) and as Captain April's one true friend.

More than halfway down the list of credits, we find our first mention of Mr. Spock. With pointed ears and an insatiable curiousity, this first-draft Spock bears *some* resemblance to his final incarnation, but at the same time he's described as "half-Martian," "reddish in color" and perhaps even brandishing "a forked tail." He is called the captain's "right-hand man," but, strangely, he's defined rather sketchily in comparison with his starship mates. A logical inference is that at this early stage, Roddenberry really hadn't quite gotten a handle on Spock as yet.

A final crewman, actually a crew*woman*, was tacked onto Gene's original proposal for rather obvious reasons. She is Captain's Yeoman J. M. Colt, a bosomy, bubbly, extremely sexually charged blonde with a "strip-queen figure" whose main activity on board the *Yorktown* would be chasing after Captain April. It would be interesting to know if Gene actually intended to include Colt throughout the series, or if she was merely tossed into the mix in an astute attempt to appeal to the prurient interest of the cigar-chomping, upper-middle-aged network suits who generally read these proposals. Either way, in time her blatant sex appeal would be watered way down, and by the time *Star Trek* had gone to series, she'd be transformed into the slightly less busty and much more wholesome Yeoman Rand.

Gene submitted his proposal to MGM with a confident, hopeful outlook. He knew he was onto something quite special, and now hoped that the studio executives would see it that way, too. They didn't. MGM did say that they were intrigued by his idea, but instead of immediately giving Gene a go-ahead, they told him that they'd like to "think about it, and get back to him." Basically, though Gene wasn't yet fully aware of MGM's intentions, he had been brushed off, flicked away with the studio's variation on "Don't call us, we'll call you."

Days passed slowly and anxiously for Gene, who still held out some hope that MGM might call in regard to *Star Trek*. Weeks turned into months, and finally, when it became sparkling clear that MGM wasn't *ever* going to call, Gene spent a few days repolishing his proposal. He even made some format alterations, the most notable being the renaming of his starship from the *Yorktown* to the *Enterprise*. Finally, when Gene felt he'd buffed his ideas to a maximum sheen, he anxiously papered every studio in Hollywood with the proposal.

He was met with a deafening silence.

Almost unanimously, the studios would praise Gene's idea, then back away for fear that producing a weekly hour-long science fiction series would prove so prohibitively expensive that even if it were to become a runaway hit, the profit potential involved would be hazy. Gene's bottom-line-massaging proposal was obviously overmatched whenever it went head-to-head with the soulless adding machines of your average studio programming executive. Actually, it's important to emphasize here that all television studios operate as businesses in every sense of the word. And while they may certainly be *intrigued* by any good idea, they will never, *ever* go out on a financial limb for purely artistic purposes.

Star Trek began to appear doomed. However, just as Gene was starting to bang his head off the office walls in frustration, *Star Trek* came back off the canvas to fight off this citywide case of unbridled apathy and found an interested studio. And, as can happen *only* in Hollywood, *Star Trek's* new lease on life was the direct result of Desilu Studios' impending financial collapse.

With studios and back lots scattered all over Hollywood, Desilu had been created by Lucille Ball and Desi Arnaz, and for years its soundstages housed such enormous television hits as I *Love Lucy, Our Miss Brooks* and *Make Room for Daddy.* For several years it was indisputably the hottest television studio in Los Angeles. However, by 1964 Desilu had suffered the slings and arrows of Lucy and Desi's divorce, and also the irrational but somehow enduring stigma attached to that particular pairing of names.

The studio's troubles were magnified by an extensive series of failed pilots that Desilu had financed and produced. Over time, this caused the studio to become rather cash-poor. They became unable to keep their soundstages manned or equipped at state-of-the-art capacity, and as a result Desilu's industry-wide reputation was rapidly tumbling to second-string status.

What Desilu needed desperately was a top-of-the-line, impressive-looking series that they could sell to a network. This would infuse the studio with some critically needed cash and allow them to use this sharp, hour-long, state-of-the-art series as a sort of weekly rebuttal to Hollywood's perception that the studio was now limping along, barely functioning at a substandard level. Failure to meet these goals would almost definitely cause Desilu, the former giant, to go belly-up.

At *exactly* this time—and in Hollywood timing is indeed everything—a man named Oscar Katz, who just happened to be Desilu's executive vice president in charge of television production, got hold of Roddenberry's *Star Trek* proposal. Keep in mind the cost-effectiveness and unique visual properties so heavily stressed in Gene's original proposal, and you'll readily understand the reasoning behind Katz's immediate enthusiasm for the project. *Star Trek*, if successful, would be the answer to all of Desilu's financial *and* perception problems. At the same time, Desilu, if up to the challenge, could allow Roddenberry to finally get his outer-space adventure off the ground. Gene signed a three-year development deal with the studio, and Katz immediately went to work trying to drum up network interest in Roddenberry's *Star Trek*. Within days, Katz had arranged a pitch meeting with CBS. However, it would turn out to be a gathering that Roddenberry would never forget . . . or forgive.

This was *supposed* to be a standard network pitch meeting. They take place almost every day, and they're generally attended by a couple of the network's bored upper-middle-management creative-executive types, who generally give a producer about twenty minutes in which to explain a given series idea. Once in a while, a producer's pitch will impress the executives enough that they'll cough up some cash, but far more often potential producers are sent away with their heads down and their tails between their legs. These pitch meetings are generally organized so that all day long, every twenty minutes, another hopeful producer is ushered in.

That is *exactly* why things seemed so odd to Gene when he got to CBS. He sat in the standard depressing, producer-packed waiting area, but he was then ushered into a conference room where no less than fifteen of CBS's top brass, including president James Aubrey, were waiting for him. They listened to Gene's pitch with rapt attention, as opposed to the standard halfhearted, sleepy-eyed lassitude. They leaned forward in their chairs. They smiled at him. They praised Gene's ideas, and *then* they asked questions, extremely *specific* questions. "How can you do a show of this broad scope on a television-sized budget?" "How can you possibly create sets and other worlds that are cost-effective *and* realistic?" "How can you be sure that a series of this nature will appeal to a *large* audience?" "How will you create believable, budget-conscious optical effects?"

The interrogation went on for hours, far longer than Gene had expected, far longer than any simple pitch meeting would merit. Gene was certainly delighted with the network's apparent interest in his project, but at the same time, he was confused . . . something about all this didn't seem quite kosher.

After nearly three hours of intense questioning, the confusion was cleared up entirely when Jim Aubrey halted the proceedings by telling Gene that he appreciated all that he'd said, but that CBS would have to pass on his series, as they were already developing a science fiction series of their own. Immediately it became clear that CBS had read Gene's *Star Trek* proposal and decided to call him into this pitch meeting for the sole purpose of picking his brain and digging out whatever secrets might help the network make *their* series a bigger and more cost-effective hit. The end result and ultimate proof of their sleazy intentions arrived on the air the following September with the CBS premiere of *Lost in Space*.

All Gene could do was shake his head in disgust.

Years later, Gene would still rail that CBS had raped him of his innovations without even paying him for his advice. His favorite line in regard to this particular subject was to equate his treatment by CBS with being horribly, violently ill. As Gene described it, you'd wait until you were feeling your absolute worst, pull yourself out of bed and drag yourself over to the nearest specialist's office. You'd have him examine you for two hours and tell you exactly what was wrong and how to treat it. Then at the end of the office visit you'd simply say, "Thank you for your time, but I won't be paying you. I've decided to treat myself."

Roddenberry began licking his CBS-inflicted wounds while across town Oscar Katz was about to make some bona fide progress. Katz had persuaded (i.e., begged) a guy named Mort Werner, who was NBC's vice president in charge of programming, to read Gene's proposal. Werner read it and liked what he saw very much, but even as he read Gene's theories in regard to the series' cost-effectiveness, the gears in Werner's head were turning, rapidly calculating a sort of mental debit sheet on what a show like this would undoubtedly cost. Katz kept the pressure on, praising Roddenberry's efforts, blowing smoke about how studios "all over town" were "falling in love with this show" but that he and Gene would really prefer working with NBC.

Werner, who had not just fallen off a turnip truck, saw through Katz's grandstanding and made a counteroffer. He explained that he really liked this *Star Trek* idea a lot, but that he'd done a little budgetary figuring and placed the cost of shooting a pilot episode at nearly half a million bucks. *Nobody* was going to rush Mort Werner into taking a blind plunge into a half-million-dollar pool. He was instead going to test the water, slowly getting wet, one toe at a time.

Instead of a half-million-dollar go-ahead, Werner suggested that NBC allocate twenty thousand dollars in "story money." NBC asked Gene to come up with three ideas, fleshed out as full stories (of about ten pages each) that would illustrate the broader, more general concepts written up in the original *Star Trek* proposal. Werner went on to structure the deal so that once Gene had written up his three stories and NBC had read them, the network had the right to either choose the story they liked best and ask Roddenberry to flesh it out as a teleplay or reject the entire series. If all went well, Roddenberry's completed teleplay would be used, upon NBC's approval, in shooting a series pilot.

Basically, it was "put up or shut up" time, because if NBC liked Gene's story ideas it was "onward and upward." If not, the network could sneak out the back door, having lost only twenty thousand dollars in story money. Werner had hedged his bets admirably, and now it was up to Gene to come through with story ideas smart enough and strong enough to persuade NBC to hand over the cash necessary to shoot a *Star Trek* pilot.

Within a week's time, the contracts were drawn up and signed. Gene dotted the I's, crossed the T's, swallowed some Maalox and unknowingly got onto the roller coaster that would continue to supply him with thrills, chills and occasional nausea for the rest of his life.

"T
CA

ith NBC's twenty grand burning a hole in his pocket, Roddenberry quickly got to work, fleshing out his *Star Trek* proposal and exterminating the small swarm of bugs still looming inside. He satisfied his own first priority by immediately stealing Matt Jefferies, one of Desilu's youngest and most talented art directors, and putting him to work full-time sketching up ideas on what the *Enterprise* should look like. I asked Matt to tell me about how he got involved with *Star Trek*, and about the work he was doing during the show's earliest days.

had been working for Desilu as a sort of assistant art director on *Ben Casey*. And during the run of that show I'd taken four weeks off, during which time I went to the New York World's Fair and visited with family in Virginia. At the end of my vacation I came back to work, walked into my little cubicle and found it empty. My drawing board and my drafting tools were gone. So I went into my boss's office and said, "I don't know where all of my stuff is, but where the hell is the next *Casey* script?" He said, "Forget it, you're not on the show anymore."

So I figured, "Well, I guess that serves me right for being a smartass and taking a month off." But as it turned out, my boss wasn't firing me at all. He said, "Some guy's coming in by the name of Roddenberry. You'll be working with him now. He's got some kinda idea for some sorta outer-space show. So your stuff's been moved into the big room."

This "big room" was in reality just a thirty-by-sixty-foot storage space that wasn't used anymore. Jefferies settles in there, alone, unpacking his stuff, until ten A.M., at which point Roddenberry arrives. The two men begin talking, get to know each other, and it becomes clear rather quickly that they are going to work well together. They hit it off immediately, finding that they share a love of aeronautics, and especially World War II B-17s. In fact, Jefferies remembers coming away from this meeting feeling quite enthused about working with Gene. "I could make him laugh," Jefferies recalls, "and we seemed like a perfect combination in that he was a real head-in-the-clouds dreamer, and I was a nuts-and-bolts man."

Gene then lectured Jefferies on the basic principles of *Star Trek*, touching upon the five-year mission, the uncharted space travel, the shirt-sleeve environment, the crew of between two and four hundred men and women, the quasi-military overtones, and the necessity to always remain believable. Once Roddenberry had explained the basic framework of his new series, the two men spoke about the *Enterprise* itself, and while Gene really didn't have a clear vision of what the ship *should* look like, he certainly knew what he *didn't* want.

R oddenberry told me, "I don't want to see any rockets. I don't want to see any flying saucers. I don't want to see any planes. I don't want to see any jets. I don't want to see any wings." At that point, he squeezed his big hands into big fists and said, "Just make her look like she's got power." And he walked out. Remember, I was young and relatively inexperienced, so when Gene left, I basically had no idea what was going on or how I was going to pull this off. But even though I was clueless, I got started right away.

The first thing Jefferies did was to spend some of Desilu's money by purchasing virtually everything he could find on Flash Gordon and Buck Rogers, buying anything he could dig up that was crammed full of rocket ship imagery. Then he came back to his office, hung all of that stuff up on one of its big empty walls and said, "There, that's what I will *not* do."

A nd then I started sketching. I knew almost immediately that the basic shape of the *Enterprise* needed to be unique and recognizable very quickly, regardless of the angle. And I knew that I wanted the starship to have a relatively plain surface, so that we could throw different colors upon it, depending on the story line and what kind of atmosphere or battle the ship might run into. I mean, we didn't know what the hell kind of colors might exist out there in space, or where they'd be coming from. So I fairly quickly settled on a neutral gray.

In regard to the basic shape of the *Enterprise*, I started playing with charcoal, pencil and paint, doodling, looking for any kind of idea. I was playing with cigar shapes and balloons, anything that stayed away from the stereotypical age-old bullet-shaped rocket. I kept this up for a good two weeks, and by the time Gene came back to check on my progress, I had all of these new sketches up on the walls. All four of my enormous walls were now covered with potential Enterprises.

So now Gene came back with a couple of NBC types tagging along behind him, and they went around the room looking closely at Jefferies' sketches one by one. Any time Roddenberry would comment positively about any specific aspect of a sketch, Jefferies would make a note of it. Any sketch that Gene passed by without comment Jefferies tore down, crumpled and tossed as soon as they left.

Now I looked at all of the sketches that they'd commented upon, and I started to sort of combine sketches, piecing together all of the elements that Gene seemed to like. About ten days later, my walls were covered again, Gene and the NBC guys came back, looked around the room and we went through the whole damn process all over. They liked a piece of one ship, a piece of another, an engine here, a shape there, it was getting frustrating as hell, not so much because of all the work, but because by now we were starting to run out of time in regard to the production schedule. I mean I was already running late in working up the sets for the pilot.

So anyway, what I finally did was to go through all of my sketches one more time, taking out everything that I liked best. Then I just put all these damn things together, cramming them all into one big ship. Y'know, I liked the idea of the engine being separated from the main hull, and the basic dish shape really appealed to me, so I played around with all that stuff. I had the engines down, the engines up, all kinds of things. Anyway, when I'd finally gotten it shaped up into the configuration I liked best, I did a painting of this particular ship, and that really stacked the deck in its favor. I had walls full of Enterprise sketches, but now sitting amid all that and looking far more attractive than any sketch was my painting of this particular Enterprise. Gene came in once more, loved the painting so much I ended up giving it to him, and the Enterprise was ready to fly. I really changed very little about the ship from that point on, and when the Howard Anderson Company was hired to do the pilot's special effects, I worked with them in creating our first miniature. It was about four or five inches long, and we made it out of balsa wood and some cardboard. When Gene approved it, we made up a three-footer, and by the time we'd started shooting, it was finished. I showed it to Gene on the set, and he loved it. At that point we started making the oxymoron, the big miniature. It was one hundred and thirty-four inches long! ◦

While Jefferies was building a starship, Roddenberry was pounding out the three *Star Trek* story outlines that NBC would read in determining the fate of the series. If the network was suitably impressed by Gene's stories, they'd pick a favorite and Gene could go on to the teleplay stage. If they were disappointed, Gene could go . . . home. The project would be killed.

With so much riding on these story outlines, Gene was even more industrious than usual, burning the midnight oil, obsessing over each page and every word. Finally, after a month of writing and several weeks of revising, polishing and tweaking, Gene handed his trio of *Star Trek* story ideas over to NBC.

Several days later, he got his answer. NBC loved his stories and wanted to make a pilot out of one called "The Cage."

Basically, this was a tale in which the *Enterprise* is lured to the planet Talos IV by what seems like a weak distress signal. When Captain April, Spock and Navigator Tyler beam down to the planet's surface, they encounter a makeshift tent city that seems to be constructed from the

debris of a downed spacecraft. They are then greeted by what appears to be a rather feeble group of survivors. The survivors explain that they're scientists, that they crash-landed on this planet almost twenty years earlier and that

**ON THE SET OF "THE CAGE,"
RODDENBERRY CHECKS OUT JEFFERIES'
THREE-FOOT *ENTERPRISE* MINIATURE.
(© 1993 PARAMOUNT PICTURES)**

they've spent the better part of two decades calling out into space for help. Strangely enough, Spock's biological readings find that these decrepit-looking scientists are actually in terrific health.

Enter Vina, the young and stunningly beautiful woman who explains that she was just an infant when the scientists' craft crashed on Talos IV, and that she'd be happy to show the captain the secret that allows these old geezers to survive in such great shape. She then leads April toward a secluded, rocky cliff, where he is immediately kayoed and dragged away by some large-headed, small-bodied aliens, disappearing into a subterranean cave.

Once inside, he apparently finds out the truth. The scientists were merely an illusion aimed at attracting a suitable mate for the seemingly lovely Vina, who is actually the sole survivor of the crash. The small, weak-looking Talosians have taken it upon themselves to care for her, and now it seems that what she really requires is Captain April.

The Talosians' actions anger the captain, but he is powerless to escape. Instead, the Talosians begin

ABOVE LEFT: **S**USAN **O**LIVER AS **V**INA, KEEPER OF THE TIN-FOIL HALLWAY. (© 1993 **P**ARAMOUNT **P**ICTURES) ABOVE RIGHT: **J**EFF **H**UNTER LAUGHING WITH **S**USAN **O**LIVER AND A COUPLE OF **T**ALOSIANS AS THEY REHEARSE HIS SURPRISE ABDUCTION. (© 1993 **P**ARAMOUNT **P**ICTURES)

offering him a series of illusions wherein he and Vina get together under different and much more pleasurable circumstances. Vina appears as a member of medieval nobility, a wild, green-skinned Orion slave girl and finally as a corn-fed well-scrubbed midwestern dream girl, arriving complete with picnic lunch.

Number One and Yeoman Colt arrive to rescue April, and after a series of defeats they finally manage to outwit the Talosians, who then tell the whole truth. As it turns out, Vina really did survive a starship crash, but she is by no means young or beautiful. In reality, she is middle-aged, and horribly deformed from the wreck. The Talosians have merely provided her with the illusion of beauty so that she might lead a happier life.

On top of all that, the Talosians explain that centuries earlier the entire surface of their planet was destroyed by nuclear war. That's what forced them to move belowground, and what allowed them to develop such

incredible mind power. However, as a side effect of the war, their race is no longer able to procreate, and that's why they've been taking care of Vina. Their ultimate goal is that one day she'll find a suitable mate and begin spawning heirs who might absorb and keep alive some of the more noble traditions of once-great Talosian society.

In the end, April allows the Talosians to provide Vina with the illusion that he has indeed fallen in love with her and decided to stay. He is then returned to the *Enterprise*, where he's whisked away, bound for what promises to be a series of weekly adventures.

Still, while NBC loved Gene's story line and agreed to move forward with *Star Trek*, the network had some reservations in that they were not entirely convinced that the actual production of Gene's project was possible, especially at a farm-club studio like Desilu. *Star Trek*, as proposed, represented a huge undertaking, requiring extremely complicated sets, costumes, makeup and above all else untried, unproven special effects. Therefore, NBC was quite uneasy about this pairing of a young rising producer like Roddenberry and an old declining studio like Desilu.

The network's biggest fear was that should *Star Trek* ever become a series, its unavoidably massive technical, production and optical demands would make it impossible for Desilu and Roddenberry to churn out episodes fast enough to meet their airdates. As a result, NBC would be watching the production closely, monitoring its cost and making sure that the *Star Trek* pilot remained on schedule.

Still, as far as Roddenberry was concerned, *Star Trek* had been greenlighted, and that was all that mattered. Gene had succeeded in nurturing his outer-space baby from proposal through the story phase, and he was now about to watch it blossom into a full-grown television pilot. *Star Trek* was still a long, *long* way from making it to the airwaves, but for now Roddenberry could savor a victory, at least for a little while.

Just hours after NBC's decision, Roddenberry got to work writing the script for *Star Trek*'s pilot. Once more Gene cranked up his creative energies. Once more the sounds of furious typing, furious swearing and furious paper crumpling filled Gene's office from dawn until dark until dawn. Smoke billowed from his office as if he were electing a pope, and draft after draft his fingers flew, writing, refining and working to ensure that his script straddled the fine line between creativity and believability.

Toward this end, Roddenberry began corresponding with a number of scientific professionals, mainly aeronautical engineers, technical craftsmen, scientists and physicists. He'd allow these guys to read his early drafts of "The Cage" and then solicit their advice as to how he might create a more scientifically accurate, wholly believable view of the future and intergalactic travel.

Far and away the most important of these contributors was an unassuming physicist from Rand Laboratories named Harvey P. Lynn. His correspondences with Roddenberry were lengthy and specific and cleared up the scientific inconsistencies found within Gene's script. For example, having read an early rough draft of "The Cage," Lynn offered specific technical advice as to how the Enterprise's shuttlecraft should launch, return and dock at the mother ship. He also argued with Roddenberry over interstellar terminology, insisting that Gene change a line of dialogue wherein April sets the Enterprise's course toward a specific "quadrant" of space. Lynn's argument was that since a quadrant inherently refers to a fourth of something, because the universe has no defining boundaries, the reference was simply meaningless. Lynn politely requested that the word "region" be substituted. Along the same lines, he'd ask Gene to do things like eliminate the word "static" from a communications officer's dialogue, insisting that no such interference was possible in outer space, and he'd get downright angry over the fact that the real-life heavenly bodies mentioned in Gene's script were chosen not because of any logical spatial relationship or hypothetical course set for the Enterprise, but simply because they'd sound vaguely familiar to viewers. As a result, he argued that if any competent astronomer were to sit down and chart the course of the Enterprise, he'd find it zigzagging wildly about the cosmos.

Lynn also noted that Gene's script for "The Cage" referred to Talos IV as having "gravity 1.3 of Earth" (about one-third stronger than that of Earth). This, he correctly pointed out, made the Talosians' oversized heads an anatomical impossibility, as a gravity greater than Earth's would, over time, significantly shrink and flatten the inhabitants' heads. This made the Talosians' large heads unexplainable, and as a result (at least to someone as technically minded as Mr. Lynn) unbelievable. He suggested that making the gravity level less than Earth's would clear up this problem quite easily.

As a last example of how Roddenberry harnessed Mr. Lynn's specific brand of genius (although dozens more exist), it was Mr. Lynn who quite correctly took umbrage at the notion of the Enterprise crew running around with "laser" guns. He is the man who suggested that Roddenberry rethink this name and replace it with one a bit less prone to criticism from scientific types, who'd soon realize that a laser probably couldn't blow up a rock or knock over a tree. Star Trek's "lasers" became "phasers" shortly thereafter.

Roddenberry's academic brain trust certainly assisted him in keeping his script believable and grounded within the basic principles of science. However, even with this valued assistance, Gene still found himself plugging away at his teleplay for "The Cage," rewriting the same scenes time and again. It wasn't that his script wasn't good; in fact, it was terrific. Instead, these revisions were due to the fact that no matter how often Gene rewrote "The Cage," he'd always come away feeling like he could make it a little bit better. Gene's personal standards of excellence were holding him prisoner at his own desk.

This was obviously the most important script that Gene had ever written, and with so much riding on it, he simply couldn't allow himself to stop polishing. Obsessing over his characters' names, he had Captain April become Captain Winter, then Captain Christopher Pike. Finally, as the time constraints of a preliminary shooting schedule began to demand its completion, "The Cage" was nearing a form that Gene could live with.

Throughout this period of frenzied script revision, Gene was also beginning to deal with many of the creative people and technicians who would ultimately turn his dreams so satisfyingly into reality. One of the first to arrive was a man named Franz Bachelin, one of Desilu's most experienced in-house art directors. Bachelin would be responsible for the overall look of Star Trek's series pilot and would also serve as Matt Jefferies' boss. However, within a relatively short period of time it would become clear that Jefferies, who was officially credited as assistant art director, would be doing the lion's share of the actual work.

Bachelin, whose designs were apparently more "beautiful" than "buildable," generally worked in watercolors, coming up with the broad strokes (bad pun intended) in regard to the interiors of the Enterprise. Once Bachelin's basic designs had met with Roddenberry's approval, it was up to Jefferies to translate these ideas into the reality offered by a limited budget and a rather run-down television studio. Jefferies explains:

> had to come up with the construction drawings to actually build these sets, and my problem was in trying to figure out just what the hell Bachelin had done such a pretty painting about. I mean in terms of construction and in terms of practicality, his paintings just didn't work; the construction crew would have gone out of their minds trying to build what he'd painted.

At any rate, as I said, I was a nuts-and-bolts man, so I took his basic paintings and used them in creating all of the ship's specific design work. I'm talking mainly about the bridge, the layout, the relationships between *Enterprise* crew member positions, the original instrumentation—all of this stuff required a massive amount of work.

Keep in mind that Jefferies was now developing all of the *Enterprise* exteriors, interiors and construction elements, and that all of his sketches had to take into account not only stylistic considerations but also budgetary, scheduling and construction constraints. Roddenberry and Desilu had both made it crystal clear that no starship set was going to be approved unless it was functional, sturdy, realistic and cost-effective. Still, Jefferies was used to working within those restrictive guidelines—that was all part of his job. However, on this particular project his creative ideas not only had to be approved by Gene (who, as producer, had final creative control), but also had to survive Gene's battery of technical advisers, each of whom could come up with any number of memos regarding the inherent feasibility and practicality of Jefferies' sketches as they related to hypothetical means of future space travel.

On top of that, since Roddenberry was still pushing for believability at every turn, every one of Jefferies' artistic suggestions had to serve a functional purpose. For example, if Jefferies were to put a light panel on the *Enterprise* bridge, it couldn't simply blink for decorative purposes; Gene would want an explanation as to its specific duty. With all this in mind, Jefferies was not so much designing the simple nailed-together sets of standard television, but in a very real sense designing a workable intergalactic spaceship.

In time, Jefferies would outclass and eclipse the creative contributions of Bachelin and go on to become *Star Trek*'s art director throughout our three seasons. He would also become a major (and perhaps the most significant) contributor to the look and feel of *Star Trek*, the *Enterprise* and the planets below, as well as to the ships, accommodations and homelands of our alien life forms. And while Matt has never officially been given the credit he so richly deserves for his creative contributions to the show, he is nevertheless immortalized within the (barely) fictional bowels of the *Enterprise*.

Specifically (and you're probably two steps ahead of me here), the long cylindrical passageway that houses most of the ship's most important and delicate circuitry, and also many of those scenes wherein Scotty yells, "I canna deeeeeew it, Captain," was proudly named "the Jefferies tube." It seems that when this *particular* area of the *Enterprise* needed a specific name in one of our scripts, Roddenberry's idea was to christen the tube after its creator.

As the weeks passed, the level of activity surrounding "The Cage" was increasing rapidly, and by midsummer, the Desilu lot seemed overrun with the artists, craftsmen and skilled technicians who were laying the groundwork for *Star Trek*. Almost unanimously, these professionals saw "The Cage" as the most intricate and complex piece of filmmaking they'd ever worked on. No project of this genre and magnitude had *ever* before been attempted on television, and that made for a studio-wide feeling of excitement, coupled with the anxiety of going where no TV production had gone before.

Problems arose every day. Gene rewrote parts of his script daily, and through it all, whenever a snag was encountered, Roddenberry and crew simply came up with a way to beat it. On *this* set you could expect the

SCOTTY HARD AT WORK IN JEFFERIES' EPONYMOUS TUBE. (© 1993 PARAMOUNT PICTURES)

unexpected, and the only *rule* was that there *were* no rules. With a premise unlike any ever seen on television, sets unlike any ever constructed and a script that called for, among other things, large-headed aliens, phaser fights and a green dancing girl, *Star Trek*'s production crew quite often found themselves making things up as they went along.

Still, though it may have appeared to the studio and to the network executives that the inmates were indeed running the television studio/asylum, there was actually a strong sense of organization and order governing the proceedings. For example, while set design and script revisions were under way, the casting process had also begun, and by now Roddenberry knew his characters so well that he had a very clear and definite sense of what he was looking for.

With Majel Barrett already set to play Number One, Lloyd Bridges was approached to play Captain Pike. However, he turned down the role and told Roddenberry in no uncertain terms that he wasn't the least bit interested in doing any kind of outer-space series—his feeling was that once any actor left terra firma, he could kiss his future credibility good-bye. Strangely enough, Bridges had recently spent several successful seasons just offshore of his beloved terra firma, splashing through a starring role in *Sea Hunt*.

With Bridges' rejection, Roddenberry spent the next several weeks trying to fill the job opening of "*Enterprise* Captain," ultimately hiring Jeffrey Hunter, a seasoned movie actor who had most recently portrayed Jesus in *King of Kings*. Joking that any actor capable of ruling over all of Christianity could easily command a starship crew, Hunter accepted the role, and after the requisite agents' haggling, Captain Pike became animate.

In the meantime, John Hoyt was hired to play Dr. Boyce, and the rest of the ship's personnel fell into place shortly thereafter. Most importantly, it is at this point in our story that my esteemed colleague and dear, dear friend Leonard Nimoy makes his entrance.

It's funny, but I realized as I sat down to work on this book that I really had absolutely no idea how Leonard initially got involved in *Star Trek*. With that in mind, I theorized that I could either make up some funny and slanderous story about the guy, or I could go over to his office and find out the truth. Since Leonard is bigger than me and loaded with that superhuman Vulcan strength, I figured I'd better play it safe and give him a call.

At the risk of making a long story longer, I should explain that when you visit Leonard's office, you're in reality visiting Leonard's office *building*—he owns the whole thing! He's a tycoon! He's huge! Over the years, he's simply grabbed Hollywood by the balls and shoved the whole town into his back pocket. He's become one of the town's major players, and he's firmly established himself as a successful producer, director, writer and actor.

So now I call him, and his secretary buzzes his assistant and the rest of his people confer and take meetings about it, and finally, after seventeen minutes on hold, I get through to Leonard, and I ask him if I can come over and chat with him about how he originally got cast in *Star Trek*. He says, "Sure." So now I drive over there, and in trying to impress my friend, I bring with me my brand-new voice-activated mini–cassette recorder, which I casually pull out of my pocket and place on Leonard's desk.

"Just a little high-tech toy I picked up," I boast, "real cutting-edge stuff."

Leonard yawns at me. Then he laughs at me, when I can't figure out how to start the damn thing. Actually, up until now I've been ashamed to admit it, but I haven't a clue how to use anything that's even the slightest bit technical in nature. So now here I am, the great space captain, sitting in Leonard's office going, "Test, uh . . . one, two . . . Test, one, two . . . " and Leonard's chuckling at me. So, since he's so smart, and since *he's* supposed to be the logical one, I decide I'll let *him* figure this out.

I slide the thing over to his side of the humongous desk, and I watch him poking around at the buttons and fiddling with a couple of knobs, and all the while he's got a sort of confused dog look on his face, staring dumbfounded at this piece of Japanese audio wizardry. Turns out he's even more inept than me. So now the two of us, who've explored unknown numbers of planets and who've saved the universe on at least 173 occasions, are sitting in an office building in Burbank, both of us in bifocals, and we're staring myopically at this simple contraption whose operating methods elude us entirely. Finally, after nearly a half-hour of grumbling and button-pushing, I realize that we haven't actually been running the tape at all—we were trying to record on the leader section.

Embarrassed, I push "RECORD" and ask Leonard about how he got cast in *Star Trek*.

had a very talented, bright, aggressive agent who was a sort of terrier. He would get hold of an idea for one of his clients, and he'd pursue it and keep chewing and chewing on it until somebody paid attention. I was known at the time for playing heavies, ethnic types, dark characters. This was before ethnic awareness, so I was always playing Mexicans, Italians, all these ethnic groups.

Anyway, at the time a man named Marc Daniels was set to direct an episode of *The Lieutenant* and he needed to cast a flamboyant movie star character, a character who wanted to make a movie about *The Lieutenant* himself, using Marine Corps facilities and personnel. Marc was extremely resistant when my name was mentioned as a possibility because he was so familiar with my typical "heavy" roles.

Y'know, he was casting a fast-talking con man, a glib guy with lots of charisma and charm, and he just didn't see me that way. But my terrier of an agent was determined, and he kept on chewing on Marc until he finally agreed to let me read for him. I came in, gave him a fast-talking patter reading, and he said "Oh, I guess you *can* do this," and I had the job. That simple.

Now, you know Roddenberry was producing the series, and Majel Barrett was also in this episode, playing my secretary. We shot the show, I had a good time and then a few weeks later my agent called and said, "Gene Roddenberry really liked what you did on *The Lieutenant*, and he just called to say that he has you in mind for a role in a sci-fi pilot that he's doing." That's how the ball started rolling.

Actually, Majel now tells me that she actually had a hand in my getting hired for *Star Trek*.

I have to break in here and tell you that shortly after I spoke with Leonard, I drove over to Majel Barrett Roddenberry's house and had a long conversation with *her*. Of course, one of the things I asked her to do was verify Leonard's story. Here's what she said:

eah, it's true. Gene said to me, "I've got this alien and I want him to look kind of satanic." I remember those were his exact words, and a thought struck me. I remembered Leonard's great angular look, and how good he had been in *The Lieutenant*, so I said, "Hey Gene, you remember that guy I did *The Lieutenant* with? Why don't you take a look at him?" And Gene's eyebrows went up, not unlike Spock's, and he smiled, and that's how Leonard got the part. It was that simple.

Two minutes later, Gene's smiling and dialing. Leonard's terrier gets a phone call, he and Gene exchange greetings, wade through some small talk and set up a preliminary meeting between Roddenberry and Nimoy. Leonard recalls:

My first meeting with Gene basically consisted of him asking me, "Will you do this role?" I was intrigued. I can't say that I fully understood it at first, but I was intrigued by what Gene told me about the interior life of the character and by the fact that he was half-human. I thought, "That creates a real friction, something could grow out of that. There's a basic tension there that's playable, particularly if it's written to." That's really what got me intrigued, and later on, when those kinds of opportunities started to present themselves, that's when the Spock character really started to work.

At the time, Gene didn't make any specific statements about how he'd write for Spock, but I did get a real sense that he knew what the potential life of the character could be, and that it might be fun to explore him.

Another interesting, almost "stop-the-presses" piece of trivia sprang up while I was researching the book. I was interviewing DeForest Kelley, and he let slip something I've never heard him say before, that *he* was actually the first person offered the role of Spock. Here's how it went:

I had lunch with Gene one day [they had just done their television pilot] and he said to me, "De, I have two new properties that I'm working on. One is based on *High Noon*, and the other is this science fiction thing, and there's a character in there who's an alien, and he's going to have pointed ears and green color." So of course I said, "Aw, geez! What, are you kidding? Get outta here! No way! Forget it! Call me when you do *High Noon*." He was talking to me about Spock . . . but the right guy got it. Leonard really was a wonderful choice.

Once the pilot's cast was in place, with sets and designs shaping up nicely and with Gene's teleplay nearing final draft status, the creative aspects of *Star Trek* and "The Cage" were both beginning to come together. However, nothing about this birth was going to be easy, and progress on the technical side of things seemed to be met at every opportunity by setbacks and delays.

For example, there's a scene in "The Cage" that I mentioned earlier where the young girl who's living on Talos IV begins to appear differently to Pike, changing her looks several times in the hope of having him find her attractive. In one of these incarnations, she appears as an uninhibited green slave girl from the planet Orion. Of course, no green woman had ever before appeared on television, and for that reason no one quite knew how to pull it off, not even *Star Trek*'s master makeup artist, Freddie Phillips. Freddie was as talented as they came in Hollywood, and he was a magician throughout the three-year run of the series. However, at this early juncture even he was having trouble.

So now Gene and Freddie have this green alien woman to create, neither one knows how to do it and of course this is not the kind of thing you'll find in a textbook anywhere—you know, "page 52, 'How to make a beautiful starlet green'" just doesn't exist in the standard Hollywood makeup texts. So once again these two extremely talented gentlemen put their heads together and just sort of guessed.

The first thing these guys did was to con the unsuspecting Majel Barrett into helping them out with "a few simple makeup tests." Next, Freddie whipped out a fresh homemade batch of disgusting green makeup that he spread liberally over Majel's now-horrified face. Still, "for the good of the show," Majel put up with Freddie's emerald concoction and put her best face forward for some screen tests. Everything went well, Freddie was once again hailed as a conquering genius and everyone was quite satisfied with the day's work . . . until they watched the dailies.

Unbelievably, when the screen tests came back from the lab, they showed Freddie's guinea pig/actress with perfectly normal skin tones. "This is fucking impossible!" screamed Freddie, who was not the least bit accustomed to unsuccessful makeup work. Freddie's tirade was undoubtedly met by a similar outburst from Gene, who in all likelihood mustered great volume and profanity in demanding a new batch of screen tests, an

improved, even greener batch of make-up and of course a greener actress.

Freddie left the screening room frustrated and immediately set about mixing up a green goulash that would put the fabled meadows of Ireland to shame. Next a new but equally unsuspecting actress was hauled in and plastered with Freddie's foul-looking, and now equally foul-*smelling*, concoction. Once again she looked mortified as the cameras rolled, and once again the test footage came back from the lab bearing the beautiful image of a lovely pink-skinned young actress.

Now I wasn't there, but I *can* tell you with some degree of certainty that by this time smoke was probably escaping from Roddenberry's ears, and large throbbing veins were probably plainly visible through Freddie's forehead. Again there was yelling, and again Freddie went back to his trailer, having lost the battle but determined to kick some serious cosmetological ass. He and his assistants now labored over a green vatful of viscous liquid mumbling to themselves and appearing not unlike Macbeth's three witches. Finally, after adding some unusual ingredients into the mix (Eye of newt? A bit of dragon's blood? Who knows?), they once again came up with a bright green batch of new improved paste, and proceeded to spackle it all over the lovely young mug of yet another horrified actress. Test footage was shot once more, and ... you guessed it, once again Freddie and Gene watched the screen with furrowed brows as a lovely young woman with a fine pinkish Caucasian complexion appeared before them.

Picture frenzied forehead-slapping and large puddles of sweat forming all over these two Type A perfectionists, nostrils flaring and vocal cords straining under the load of warp eight yelling. Now you've got a sense of what it was like inside that screening room. Finally, a dejected Rodden-berry calls the film processing lab to see if they can suggest any filter or lighting tricks that might make an actress appear bright green on film.

"What?" stammers the quite obviously terrified lab technician. "I've been working overtime the last three nights trying to correct your actresses' lousy green skin tones. . . . I had no idea you wanted them green, I just thought you had hired a shitty cinematographer."

You'd think that must be the end of the story, but I've got to jump forward in time to tell you that during the filming of "The Cage," when lovely young actress Susan Oliver had the dubious distinction of wearing this green makeup all over her body, it had the unwelcome side effect of making her feel extremely fatigued. When her condition became apparent on the set, a doctor was quickly called in. However, nobody bothered to explain the situation to him in detail. All he knew was that there was a woman who needed to see him right away. He rushed over to the set, asked for Susan Oliver, sprinted to her trailer, threw open the door and beheld his patient: an exhausted-looking, nearly nude woman who just happened to be green. I'm told that he let out a bit of a yelp, stumbled through an introduction, then obviously began stalling for time while he tried to figure out what might turn an otherwise healthy young woman green. Finally, after all had been explained, a quick shot of Vitamin B got Susan through the shoot ... although I'm also told that finding an unpainted bit of Susan proved tricky and embarrassing.

Throughout the entire green woman fiasco, Freddie Phillips was also burning the midnight oil while he went about creating something that would prove far more enduring than his green woman . . . Mr. Spock. Gene

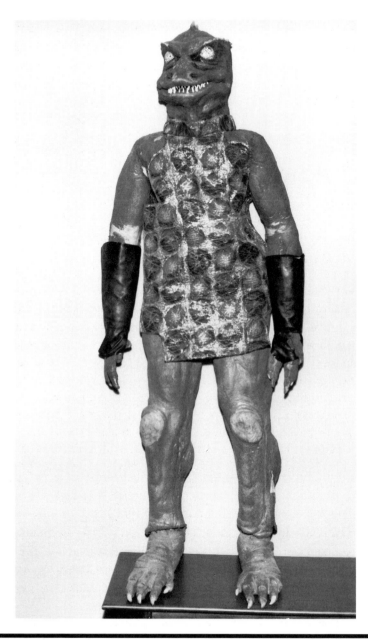

THE **G**ORN CREATURE . . . JUST A BIT LESS REFINED THAN **S**POCK'S EARS.
(© 1993 **P**ARAMOUNT **P**ICTURES)

had given Freddie some broad ideas as to Spock's look, but it was now up to Freddie to refine and improve upon Gene's basic ideas. Surprisingly, this was to become a major problem for Freddie, Leonard and Gene. And since this is a subject where *my* perspective is truly only second best, I suggest we get the real story of Spock's ears from Spock. Here's how Leonard tells it:

There's a very interesting series of events in regard to this subject, and a small story of heroism that had to do with Freddie Phillips. When it came time to experiment with Spock's look, what Gene gave us as a sort of mandate to work on was the internal life of the character, and a very generalized vision about his appearance. Pointed ears and strangely colored skin . . . those were the two leads he gave us to work with. In fact, he suggested that the skin might be a bright red.

The problem with that was that in the mid-sixties there were still a lot of black-and-white TV sets in use in the country. We were still really in a crossover period between black-and-white and color, and red skin viewed on a black-and-white set would simply look black, and that was not the connotation that Gene was looking for. He wanted Spock to appear obviously alien, not black. So that eliminated the red, which I was relieved about. So now Freddie and I sat in front of a mirror for quite a number of sessions, maybe a dozen or so, each lasting three or four hours, and we spent all of this time just looking, experimenting with the ears, experimenting with the eyebrows, experimenting with the haircut.

And I remember there was a special-effects house that worked literally out of a garage on Hollywood Boulevard . . . a couple of young guys. They ended up being contracted by the studio to make all of *Star Trek*'s grotesqueries, monster heads, monster hands and feet, that sort of thing. You know, they would create things like the Gorn creature from "Arena." Anyway, at this point in time I was sent to them for the Spock ears. And I went through the procedure, the plaster-cast mold of my ears, and then they made up a sculpture of what the ears would look like. Next they made the prosthetic ears, sent them to us, and Freddie was dismayed. I mean, he was an extremely painstaking, meticulous craftsman, and he said, "We're going to have a big problem because they're not using the kind of rubber that's necessary for really fine appliance work." His feeling was that in any close-up, these ears would be noticeably mismatched to my own skin in texture and tone. They'd just look phony.

The problem here arose from the fact that Desilu's production heads had made a deal with an inexpensive effects house without ever checking the company's work. With that in mind, they had no idea that this company would be incapable of performing the very delicate sort of work required in creating Spock's ears. Instead, they just looked at the bottom line and cooked up the contracts for a sort of package deal. You know, "Desilu will pay you $5000, you give us three giant Martians, a salt vampire and two pairs of ears," that kind of thing.

Still, although they were consistently coming up short, this company just kept coming back with more and more ears, and Leonard and Freddie kept meeting in rundown dressing rooms where Freddie would try his best to attach these things to Leonard's head. Freddie would quickly start muttering and cursing, gluing and patching and pasting, until it became obvious that this was a no-win situation. At that point he'd storm off to Desilu's bean-counters, saying, "These ears just aren't going to work! I need to go to an appliance lab to do these properly!"

The production managers would then look up from their ledger sheets, with beady eyes widening and eyebrows rising, and they'd gasp, "But that's going to cost us money." And Freddie would reply, "Yes, it is. To have the first pair made properly would cost six hundred bucks. After that, each ensuing pair will cost about one hundred to one hundred and fifty. But to pay for the labor

LEONARD SHOWS OFF HIS NEW, IMPROVED EARS TO RODDENBERRY. (© 1993 PARAMOUNT PICTURES)

involved in casting a new pair, making the molds, and actually creating the first ears, it's gonna run us six bills."

At this point, the production department would just yank the purse strings closed, saying something like, "We're already paying *one* company to make these ears . . . you just tell them to get it right!" This basic scenario became a regular occurrence until they were just three days away from beginning to shoot the first pilot. That's when Freddie cracked. Leonard explains:

We had just gotten yet another pair of ears, and I went to the makeup department, sat down in the chair and almost immediately Freddie begins cursing, because this new set of ears looked grotesque rather than sleek, cool and sophisticated. They were "creature" ears, gross instead of intellectual.

So now Freddie begins muttering to himself again, and finally he explodes. He just ripped these ears off my head, threw them mightily into the nearest wastebasket and said, "THAT'S IT. THAT'S FUCKING IT!!!" Then he got on the phone, called a guy over at MGM named Charlie Schram and pulled a few strings.

Charlie worked in the makeup department at MGM, and he had a great reputation as a makeup artist and as a first-class appliance maker. So now Freddie calls him and he says, "I've got a guy here who needs ears that are a cross between Peter Pan and Mephistopheles, and I need them by Friday." Charlie says, "No problem! Come on down." And the next thing I know, I'm in Freddie's car driving, actually speeding, over to the MGM lot.

We got to Charlie's lab, and the difference was like night and day. I was in and out of there in forty-five minutes. We started shooting three days later with a new, comfortable, great-looking set of ears. Freddie had made an end run around the budget crunchers at Desilu, and gotten the job done to his satisfaction.

At this point, I should probably take a moment to say that Spock's ears fascinated me throughout the series, and they continue to do so even today. I mean, I've *always* been impressed with the artistry of the makeup, but at the same time there's a whole other side to the situation that I've never explored. For example, if I were in Leonard's position and Roddenberry had come up to *me* saying, "You've got the job. Oh, and by the way, you're going to be wearing this pair of pointed ears," I'd be thinking, "Oh, shit! No way!"

I'd have felt that way because as an actor there's a very thin line between using those ears as a device aimed at broadening your character and just looking silly. Going into the series, Leonard certainly knew that the ears would give him a different look, but at the same time he also must have been aware that the whole appearance might just backfire. People could very well have laughed at him. I spoke with Leonard about my feelings, and I asked him if he'd ever had any similar thoughts. I wasn't surprised by his answer.

> During the period when we kept on getting the bad ears, I went to Gene because I was nervous about exactly what you just mentioned, and I began to ask myself, "Do I really want to do this?" So I went to a friend of mine, Vic Morrow, who was shooting *Combat* at the time, and I told him about the ears and about what was going on with them, and I expressed my fear. I asked him, "What will happen if I do this? What if this doesn't work? And what about my future?" And Vic came up with an idea. He said, "Well, how about having them do a makeup job on you that is so complete that no one will ever know it's you? That way, when the series is over and done with you can come out of it, and there will be no connection between your face and that character." He made sense, but here of course is where my actor's ego kicked in. I said, "But what if the character's wildly successful? I'll definitely want people to recognize that it's me, and I'll absolutely want the identification with Spock."

At this point, Leonard *could* have simply asked that Freddie give Spock a sort of interstellar rhinoplasty. You know, slap on a funny nose and a few prosthetics, a real Ferengi sort of thing. That way no one would ever know who was under there. Instead he decided to talk through the situation with Gene.

> I went to Gene and said, "I'm really afraid of this, we could be creating a character that's going to be perceived as unintentionally funny or grotesque or something," and Gene just said, "Keep working on it." And at face value, that sounds like a brush-off, but in reality this was a kind of abiding concept that Gene had, one that I respected a lot.

Gene felt that you start out with a vision that's powerful and full of rich ideas, and if you let it erode here and there simply because this person tells you, "It won't work" or that person says, "I don't think this is right," you'll just end up with a bland, blank concept that's no longer interesting, exciting or even reflective of what you set out to do.

So Gene was very firm about making the Spock character, and all of Star Trek, work.

On the other side of the coin, Gene loved to tell *his* version of the same story, talking at length about how Leonard came to his office extremely worried about the Spock ears. Apparently, during the period of time when Leonard kept on getting the unsatisfactory earpieces, the production crew began making jokes at his expense. This was to be expected, in that if you're working with a crew, *any* crew, and you show up each day sporting a different but equally weird-looking set of ears, you're going to get razzed. It's simply part and parcel of the ribbing that is indigenous to almost every Hollywood set.

The set of "The Cage" was no exception, so Leonard very quickly was given such subtle, witty and pithy nicknames as "Dumbo," "Pixie-man," and "The Rabbit." He was also greeted on a regular basis by would-be stand-ups shouting, "Hey, nice ears." As you might have guessed, this did not sit well with the already uneasy Vulcan-to-be. Then, as Roddenberry told it, one day there comes a knock on the Great Bird of the Galaxy's office door. Gene opens up, and in walks a perturbed and extremely nervous Nimoy.

"Gene," he says, "I've worked very hard at becoming a serious and credible actor, and I've come to a decision . . . it's me or the ears. If Spock has to remain a freak, I don't want to play him."

This was less than a week before shooting was to begin, and there was no way in the world Gene could afford to lose an important cast member, so he did his very best to change Leonard's mind. Over the course of a half-hour the pair delved into and dissected the intrinsic depth, intelligence and dignity of Mr. Spock, speaking about the unique set of challenges that *playing* such a character could present to the truly consummate actor. Nimoy was already beginning to waffle when Gene hit him with the knockout punch. "Leonard," he said, "play the role. If the first thir-

teen shows go by and you're still unhappy about Spock's ears, I swear to God, I . . . personally . . . will write you an episode wherein we give him a fucking ear job, and he ends up looking just like everybody else."

At this point Leonard burst out laughing, Gene cracked up alongside him and for the rest of the day, at any given time and completely out of context, either one of the pair could be found trying vainly to suppress a deep-rooted laugh.

Though Leonard did indeed have some reservations about the appearance of Spock, Roddenberry was absolutely determined that the character remain blatantly alien. In fact, there was a premeditated and extremely important reasoning behind Roddenberry's insistence that Spock retain such an unusual, otherworldly appearance. You see, Gene was dead set upon including a character among the recurring cast who with every appearance on screen would serve as an unmistakable reminder to the audience that they were now in the twenty-third century, emphasizing that this ensemble was not just international, but interplanetary. Obviously, Spock was to become that highly visible alien.

However, as uneasy as Leonard may have been in regard to Spock's appearance, he wasn't nearly as upset as NBC. Remember, those were the days when virtually everyone on television was of the suburban middle class and white. Actually, television's population wasn't so much white as it was white bread. I mean, where else but on a sitcom or TV drama of the late fifties or early sixties did a "typical father" come down to breakfast on a Saturday wearing a suit and tie? Where else did mothers wear starched, puffy

ABOVE AND OPPOSITE: **T**HE NETWORK'S AIRBRUSHED PHOTOS OF THE PLUCKED AND ROUNDED SPOCK. (© 1993 PARAMOUNT PICTURES)

skirts, high heels and pearls while ironing? The cathode tubes of the time were chock-full of these Waspy, terminally suburban characters who answered to names like Ozzie, Princess, Wally and "The Beaver." This is what the networks were used to, this is what made them feel comfortable.

Now all of a sudden along comes this new guy named Roddenberry, and he's throwing (gasp) black people and (gasp) strong, aggressive career women into his pilot. On top of all that, he's *also* throwing into the mix a green-blooded, pointy-eared, strangely coiffed alien. "What will they say down in Dixie?" quivered the network's marketing department. "What will the sponsors say?" This was the mind-set, and this is what Roddenberry had to fight against.

Almost from day one, battling over Spock's very existence became a constant vigil. One of the most heated skirmishes pitted the network against Nimoy and Roddenberry, and it turned these still-unfamiliar working acquaintances into allies fighting against a common foe. Leonard tells it like this:

I remember a lot of posturing around the Spock character early on, in which Gene was extremely supportive. NBC put out a brochure about the production. It was a sort of fold-out display of information about the series, and it was about to be sent out to advertising agencies, hoping that they in turn might bring in some potential sponsors. In a nutshell, it was a sales brochure, with a thumbnail sketch of what the series would be about. •

It also featured some discussion of the main characters, and there were a few production stills sprinkled into the mix. One or two of those shots featured the Spock character, but on first glance something about him didn't look quite right. Upon closer examination, it became obvious that Spock's pointed ears . . . were gone.

It was clear that the photos had been retouched and that the pointed tips had been taken off Spock's ears, and that his rising eyebrows had been airbrushed out, then drawn back in so they'd appear normal. All he was left with was the odd haircut. I was baffled by it, and I remember feeling threatened by it because I thought something was wrong. I mean somebody somewhere at NBC had made a conscious decision to do this. I called Gene, and asked him about the ears and he told me it was a manifestation of the fear in the sales department at NBC that a major alien character in a series might frighten off some potential advertisers if he was seen to have a devilish appearance.

The concept in those days was that each of the major characters in a television series had to fulfill a very specific function, and that was to attract a very specific portion of the audience which would identify with them. The mothers had to be attracted to the lady in the show. The fathers in the audience had to be attracted to the leading man, empathize with him, see him as a potential and desirable friend. There was usually a child thrown in for the kids in the family, and an animal for the pet lovers.

All of this led the marketing types to ask themselves, "Who the hell's going to identify with the guy with the pointy ears?" This is a threatening character, they decided, and thus, with some nifty photographic tools, they lopped off the tips of Spock's ears. Not only that, they'd plucked his eyebrows!

I asked Gene, "Where does that leave me in terms of the actual show? Suppose the thing sells? What are we gonna do?" And Gene reassured me and told me not to worry about it. "The character," he said, "will remain intact." He was very clear about this.

Shooting dates for "The Cage" were now approaching rapidly, but the production was beginning to come together rather well. Gene feverishly continued to polish his script while Franz Bachelin and Matt Jefferies continued to work their magic, now overseeing the construction on the incredible array of sets that were rapidly beginning to cover every last inch of Desilu's tired, squeaky, antiquated and truly inadequate soundstages. Freddie Phillips continued to create his universe full of scientific miracles and every day now new and important crew members were coming aboard.

First and foremost among these was Bob Justman. Stolen away from *The Outer Limits* and hired as an assistant director, Bob would in fairly short order become one of the most important people ever to grace our soundstages. He was and continues to this day to be a remarkably talented and incredibly likable professional who somehow managed to suffer every one of the unavoidable slings and arrows of network television without ever losing perspective or his formidable sense of humor. He was also (with apologies to James Brown) the hardest-working man in show business, routinely overseeing, documenting and ultimately solving many of *Star Trek*'s production problems and toiling through months of eighteen-hour days and seven-day workweeks.

Bob's incredible talents and infectiously joyous demeanor quickly allowed him to rise to the position of associate producer and, in our third season, co-producer. For now, though, since Bob will show up throughout the rest of this book, it will have to suffice to say that this shaggy, lovable sheepdog with a mustache had his foot in the door, and we would ultimately all be better off for this.

Bill Theiss, who'd go on to design virtually all of *Star Trek*'s costumes, also signed on at this point. He immediately began work creating the uniforms of the *Enterprise* crewmen and designing the Federation breast patch, which would, over the course of the next twenty-five years, become globally recognizable, as well as the cornerstone of a billion-dollar merchandising juggernaut.

Bill's main guidelines in creating the *Star Trek* costumes would be monetary. Since he usually couldn't cut corners by simply borrowing costumes pulled from Desilu's wardrobe department, Bill and his crew had to make all of the show's wardrobe by hand. The unavoidable labor costs involved in such an undertaking led Bill toward working as cheaply as possible. With that in mind, velour, which was cheap and easy to work with, and female skin, which was free and easy to look at, became two of his most often utilized trademarks.

Joe D'Agosta, a casting director who'd worked with Gene on *The Lieutenant*, also helped out in the casting of this pilot. Since the cancellation of *The Lieutenant*, D'Agosta had been working full-time at Fox. However, when Gene phoned his old friend asking for help, D'Agosta was only too happy to get involved.

Since I couldn't leave my staff job at Fox, I actually did the casting for the pilot over the phone. I dealt with Leonard, and Jeffrey Hunter, but the best thing we did was to cast women as the "frail, fragile-looking Talosians." We brought in these three

OPPOSITE: GENE AND HIS TRIO OF CROSS-DRESSED TALOSIANS. (© 1993 PARAMOUNT PICTURES)

ABOVE: JOE LOMBARDI, JUST BEHIND THE ORIGINAL *ENTERPRISE* BRIDGE SET, RUNNING THE SHIP'S ORIGINAL ELECTRIC WIRING . . . AND *YOU* THOUGHT WE USED DILITHIUM CRYSTALS. (© 1993 PARAMOUNT PICTURES)

RIGHT: GENE CHECKS OUT ONE TALOSIAN'S ABILITY TO THROB ON COMMAND. NOTE THE LOW-TECH RUBBER TUBING AND AIR BLADDERS THAT MADE THIS POSSIBLE. (© 1993 PARAMOUNT PICTURES)

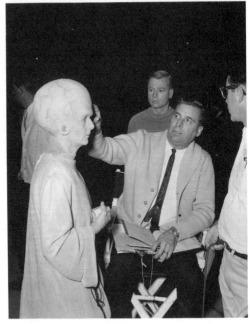

lovely middle-aged actresses, and Gene had Bill Theiss bind their breasts with Ace bandages, and then Bill dressed them in loose-fitting tunics, which made them appear even weaker. Next, Freddie Phillips put big veiny bald heads on them so they'd appear super-intelligent, and we were set. It worked beautifully. You really have to look close to catch on that the Talosian men were actually women.

Operating the camera was Jerry Finnerman, who would go on to become *Star Trek*'s cinematographer throughout our first two seasons. Rounding out the technical crew and providing special effects were Desilu veterans Joe Lombardi and

THREE DIFFERENT PERSPECTIVES OF "THE CAGE": (OPPOSITE) ON THE SET, (LEFT) ON THE PHONE—RODDENBERRY AND HUNTER SIMULTANEOUSLY CALL THEIR AGENTS—AND (BELOW) ON THE BRIDGE. (© 1993 PARAMOUNT PICTURES)

RODDENBERRY MEETS WITH HIS KEY CAST MEMBERS: (ABOVE LEFT) **G**OING OVER THE SCRIPT WITH **J**OHN (**D**R. **B**OYCE) **H**OYT; (ABOVE RIGHT) EXPLAINING A CONTROL PANEL TO **M**AJEL AND **L**EONARD; AND (OPPOSITE) GOOD-NATUREDLY PINCHING **J**EFFREY **H**UNTER'S LEFT NIPPLE. **A**CTUALLY, HE'S EXPLAINING THE SIGNIFICANCE OF **C**APTAIN **P**IKE'S **F**EDERATION COMMAND INSIGNIA. (© 1993 **P**ARAMOUNT **P**ICTURES)

Jack Briggs. Briggs took care of the props, most notably building the very first phaser weapons, and Lombardi spent much of his time configuring the original wiring of the *Enterprise* bridge, although he was also responsible for the air pumps that allowed the veins in the Talosian heads to throb on command.

Finally, with cast and crew in place, and with NBC's approvals on what seemed like the 478th draft of Gene's script, *Star Trek*'s pilot was ready to roll, and on December 12, 1964, that's exactly what happened. Desilu's studio lights were fired up, and for the better part of the next twelve days, history was made. Throughout the production of "The Cage" there was a general feeling that this project was turning out to be something quite special. For that reason, no one was all that concerned about the minor but mounting budgetary overruns. Finally, when the requisite happy ending and fade to black were in the can, it was time for Gene's budget to get blown completely out of the water, thanks to a series of nightmarish postproduction disasters.

Having never attempted a project like this before, it became necessary to spend a large amount of time creating and then fine-tuning all of *Star Trek*'s optical effects. The *Enterprise* had to fly smoothly and gracefully. The transporter had to work with authority and without a lot of cutesy sparkly gimmicks. The phaser, and in this case phaser cannon effects, had to be believable and not the least bit hokey.

As with the rest of this pilot, nothing came easy. Postproduction delays and cost overruns eventually climbed to the point where Gene's *Star Trek* pilot came with a $686,000 price tag attached. That's a lot of money, even by today's standards, so you can easily imagine the amount of *agita* it churned up over at the penurious offices of Desilu.

Still, when all was said and done, "The Cage" was a magnificent piece of filmmaking. Visually stunning and impressively intelligent, it was a cinematic triumph of unquestionable stature. The film was airmailed to New York, and shortly thereafter, in a swanky screening room high atop Rockefeller Center, NBC's powers-that-were got together for a special premiere screening. The

ROLL 'EM! G**ENE SUPERVISES SHOOTING ALONG WITH DIRECTOR** R**OBERT** B**UTLER AND DIRECTOR OF PHOTOGRAPHY** W**ILLIAM** E. S**NYDER.** (© 1993 P**ARAMOUNT** P**ICTURES**)

lights dimmed, images began to flicker and within seconds those dozen NBC suits had been transported to the outermost reaches of the universe.

With eyes transfixed, and paying rapt attention, NBC's top dogs hung on *Star Trek*'s every frame. When it had ended, the group applauded, and unanimously agreed on two things. First, that "The Cage" represented some of the finest work ever done for television, and second, that as far as NBC was concerned, it stunk as a series pilot. The network decided to pass.

NBC felt that "The Cage" lacked sufficient action and was far too sophisticated for the run-of-the-mill American television viewer. While the network was extremely impressed with the creative and technical qualities of the pilot, they simply felt that no normal TV viewer wanted to watch the idiot box and think at the same time. NBC labeled "The Cage" "too cerebral" and made it clear that the network would have been far more comfortable accepting a less ambitious offering, one that more closely resembled their own existing dramatic television series. NBC was looking for car chases, shootouts, fistfights and gratuitous sex, with the idea that these were the things that accounted for surefire ratings success. "The Cage" had *none* of those things. Instead, it was smart, beautiful, intellectual and thoroughly engaging. In other words, a flop.

Though the creative content of "The Cage" accounted for the main reason behind NBC's rejection of the pilot, it was by no means their only motive. For example, the network disliked many of Gene's main characters. Number one on their list? Number One, the strong, competent, intelligent female officer. It seems that NBC held some test screenings of the pilot, and as you might expect, most men absolutely hated her. As you probably *wouldn't* expect, *women* hated her, too. They called her "pushy" and "annoying," and seemed to feel that any female officer of her stature would probably just screw things up most of the time. They also felt that Number One probably shouldn't be trying so hard to fit in with the men. Retrospect, it would seem, is not always pleasant.

Still, the network's distaste for Number One was fully eclipsed by their continued and absolute loathing of Spock. To them, Spock was simply a childish, pointy-eared Martian who made the entire show look silly.

Last, and at the heart of the network rejection, NBC had been promised a "*Wagon Train* to the stars," but instead they'd received a rich, complex and multilayered story wherein the broad concepts of truth, beauty and the basic human condition were studied and spread out for viewer contemplation. In a nutshell, while they were indeed impressed by this stellar accomplishment, they felt that the American public was too lazy, too complacent and just too dumb to appreciate such tales, especially on a weekly basis.

However, instead of dumping the project, NBC did the unprecedented, giving Gene the go-ahead to film a second pilot that they hoped would be more appealing to the network's sensibilities. Thus, having pushed, strained and struggled for nearly two years, and having finally accomplished his monumental feat, Gene was basically told, "Start over . . . and do it right this time."

And now, even in the midst of Gene's tremendous disappointment and undeniable gut feeling that his efforts of the past two years had garnered him nothing, Roddenberry wasted no time making preliminary preparations for Star Trek's second chance. Almost immediately he began writing, wheels were set into motion and it became quite evident that Sisyphus Roddenberry was ready to push that big fat rock up the great big hill one more time.

If only it were that easy.

WHERE NO MAN HAS GONE BEFORE

The network told me to get rid of Number One, the woman first lieutenant, and also to get rid of "that Martian fellow" . . . meaning, of course, Spock. I knew I couldn't keep both, so I gave the stoicism of the female officer to Spock, and married the actress who played Number One. Thank God it wasn't the other way around. I mean Leonard's cute, but . . .

—GENE RODDENBERRY

Despite NBC's rejection of the first pilot, Roddenberry and Desilu had won a victory, having proven themselves effective, competent and completely capable of pulling off a project of *Star Trek*'s magnitude. Couple that with NBC's enthusiasm over the production values of the first pilot, and you'll understand the reasoning behind NBC's willingness to go out on a limb and give *Star Trek* a second chance. However, having taken a $686,000 pummeling on the first pilot, NBC also made it crystal clear that this second at bat would come with a number of strings neatly attached. First, they insisted that this second pilot should be filmed solely upon the basic preexisting sets built for "The Cage," emphasizing that they would by no means authorize *any* production costs exceeding the three-hundred-thousand-dollar mark. Second, NBC asked that Gene pink-slip nearly everyone in the cast. And third, they asked that Gene drop several key characters, among them Number One and Spock.

Gene knew he could scrape by with a three-hundred-thousand-dollar budget, he could live with NBC's decree that he ax most of his cast, and he could even bring himself to drop most of the characters in question. However, he felt quite strongly about retaining his token Vulcan, and so for the first time Roddenberry chose to bite the hand that fed him, going head to head with NBC's highest-ranking execs.

You already know that Gene wanted Spock around the *Enterprise* bridge as a constant visual reminder that this series took place in space, but the reasoning behind his stand against NBC went much deeper than that. Spock, he felt, was a complex, multilayered and extremely important character whose basic inner turmoil and unalterably alien presence could provide a strong focal point for any number of dramatic possibilities. This was something Gene truly believed in, and he was not a man who could be coerced into diluting his vision.

Finally, when the unstoppable force known as Gene Roddenberry went one on one with the immovable object that was NBC, the result was an intense and uncomfortable series of meetings. They took place over several days and were full of forced smiles, clenched teeth, dangerously high blood-pressure levels and above all else the complete unwillingness of either side to back down. Ultimately, when the length and intensity of the standoff were beginning to wear down both sides, Gene and NBC met each other halfway, with a compromise. Spock could stay, said NBC, but Gene was told that he absolutely, positively would not be allowed to focus much attention upon him. Spock, according to NBC, would be seen, not heard, and treated as a sort of living, breathing set decoration. At this point, Gene employed the age-old producer's trick of nodding, smiling through clenched teeth and muttering under his breath at a just barely inaudible level. As you might expect, he had no intention of obeying their edict.

However, the rest of the cast was not so lucky, and an entire Starfleet crew of actors bit the dust. One of those actors, as it turned out, just so happened to be Gene's girlfriend. Thus Roddenberry found himself with the unenviable task of firing his own mistress. I asked Majel to tell me how she got through that, and how she coped with being let go.

Gene was very serious. He sat down with me and said that he knew this was going to break my heart, but that the network had given him orders to get rid of the characters of Number One and Spock. Then he explained to me that he figured he could probably fight to save one character, but not both. He told me about how badly he wanted to keep Spock, and about how important that character could become to the series. He tried to be very nice about it, and he also said, "We'll work you into it. Somehow or other, you'll be in the show."

And I just sunk. I had wanted the role so badly, and it was everything that I'd wished for . . . I mean, Gene wrote it for me, for God's sake. So being let go was devastating, terrible.

But Gene said, "This is what I feel I have to do." I'm sure that I cried, but I didn't want Gene to see my disappointment. He told me, "I really think I can sell this thing, but I'm going to have to give in, in some way or another." Then he repeated that "we'll find a way to put you into it."

"Obviously it won't be the same!" I told him, but at the same time, I guess love was winning out. Yes, it hurt. It was devastating at the time, but it wasn't anything that broke me up so badly that I couldn't continue. It's not like I just stopped trying, or that I stopped loving Gene or anything.

One of the few cast members spared the wrath of the network was Jeffrey Hunter, but strangely enough, he never made it to the second pilot either. For years, the "official" story's been that Hunter turned down the role of Captain Pike due to a film commitment. That, however, just wasn't the case. In truth, Hunter wasn't so much "unable to commit to the series" as he was fired.

Apparently there were problems with Jeffrey. Not while he was shooting or on the set or anything like that, but afterward. They started when the go-ahead came in for the second pilot, and Hunter's wife, who was an ex-model, suddenly started coming to production meetings. Evidently she hated the first pilot, and as a result she began to frequently storm into Gene's office, loudly making demands like "from now on, my Jeff must only be shot from certain angles," and apparently it became "Jeff wants this" and "Jeff demands that." Gene later told me that he'd much rather be dealing with Jeff and his agent, or even Jeff and a gorilla, than Jeff and his wife. He continued that there were so many tantrums, restrictions and ultimatums being laid out on the table that he finally thought, "Well, I can't possibly do an entire series like this. They'll drive me nuts."

Now, without a script, without a cast, without a captain, and without the luxury of adequate preproduction time, Roddenberry once again found himself back at the proverbial square numbered "one." A lesser talent would have also found himself up the proverbial creek without a paddle, but Gene was nothing if not a master of accomplishing the impossible.

Already helping Gene in his quest were a handful of brilliant crewmen. In fact, many of the production magicians who'd worked wonders on Star Trek's first pilot were now performing their wizardry once more on the second. Bob Justman, now an associate producer, was already hard at work, juggling and organizing budgets, set construction sketches, script revisions, crew logistics, equipment, lighting concerns and at any given time about a half-dozen other duties. Bill Theiss and his crew were once again making like the shoemaker's elves, designing and constructing incredible costumes that seemed to magically appear each morning, but that in reality were the end results of a long night's work. Matt Jefferies was by this point responsible for all of the show's art direction work, and he and his crew were continually amazing everyone with sets that were bigger, better, more creative, more beautiful and cheaper than ever before. With these guys by Gene's side, this formidable task wasn't so much a team effort as it was an all-star-team effort.

As his production crew began work, Gene set about casting his new captain, his new leading man, and of course the very first person he called was . . . Jack Lord. Yep, *that* Jack Lord, the *Hawaii* 5-0 guy. Luckily for me, Jack apparently demanded 50 percent ownership of the show, and there was just no way Gene and Desilu were going to let him have it. So, unable to reach an agreement, Gene was forced to keep searching. That's when my phone rang.

I was in New York, where I'd been working pretty steadily. Over the course of the last several years, I'd been lucky enough to land a good handful of leading roles on Broadway, in films and scattered about what's now referred to as TV's Golden Age. I'd done a couple of *Twilight Zones*, and an *Outer Limits*, both of which had been well received, and after twenty years of barely scraping by in the paycheck-to-paycheck world that is home to nearly all professional actors, I was rapidly becoming a familiar TV face and a sought-after leading man.

So now Gene telephoned me, and at that time, I have to admit, I had no idea who he was. But he told me about what was going on, and asked me to come to Los Angeles and watch the first pilot with him. And I remember as I watched it I was impressed by a number of things. The green girl, and Leonard (who smiles . . . *twice*), and Majel Barrett as Number One, and I thought it was extremely innovative and extremely inventive. Gene then told me that NBC didn't put it on the air because they wanted him to recast it, rewrite it and do a more action-packed, less thought-provoking pilot. At any rate, Gene explained that NBC saw something there that in their minds merited a second shot at creating a pilot episode. We talked at great length about the possibilities, potential drawbacks and proposed direction of the series, and as we parted, I can remember Gene saying, "You're my leading man." Now, since I don't want to sound as if I'm patting myself on the back, I'll let *Star Trek*'s casting director, Joe D'Agosta, do it for me.

As an actor, Bill was of a higher echelon, and hiring him was really a coup. He was coming out of *Judgment at Nuremberg* on Broadway and a television series called *For the People*, and everything he was doing, whether it was on stage, on film or on television, was highly prestigious. I couldn't believe we got him.

Modesty prevents me from commenting on what Joe just said, but I would like to go on the record that in my opinion, Joe is one of the most intelligent, perceptive and credible men I've ever worked with. However, I should explain that not *everything* I was doing was "highly prestigious." For example, just prior to shooting *Star Trek*'s second pilot, I spent several weeks filming another pilot, *Alexander the Great*. I played Alex, and I must admit that this may have been one of the silliest concepts in the history of television. I mean, this show could best be described as *Combat* in drag.

Here I was, a grown man, running around make-believe battlefields while wearing fitted cotton sheets and sandals and shouting things like, "Come on, men, we must experience the glory of taking this hill! Hiiiiii-YOOOOOOOO!!!" Thankfully, this Alexander the Great died even younger than the real one, and I was able to focus my full attention upon *Star Trek*, a show in which I'd actually get to wear pants—strange-looking short-legged bell bottoms, but pants nonetheless.

Meanwhile, back in Rockefeller Center, NBC's programming executives, having been disappointed in "The Cage," were taking no chances when it came to the story line for *Star Trek*'s second pilot. This time, instead of simply asking Gene for three ten-page story outlines, they asked him to hand in three completed one-hour shooting scripts, making it clear that they were looking for stories that were action-packed, clearly defined, easily understood and loaded with fast-paced adventure. Roddenberry immediately set to work, pounding away on a story entitled "The Omega Glory," and in between paragraphs he made a few phone calls and brought into the fold two writers who would go on to pen a good number of our very best shows. In fact, as it turned out, all three potential pilot scripts would in short order be turned into *Star Trek* episodes. Stephen Kandel came in to pen the now-classic "Mudd's Women," and Sam Peeples gave his

battered Smith-Corona manual a workout in coming up with "Where No Man Has Gone Before."

I should also explain that even as Gene was priming Kandel and Peeples on the basic dramatic principles and character backgrounds of Star Trek, he was altering them daily. For example, he'd decided to blatantly defy NBC's "hide Spock" edict by allowing his Vulcan to come aboard the Enterprise as a first lieutenant, filling the ship's now-vacant second-in-command position. It is a position of far more importance and visibility than he's promised NBC's programming types, but it makes perfect sense dramatically and structurally.

At the same time, more exacting changes are being made. The captain's last name, for example, is being agonized over as if it were a matter of life and death. Heroic-sounding last names like Hannibal, Hamilton, Timber, Boone, Flagg, Drake and even Raintree are all considered but Kirk, of course, finally wins out. Also, new crew members are being written into the show's bible. First aboard is Mr. Sulu, who will function as the ship's biophysicist (he won't become helmsman and weapons officer until the actual series gets under way). George Takei recalls the series of events that conspired to land him the role.

I was living in New York and I was doing fairly well, because I'd been lucky enough to get a part in a play. It was a musical called *Fly Blackbird*, and it ran for almost six months. However, when the play closed I began really struggling. I got nothing, no jobs, no auditions, nothing. And when you're struggling, you do whatever you can to survive. So my roommate had an aunt that catered these posh parties in Sutton Place, and for unemployed actors, these things were great. You'd go in for one night, hang up jackets, serve some food, clean up and go home. They paid well, and I always used to bring home the leftovers as a kind of bonus.

At the same time, it was very hard for Asian actors to get cast in anything other than the role of a servant, and I'd made a vow to myself that I'd never play that sort of demeaning character. I felt like I had a real responsibility to try and fight that stereotype. In fact, in the middle of all this struggling, I actually turned down a role on Broadway because it was just another Oriental servant's role.

However, that night I was back there in Sutton Place, with my little black bow tie and my little white jacket, standing at the front door, accepting all of these fur jackets and lugging them up to the coat room. I was able to survive this paradox by telling myself, "This is not real. I'm *really* an actor." Y'know, I convinced myself that in real life I was just *pretending* to be a servant. At the same time, acting as a servant would have somehow seemed far more real, and far more degrading.

Still, as time passed, I began doing some live television, but because this was the early sixties, New York's television industry was drying up. With that in mind, when I landed a part in an episode of *Perry Mason* that was going to be shooting in Los

Angeles, I took the opportunity to move there. Shortly thereafter, I had my first interview for *Star Trek*.

At the time, I was represented by Freddie Shiamoto, the only Japanese-American agent that existed at that time. He called me, told me about the job, told me that it was a science fiction pilot and that it could lead to a running part and steady employment. That got me really excited. And whenever I really wanted a part, I would drive up to Griffith Park and run. Somehow that would put everything in perspective. So I went in and met Gene and read for him, and things seemed to go really well. This got me even more excited about the part, and as a result I started running myself to death, all the time hoping and praying that I'd gotten the job. Two days later, I've just come back from a run and I'm still hot and sweaty when my phone rings. It's Freddie, and he says, "We got it." I was thrilled. The next day I had to go down to the studio and meet with Bill Theiss, who needed my measurements, and while I was there, I remember, I got to meet Bruce Lee. He was standing outside the *Green Hornet* set, fooling around and going through a whole series of amazing kung fu moves. As I stood there watching him, I got really excited about working as an Asian-American actor in a role that wasn't at all stereotypical, and that might prove inspiring for people like us.

Jimmy Doohan was hired next, having been specifically recruited for his role by the pilot's director, James Goldstone. Goldstone had worked with Doohan in the past and knew of his uncanny mastery of many different accents. With that in mind, when Roddenberry expressed an interest in finding a crewman whose speech patterns would clearly represent the international makeup of the *Enterprise* crew, Goldstone immediately suggested Doohan. A meeting was arranged, Doohan ran through a solid half-dozen different accents, and Roddenberry picked Scottish and offered Jimmy the role. Shortly thereafter, an actor named Paul Fix was hired to play Dr. Mark Piper, who was a fairly ill-tempered and cantankerous foreshadowing of Dr. Leonard "Bones" McCoy.

As summer approached, Gene was putting the finishing touches on his script, as well as rewriting Stephen and Sam. Finally, after several weeks and dozens of drafts, all three scripts met with Gene's satisfaction. He sent them to be copied, then over to NBC, where Mort Werner and Grant

Tinker each read all three. The scripts were tight, action-packed, dramatic, exciting and not nearly as cerebral or philosophical as "The Cage." Gene's new script direction paid off handsomely, as NBC was quite pleased with not just one of the new scripts, but all of them. Finally, after some discussion, they'd decided that Peeples' "Where No Man Has Gone Before" would become pilot number two.

You know the story: Gary Lockwood guest-stars, playing Lieutenant Commander Gary Mitchell, an old and dear friend of Captain Kirk's, and because of some exposure to unknown radiation, Mitchell gains telekinetic superpowers and loses his sanity. And the situation intensifies to the point where Spock ends up saying, "You have to kill him, Captain, there is no alternative." And Kirk's saying, "I can't do that, he's my friend, I have to save him. I have to protect the ship. I've got to find a way out of this." Basically, Kirk's been put in a trap. The fates have conspired to lock him into a situation where his own sense of responsibility and duty demand that he destroy a friend. It was a very simple story, and the dilemma was very clear: What is Kirk going to do? It was powerful, exciting and full of human drama.

On top of all that, Gene and Sam Peeples had conspired to make sure that this pilot would simply wipe out the previous criticisms of "not enough action." "Where No Man Has Gone Before" was totally action-packed, with demigods blasting their enemies to bits and chases, avalanches, explosions, phaser fights and fisticuffs galore. Sally Kellerman guest-starred, and as you can imagine, she supplied *plenty* of sex appeal. All of these elements were consciously conceived and aimed at pleasing the network brass, but as we began production on July 21, 1965, we found that shooting would prove quite eventful—and a lot of fun to boot.

For example, toward the end of the pilot, there is a long fight sequence between me and Gary Lockwood, and we spent the better part of a morning shooting it. So Gary and I are battling and struggling and tumbling around the set, and the whole time we're going at it, Sally Kellerman is standing off to the side and doing her best to look worried about us for the cameras. Anyway, Lockwood and I are rolling around like a couple of maniacs, and we finally get to the big finish, where I'm supposed to come up with a mighty heave and toss Gary off me. We did all that pretty well and Gary landed perfectly at Sally's feet, but at exactly that moment his pants split open big-time, making the entire cast and crew fully aware of the fact that he wasn't wearing any underwear. So now all that is Gary Lockwood from the waist down is flapping in the breeze, and he looks up at the double-taking Sally and says, "Smile, you've just had your picture taken."

However, Sally isn't the least bit flustered by Gary's ad-lib, and instead of getting shocked or embarrassed, she gets even . . . more than even. She stands over Gary and even as he's saying, "Smile, you've just had your picture taken," she's wearing an absolutely wicked smile on her face. She then looks down, surveys Gary's . . . uh . . . situation and replies, "With that little brownie?" Gary goes boiled-lobster red, while over on the other side of the set I'm rolling, teary-eyed, breathless, laughing hysterically and pondering whether it might actually be physiologically possible to bust a gut.

I also remember that shortly after we'd all regained our composure, I was attacked by a mob and badly injured. You see, all over Hollywood, even today, large colonies of wasps are happily making their homes in the extremely high rafters and catwalks of unused soundstages. It's an ideal environment for the little bastards, and they will miss no opportunity to construct their homes in any suitably unoccupied space. Our set was no exception, and as we began our fifth day of shooting, we were all still blissfully ignorant of the fact that we were being watched.

Suddenly, however, as the heat of our lights drove the wasps into a sort of mass psychosis, an ominous buzzing became noticeable. A collective chill ran down our spines, and we all sort of searched the sky for a clue as to the unknown sound. Let me put it this way: If you've ever seen Alfred Hitchcock's *The Birds*, just simply erase the birds and substitute big black angry wasps. Same anxiety, same calm before the storm and ultimately the same sort of unprovoked attack.

Literally in midscene, as I exchanged lines with Sally Kellerman, they swarmed down kamikaze-style onto the stage, causing everything human within one hundred yards to panic. Enormous Teamster types, who generally talk tough and put up a ferocious front, suddenly dropped their cigarettes and coffee and took off, running and screaming like schoolgirls, beer bellies flapping as they sprinted. Sally and I, who were of course in the center of the wasp-attracting lighting devices, were at ground zero. We ducked, we covered, we ran, but neither of us made it out without getting hit. Sally took a couple of stings to the . . . um . . . let's just say "lower back," and I took a nasty hit to the left eye.

Exterminators came running in and, with atomizers blasting, committed their mass bugicide in a matter of minutes. Unfortunately, however, my eye had swollen up to softball-sized proportions. There was nothing we could do. I was sent home and, since this attack took place on a Friday, had the luxury of hiding out there until my eyeball once again appeared human. Actually, when Monday morning reared its ugly head and I reported back for work, my eye was still fairly swollen. For that reason, the next time you happen across "Where No Man Has Gone Before," look closely, and throughout the middle part of the show you'll plainly see the painful results of the attack.

I also remember that we shot this pilot episode *extremely* quickly, and I got the particulars from Bob Justman.

We shot the second pilot in only eight days. It was astounding to move so quickly, but we had to do it because Desilu was one cheap outfit. We had to finish within a certain amount of days or we'd end up over budget, and the studio had made it quite clear that they wouldn't be the least bit happy about that.

It got to the point where we were shooting about thirty setups each day, and on our last day of shooting, to avoid adding an extra day of production, we actually shot two days' worth of footage. I remember we were going crazy trying to finish on time.

At any rate, when the smoke had cleared, we finished shooting "Where No Man Has Gone Before" a day late and twelve thousand dollars over budget, and it was absolutely wonderful, crammed with a lot of the things that would go on to become the very best traits of the series. It was exciting, dramatic and although the *Enterprise* crew was running around in some godforsaken galaxy on some strange alien planet, the script never got carried away with technology or the science fiction aspects of the story line. In the end, "Where No Man Has Gone Before" was a story about people, and it was clear from the start that there was a certain chemistry beginning to form between these characters that could become extremely compelling over time. I felt that Spock and Kirk in particular shared a very interesting dynamic, and Leonard felt the same way.

> really thought that there was a chemistry between us that made a lot of sense. I didn't know where I was with Jeff Hunter. I was floundering when I was working with him. Jeff was playing Captain Pike as a very thoughtful, kind of worried, kind of angstridden, nice guy, thinking his way through a problem, and I, as Spock, couldn't find a space. He wasn't doing anything wrong, he was just playing the role the way he would play that particular role. Now, either because I couldn't get a handle on Spock or because the writers couldn't get a handle on the difference between Pike and Spock, Spock came off as sort of this weird guy out there who said and did what first officers do. "Sir, the guns are ready," whatever. Spock was not defined.
>
> But Pike didn't have the clarity or precision of character against which you could measure yourself. For lack of a better metaphor, on a bright sunny day, the shadows get very clear. On a gray day, it's hard to find the light switch.

We finished shooting "Where No Man Has Gone Before" in the midsummer of 1965. However, due to the fact that Gene Roddenberry was simultaneously producing two other television pilots for Desilu, there would be significant downtime prior to Star Trek's completion. Gene's first assignment was to write and produce the pilot episode of a police story entitled . . . Police Story. It was a fairly ordinary pilot, and is notable mainly in that it brought Gene into contact with several of the actors who'd ultimately become Enterprise crew members. Grace Lee Whitney, who would become Yeoman Rand in our first season, played the unlikely part of a police martial-arts instructor, but more importantly, DeForest Kelley continued his working relationship with Roddenberry by playing a rather crabby, easily annoyed criminologist who spends a lot of time in the police lab. Hmmm.

As soon as Police Story had wrapped, Gene began producing a rather terrible pilot entitled The Long Hunt of April Savage. Grim and deadly serious, this proposed Western series would have followed the exploits of a guntoting, revenge-seeking loner as he rode alone throughout the wide-open plains of the old West (a cowboy named "April"?). Take a look at the pilot episode's title, and you'll have a pretty good sense of the project's truly unpleasant tone. It was called "Home Is an Empty Grave," and as you might expect, this pilot came and went quietly, untouched by the networks.

By the time Thanksgiving had come and gone, Gene was once again working full-time on Star Trek, wading through the postproduction of "Where No Man Has Gone Before," and by the time we'd rung in the New Year of 1966 and shaken off the hangovers of the night before, the pilot was completed. Again the film was shipped off to NBC's New York head-quarters, and once more the network executives huddled around a film projector, screening Gene's final product.

Gene's second Star Trek pilot held its audience captive, exactly as his first one had, and it received an identically enormous round of applause upon its completion. However, this time the network types were so impressed by the action, adventure, special effects and explosions of the pilot that they completely overlooked the fact that the content of Gene's pilot was still quite a bit more substantial than network standard.

In short, they were thrilled by "Where No Man Has Gone Before," and within weeks NBC had officially added the program to their upcoming fall lineup. I got a call from my agent the next day telling me that Star Trek was a go, and I must tell you, I was thrilled. Thrilled with the victory, thrilled with the promise of steady work (no small prize for an actor) and thrilled that I was about to gain national exposure by working in such a quality vehicle. I made a quick congratulatory call to Roddenberry, then immediately celebrated by painting the town red, which in my case meant taking my daughters out for hot dogs and large Cokes. It was a day I'll never forget, and a day that officially began one of the most labor-intensive, backbreaking and happy periods of my life.

AMASSING THE TROOPS

This is absolutely, positively, never, never, never gonna work . . . it can't happen. No way, no how, no sir.

—TYPICAL BOB JUSTMAN

What do you mean, "it can't happen"? . . . We have until lunch.

—TYPICAL GENE RODDENBERRY

O nce NBC had officially green-lighted Star Trek, less than a week passed before the show was firing on all cylinders. Roddenberry, of course, began work immediately, and one of his first duties was also one of the most enjoyable. With his size 12-EEEs resting comfortably atop his desk blotter, Gene leaned back in his chair, tucked his telephone neatly between shoulder and ear and rang up many of the same talented crewpersons who'd suffered so nobly through the show's two pilots. Smiling, Gene informed his crew of Star Trek's thirteen-week commitment and then offered each member a full half-season of sixteen-hour days and hundred-hour workweeks. Surprisingly, Gene's offers were almost unanimously accepted.

However, even as Star Trek was amassing its talented crew of highly competent professionals, Roddenberry had become absolutely insistent upon taking sole responsibility for the first half-season's episodes.

RIGHT: **G**ENE, EARLY IN OUR FIRST SEASON, HOLDING ON TO THE SHOOTING SCRIPT FOR "MUDD'S WOMEN." (© 1993 PARAMOUNT PICTURES)
PRECEDING PAGE: TED CASSIDY AND SHERRY JACKSON, "BEAUTY AND THE BEAST." (© 1993 PARAMOUNT PICTURES)

At this early stage, with only "The Cage" and "Where No Man Has Gone Before" to illustrate the basic premise of Star Trek, Gene felt that there was no way anyone but himself could entirely understand his concept of what Star Trek should be.

With that in mind, Gene began personally attending to each creative detail of every Star Trek episode, refusing to let his vision be compromised so that he could partake of such luxuries as sleep, food or a personal life. Instead, Roddenberry forced himself to revise and often totally rewrite each of our first thirteen scripts, always demanding that each new draft fit the creative, structural and dramatic guidelines he'd established almost two years earlier.

Gene's meticulous sculpting of our story lines and well-reasoned script construction served to immediately and clearly define the relationships between the Enterprise crewmen. It also established the primary functions and inner workings of the U.S.S. Enterprise herself, and gracefully illustrated the basic foundation and backstory of the show.

As a result of Gene's painstaking attention to detail and carefully calculated script-doctoring, the Enterprise never just floated aimlessly in space. Instead, she immediately had a definite plan of action, a specific five-year mission. Furthermore, her crew was never simply portrayed as a random bunch of astronauts thrown together in a spaceship, as even our earliest scripts made it clear that the Enterprise was populated by a highly trained, specifically chosen and supremely talented corps of explorers.

Each crew member was quickly fleshed out as possessing his or her own unique personality, talents and specialized duties. However, Star Trek's initial scripts also made it clear that each member of the Enterprise crew was also functioning as part of a bigger picture, working and interacting for the common good, always amid the quasi-military procedures and ranking systems of "the Federation."

This attention to detail allowed Star Trek to hit the ground running, avoiding the kind of early-season confusion that often muddies a new series. It also permitted Star Trek's characters, stories and science fiction themes, no matter how fantastic, to somehow be perceived as credible and firmly grounded in reality. As a result, Star Trek, no matter how wild or incredible the plot, somehow managed to remain believable, thus fufilling Roddenberry's fondest wish.

Throughout this early burst of frenzied creativity, Gene also began attending to the budgetary, scheduling and production aspects of the show. Toward this end, he immediately started meeting with key personnel to communicate some of his earliest creative ideas, trusting that they would somehow be able to transform his dreams into a weekly hour-long television show. First and foremost among these trusted accomplices was associate producer Bob Justman.

If Gene was the Captain Kirk of the *Star Trek* production crew, boldly (and blindly) going where no producer had gone before, Bob Justman was his Scotty: brilliant, talented, immensely likable, and one of the most stubborn men ever born. To further illustrate the Montgomery Scott metaphor, I should explain that from day one through the end of the series, when presented with any unusual budgetary or production-oriented mandate, Bob's first response would almost certainly be along the lines of "There's no wa-a-ay, we need more time, we need more money. Our budget just can't handle that kind of pressure." Cementing the similarities between himself and *Star Trek*'s engineering miracle worker was the fact that after any given bitch session, Bob could ultimately be counted on to come through brilliantly.

Re-hired by Gene just one day after NBC had given him the official go-ahead, Bob immediately got to work juggling a budget that demanded that each episode of *Star Trek* cost no more than $193,500, less than one-third the total of the original pilot.

With his trusty adding machine crunching numbers with each pull of its handle, Bob mapped out a strategy. He found that to stay within budget each episode would have to be shot in just five days with precious little time for rehearsals or last-minute emergency shooting. Obviously, there was no way anyone was getting a day off until this thing was finished.

As Bob began penciling, erasing and swearing over his budget sheets, several more of *Star Trek*'s unsung heroes began reporting for duty. Matt Jefferies, now officially and deservedly credited as art director, was also meeting with Gene on a daily basis, and his first directive was to immediately begin sketching, revising, rethinking and redesigning the interiors of the *Enterprise*. Jefferies' goals in tuning up the ship would be to add more detail to the *Enterprise* bridge, transporter room and sick bay, and also to create several easily constructed, easily stored, reusable sets that could

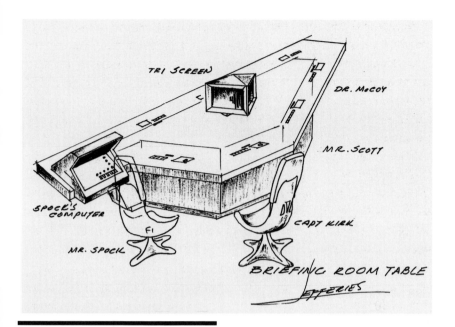

TRI SCREEN

DR. McCOY

MR. SCOTT

SPOCK'S COMPUTER

CAPT KIRK

MR. SPOCK

BRIEFING ROOM TABLE

JEFFERIES

A couple of Jefferies' early designs for the interiors of the *Enterprise*. (Courtesy Walter M. Jefferies)

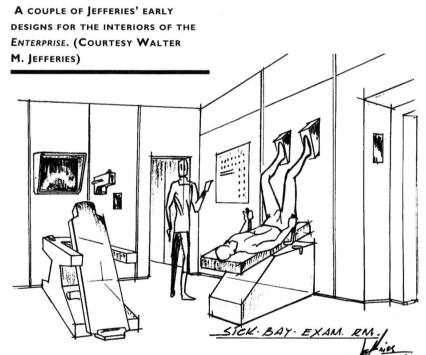

SICK·BAY·EXAM·RM·

Jeffries

be hauled out and set up on an as-needed basis. Kirk's quarters, the ship's recreation area, our briefing room and the engineering decks were generally constructed from these very "kits." As the weeks passed and our first shooting scripts began to filter in, Jefferies also got to work on his alien-planet-building chores.

Back on the lot as well was Bill Theiss. He'd already begun revising the uniforms worn by the *Enterprise* crew and roughing out ideas for the costumes worn by our first handful of guests. Even at this early stage of the game, there was no mistaking Bill's fondness for flashing female flesh, as he almost immediately pulled the pants off our female crew members, and replaced them with short (and I mean *short*) miniskirts. Even within our first handful of episodes, Theiss had begun his series-long habit of keeping our guest actresses chilly . . . and nearly naked. One look at Mudd's women or at the "dress" that Sherry Jackson's barely wearing in "What Are Little Girls Made Of?" proves this point quite nicely.

Meanwhile, a man named Irving Feinberg began his long and esteemed tenure as *Star Trek's* Propmaster of the Universe. Feinberg would quickly become unsurpassed at digging up all of our weirdest intergalactic props, but at this point in time he was still getting a lot of advice from Gene. For example, I can remember that when some live greenery Irving had rented

didn't look alien enough for Roddenberry, Gene remedied the situation by simply yanking the plants from their pots, smacking and shaking the dirt from their roots and turning them upside down. The plants' roots became "branches" and the result was messy, but quite effective.

Another instance of Roddenberry's tutelage of Feinberg occurred during the production of "The Man Trap." This show's storyline centered around a monstrous creature with an equally monstrous appetite for salt. As a result, the script called for several salt shakers, one of which Kirk would end up using as bait for the beast. With that in mind, Irving went out and scoured L.A. looking for the most futuristic shakers available. Finally he came up with several pairs of oddly shaped Swedish chrome-plated numbers, which Gene immediately rejected.

"For this story," Roddenberry explained, "the salt shakers have got to *look* like salt shakers or else nobody will get the point. But you know, these chrome jobs are really interesting. Let's use them as McCoy's operating instruments." As a result, De Kelley spent three seasons healing large numbers of injured crewpersons and aliens with medical tools far more suited to the kitchen than the surgical table.

With Gene's input, Irving quickly got a handle on the kind of props needed for *Star Trek*, and in short order he became a wizard at finding or

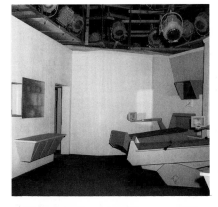

concocting whatever we needed. In fact, our *most* bizarre and unique *Star Trek* props quickly became known around the set as "Feinbergers," as in, "Oh, there's an alien dinner banquet in this episode, better get a nice assortment of Feinbergers."

Over in a workshop at Desilu, a man named Jim Rugg was hired to create all of *Star Trek*'s special effects, and he was already overwhelmed with responsibilities. Even at this early juncture, you could find Rugg working overtime building all of *Star Trek*'s weapons and gadgetry (communicators and tricorder included), as well as wiring all of the new and improved working panels aboard the *Enterprise*. In short, if it blinked, beeped, moved, lit up or even exploded, it was rigged by Jim Rugg.

Back in the office, Gene also hired a guy named John D. F. Black. Black came aboard as an associate producer, but unlike Bob Justman, he worked in a mainly creative capacity. During his tenure, he would write one terrific

OPPOSITE: **R**IGGING THE GADGETRY
AND WIRING OF THE *ENTERPRISE* SICK
BAY . . .
THIS PAGE: . . . AND THE BRIDGE.

episode of Star Trek ("The Naked Time"), but his main responsibility was to work with the show's freelance writers, guiding them through the creation of their scripts and then conferring with Roddenberry to make sure they were suitable and consistent in regard to Star Trek's creative guidelines. Black very quickly became a well-respected and well-liked member of the Star Trek staff, but he also became one of the first victims of Gene Roddenberry's practical jokes.

Pranks seem to spring up on every Hollywood set, and they serve to break the tension of long workdays and hectic schedules. Our Star Trek set was no exception, and one of the chief perpetrators was also the man in charge. In fact, Black had been on the job less than a week before Roddenberry unleashed his mischievous scheme.

The story begins to unfold as Black, who's sitting at his desk rewriting a script, hears a knock on his office door. "Who is it?" he calls out, still typing.

"It's me, Gene," says the oversized man who's already bounded into Black's office. "I have to run over to the set for a couple of hours, so I need to ask you a big favor."

"Sure, what is it?" says Black, who's still new on the job and eager to impress his boss.

"Well," whines Gene, "this friend of mine has a daughter who wants to be an actress, so I told him that she could come in and audition for us sometime. Anyway, she just called me. She's in the parking lot. She drove in from San Diego, and I can't just tell her to go away. Can you just let her read for you, then give her a polite brush-off?"

"Uh . . . yeah, sure," says Black.

"Great, thanks a million."

At this point, Roddenberry leaves Black's office, smiling. Black shrugs, then goes back to his script and continues working until he's interrupted by another knock. "Are you Mr. Black?" says the attractive blonde woman in the doorway.

"Um . . . yeah," says the pleasantly surprised Black.

"Mr. Roddenberry told me that you were the man who could get me a part in Star Trek," she says, extending her eye contact to an uncomfortable stare.

"Uhhh . . . that's true, but I should tell you, we don't really have a whole lot of roles available at this time."

"Hmmm," she says, taking off her left shoe. "Is that so?"

Off comes the right.

"Uhhhhhhhhhh . . . uh, yeah," says Black, who's now hunched over his typewriter, trying his best not to notice that she's now begun unbuttoning her dress.

"Well," she says, "maybe we can work something out. I really am good."

The dress now drops, revealing a bikini that would have made even Bill Theiss blush, and the "friend's daughter" now slowly begins working her way around the desk toward Black.

"Wait a . . . hold on . . . uh . . . whoa." Words have suddenly failed this particularly talented writer.

"I'm sure we can think of something," says the actress as she climbs into his lap.

Black's gone white, and as he gurgles, Roddenberry comes bursting through the office door, accompanied by me, Bob Justman and about a half-dozen other production crew types. We've all been tipped off by Roddenberry, and as a result we've been piled up just outside the door, listening to Black squirm and waiting for the best possible moment to bust him. Roddenberry shuffles through some phony paperwork as we enter.

"Hi, Bob, I got back early and I thought we all should have a meeting about . . . OH MY GOD!!!" he cries, screwing on his most mortified expression.

"Wait . . . uh, Gene, it's not . . . "

"Mr. Black, I don't know about your past, but this is *not* how we interview actresses on *this* show . . . your behavior shocks me, and I am deeply offended by your lack of professional decorum."

And now, as we're all trying our best not to laugh, the phone rings. Black picks it up and immediately recognizes the voice of his wife. "Hi, honey," she says pleasantly, "How's the new job?"

That's it. Black's eyes roll up into his head, he's ready to die and we just can't hold it any longer. Great guffaws begin bursting all over the room, and in no time this entire group of grown (if not entirely mature) men begins rolling with laughter. The scantily clad "friend's daughter," who's of course been hired by Roddenberry, then runs off to get dressed, giving Gene a thumbs-up as she exits. Black realizes that he's been set up, and begins yelling at us, swearing at us, laughing and tossing pencils at us

DOROTHY FONTANA'S FIRST *STAR TREK* CREATION . . . CHARLIE **X.** (© 1993 PARAMOUNT PICTURES)

from behind the desk. We scatter, slapping Gene on the back and congratulating him on a joke well done.

Black survived his opening-day prank, and over the course of the next several weeks, he and Roddenberry began screening prospective writers for the show. However, instead of just hiring veteran TV writers, they also contacted some rather well-known names from the world of literary science fiction, ultimately luring many of them to the show. Story meetings were then set up in which these writers would pitch their ideas for possible episodes, and Gene would then pick a favorite, hiring the writer to develop the agreed-upon rough idea into a detailed story outline of about a dozen pages. For this the writer would receive the whopping sum of $655. With this basic arrangement in mind, I asked Dorothy Fontana to relate some more specific examples of the process through which *Star Trek*'s earliest scripts were written.

When we got the news of Star Trek being picked up by the network, we didn't have a party or anything, we just had a quick drink in the office, and almost immediately Gene started getting writers in for stories. Already he had roughed out the basic ideas for a handful of scripts that he would write himself or assign to writers. Gene also asked me which story I'd like to write, and I chose "Charlie X."

But we also had some of the very best science fiction writers in the world coming in to pitch stories. Harlan Ellison came in, Jerome Bixby, Ted Sturgeon, Richard Matheson, Jerry Sohl, Robert Bloch, George Clayton Johnson, all of these were well-established science fiction writers who had come up with some great published stuff, as well as worked on shows like Outer Limits and Twilight Zone, so some of these guys had strong television credits, too.

Gene began by assigning a lot of those very early scripts to those writers with a science fiction background. At the time I was still manning the secretarial desk out front, so I'd sit in on the writer meetings whenever Gene wanted some notes taken. That's how I got to witness the process so many times.

Basically, a writer would come in and pitch a handful of rough ideas. One particular meeting that I remember quite well involved Paul and Margaret Schneider, who came in wanting to do a science fiction version of a theatrical movie that was quite popular at the time. It was a World War Two submarine drama entitled The Enemy Below. Specifically, it was about an American destroyer commander up on top, and a German submarine commander down below, and throughout the film they played this strategic game of cat and mouse, each trying to outmaneuver and ultimately destroy the other. As an added dramatic element, the two captains would communicate over the radio but never see one another until the very end of the film.

They wanted to take this basic idea and translate it into science fiction terms with Kirk substituted for the destroyer captain and the Enterprise substituted for the ship. On the other side, the German submarine became a Romulan ship. And I can remember that Gene liked the idea, but he didn't want it to be exactly patterned after the movie. Instead, he felt that the idea of two captains, both honorable men, both fighting for what they perceived to be right in a disagreement over the Neutral Zone, should pro-

REHEARSING FOR **"B**ALANCE OF
TERROR.**" N**OTE THE UNVULCANLY
VICE TUCKED AWAY IN **L**EONARD'S
LEFT HAND. (© 1993 **P**ARAMOUNT
PICTURES)

vide the real basis of the story.
The human drama within this
battle of wits and will was what
really intrigued him. And through
the give-and-take of the meeting,
the rough idea was hammered
out and provided with a basic beginning, middle and end. The
general flow and arc was in place. This meeting provided the basis
for "Balance of Terror," which turned out to be one of our very best
episodes, and it's fairly illustrative in regard to the process by
which Star Trek's basic story ideas would evolve.

In a week or two the writer's ten-to-twelve page story would arrive, and
Gene, John D. F. Black and Bob Justman would all comment upon the feasibility and potential of the project. A round-robin of memos on the subject began at this point, with the circle of correspondents expanding to
include Matt Jefferies, who'd be on the lookout for proposed sets that
might be unbuildable, unaffordable, unable to fit within the confines of
Desilu's Stage 10 or just plain unphotogenic.

Bill Theiss would also give it a once-over, trying to get an early warning
as to whether any very unusual or difficult wardrobe requirements might

be involved. Irving Feinberg would take a similar look, trying to get a jump on propping the show, and Freddie Phillips would scan it, too, just in case there were any one-eyed purple furry aliens or equally labor-intensive makeup jobs lurking within its pages.

All of these guys would offer comments as to the general feasibility of the script, and then the original trio would decide (though Gene would have final say) on whether to move forward into script form, ask for a major revision or simply give up on the story altogether. Once the basic story had been approved, the writer would go off and spend the next several weeks hammering out the first draft of his full-blown script. When that was complete, it would be handed in, run through the mimeo machines, read by Roddenberry, Black and Justman, then ultimately discussed in a whole new round of interoffice memos.

Black and Roddenberry would generally pick over character motivation, dialogue and creative and dramatic punch, but Justman was equally important in the molding of Star Trek's scripts, in that he would scrutinize each teleplay from production and budgetary standpoints, looking out for the kind of script elements that could ultimately blow up the show's budget or cause delays in shooting. Oversized casts and sets and expensive special effects were among his most frequently flagged potential problems.

Justman would also ensure that each new script was written within the confines of Star Trek's structural format, checking to see whether the scenes allowed for the insertion of commercial breaks and whether the script was overly long or short.

After the three men had each read the first draft, Black would meet with the writer to discuss the teleplay and ask for specific revisions. Once those changes had been completed, the writer would get paid the remainder of his fee, which in 1966 totaled about four thousand dollars. Any further revisions or rewrites would be done by Black or, more likely, Roddenberry.

By the time June had arrived, a handful of Star Trek's original scripts had reached second-draft status, and as such they were currently being re-revised by Gene and John. However, though these freelance scripts had now become "in-house rewrites," they were nonetheless still subjected to the unmerciful wrath of Bob. Justman would read each revision of every script, always keeping an eye out for potential production difficulties, timing problems and visual ideas that he felt wouldn't translate well onto the small screen. Once he'd finished, Justman would write out a long, no-holds-barred memo detailing his numerous thoughts. Some examples of Bob's typical suggestions follow, all in regard to the various drafts of the script for our fifth production, "The Enemy Within."

Desilu Productions Inc.
To: *John D. F. Black*
From: *Bob Justman*
Date: *April 22, 1966*
Subject: STAR TREK

"THE ENEMY WITHIN"
by RICHARD MATHESON

Firstly, I would like to state that I feel there are too many speaking parts and extras in this story. If there were a great need for many speaking parts, I would understand it, but this is not the case. Also, how about letting some of our regulars have some of the speaking parts that are necessary to the story? Such as SULU and SCOTT.

On the first page of the teaser, do we need to establish 16 crew members down on the surface of the planet? Five lives are important too. Sixteen lives are more than I feel we can afford for this segment.

I feel the teaser is too long.

On page 14, KIRK'S DOUBLE looks at JANICE'S wristwatch. Does she wear a TIMEX or an INGERSOL? Is it set to Eastern time, or Pacific?

On Page 17 SPOCK finds the storage room door ajar. When is a door not a door? When it's ajar. However, our doors on board the Enterprise are never ajar. They are always closed or open.

On Page 45, McCOY'S second speech is schmucko. I don't think "half of KIRK'S cellular structure is missing" or "half his blood," I just think the poor fella is emotionally deprived.

I refer you to the bottom of page 45 and the top of page 46. Boy, is our CAPTAIN KIRK heroic? You bet he is!!

In scene 23, we find KIRK throwing cold water on his face. We have no provision for a bathroom or fire hydrant in Kirk's quarters.

Who is LT. MARSHALL? He's not listed in the cast list at the beginning of the script. Who is LT. DAY? Who is LT. KILEY? Who stole my heart away? Who made me dream all day? Dreams I know can never come true.

Someday I hope to be able to write memos that are full of sweetness, and light, and optimism, and faith and hope and charity and all the other chozzerai [YIDDISH FOR "CRAP"] that I have been unable to corral up to now. I really do like to be a happy individual. Maybe I'm in the wrong business? Maybe I'll just raise chickens.

Regards.

Upon receipt of Bob's troubleshooting memo, Gene would make yet another round of changes, reconfiguring the script, tearing it apart creatively and structurally. Then, revising like a man possessed, Gene would clobber the keys until he felt confident enough to declare that the script had reached "final draft" status.

Meanwhile, throughout this period of repeated script revision, thousands of man-hours were being spent preparing to shoot this long-awaited script. For example, as soon as Matt Jefferies had finished reading any story outline, he'd immediately begin to visualize the specialized sets that the particular episode would demand. He'd then spend some time doodling, trying out a number of different ideas. When he'd settled on a favorite, he'd draw up some preliminary sketches and meet with Roddenberry, Justman and the upcoming episode's director, soaking up their feedback and, with luck, their approvals.

Once his sketches had been authorized, Jefferies would hit the drafting table, creating detailed blueprints and construction plans. He'd then meet with the show's construction crew, and after a quick review, they'd begin building. Next, even as the first nails were being whacked into place, Matt would confer with the show's set decorators and discuss the necessary furnishings and dressings (drapes, rugs, plants, etc.) for each new set.

Once Jefferies had finished describing the basic "look" he was after, it was up to our set decorators to go out and dig up the appropriate trap-

EXT. TEMPLE - CRATER'S CAMP
THE MAN TRAP
#06

ANDROID LABORATORY
"WHAT LITTLE GIRLS ARE MADE OF"
#10

+20²
+17²
+14² (CRANE)
+10²
+4²
+2² - 3²
paint block
STG FLR.
INT. CAVERN
"WHAT LITTLE GIRLS ARE MADE OF"
#10

SUBTERRANEAN CHAMBER
"RETURN of the ARCHONS"
#22

pings. This is a tough job on *any* series, but when you take into consideration the fact that *Star Trek* created whole new sets every week, that our
budget was minuscule and that each of these sets had to believably reflect
the premise that we were a couple hundred million light-years away from
the nearest furniture store, it became a giant headache.

Throughout our first season, this task was taken care of by two guys
named Carl Biddiscombe and Marvin March, who'd spend the better part
of each day digging through musty thrift shops, plastic mills, army surplus
warehouses, local junkyards and the entire Desilu lot in search of the
unusual appointments that our sets demanded. Further, on the frequent
occasions when all of those particular channels had proven fruitless, it
was not at all uncommon to find John and his crew rummaging through
the Desilu trash bins, looking for anything that might prove useful. Odd
plywood shapes that the carpenters on other shows might have thrown
out, castoff sheet-metal remnants, discarded fabric remainders and even
the large cardboard tubes that this fabric came wrapped around were all

SCALE: ¼" = 1'·0"

RUINS —
CRATERS CAMP
6149-6

frequently recycled for our sets and considered by these guys as prized buried treasures. I mean, I can remember standing around the studio lot when all of a sudden you'd hear this loud, gleeful yelp rising up out of a Desilu Dumpster. If you were to look inside the thing, you'd find Biddiscombe, March and a couple of assistants smiling and congratulating one another as if they'd struck gold instead of garbage.

"Alright! Paint those whatchamacallits purple!" March would bellow. "We'll hang 'em on the wall and make them look like . . . something. Doesn't matter *what* they are, so long as they look weird."

Still, as this crew of grown, intelligent men cavorted about the oversized Dumpsters of Desilu, it was obvious that they were all having a pretty good time, and that every one of them was being really creative and looking for interesting ways to make mundane castoffs look futuristic. Their level of enthusiasm was extremely high, and they really seemed to enjoy solving problems such as "What do Romulans sit on?" and "What would you find on the walls of Kirk's quarters?"

As a footnote, I should add that throughout our first season, these guys were also responsible for operating the "automatic pocket doors" of the U.S.S. *Enterprise*. Standing behind the walls of our set, with one member of the crew on either side of the doorway, these guys would be given one cue to open the door and another to close it. Sounds simple, but my crooked nose will provide evidence of the fact that we often screwed it up.

As the sets were beginning to take shape, Bill Theiss and his crew could generally be found running around the lot, costuming anything and everything that moved. This was due to several factors. First, every *Star Trek* script was populated with a rather large contingent of guest characters, each of whom needed at least one, and often several, custom-made costumes. Since none of these costumes could be rented from traditional wardrobe houses or found within the warehouse at Desilu, practically every piece of clothing that ever walked across our sets was tailored by Bill Theiss or one of his assistants.

Adding to the hectic pace of our wardrobe department was the fact that the *Enterprise* always seemed full of crewmen who'd show up for one episode, then disappear back into the bowels of the ship, never to be seen or heard from again. Of course, our "red shirts" also racked up an extremely high mortality rate.

ABOVE: A PERFECT EXAMPLE OF BILL
THEISS'S CREATIVE TALENTS IS WORN
BY LESLIE PARRISH IN "WHO MOURNS
FOR ADONAIS?" HER GOWN WAS
STUNNING, BUT SO SKIMPY THAT IT
HAD TO BE ATTACHED TO HER . . .
UPPER HALF WITH GENEROUS
HELPINGS OF DOUBLE-FACED TAPE. AS
A RESULT, SHE WOULD LOSE CHUNKS
OF SKIN WITH EACH COSTUME
CHANGE. RIGHT: ALSO, MODESTY
FORCED LESLIE TO REHEARSE HER
ENTIRE EPISODE WHILE WEARING THIS
RATHER RATTY BATHROBE. (© 1993
PARAMOUNT PICTURES)

As a topper, it would become quickly apparent that our *Enterprise* uniforms shrank with every dry cleaning. As a result, by the time any of our pullovers or miniskirts had gone through the laundry two or three times, they'd reached unwearable status. With that in mind, the entire stockpile of crew member uniforms that Bill had been so diligently compiling since day one would become completely useless by the end of our first two weeks of shooting. This basically doubled the workload for Theiss and his crew throughout *Star Trek*'s first season.

For all of these reasons, the Theiss *work*shop often looked more like a *sweat*shop, with an ever-present row of overworked seamstresses hunched over sewing machines, bobbins bobbing madly, while they masterfully (albeit thanklessly) created costumes one after another after another. Still, despite the insanity of the surroundings, Theiss and his crew managed to always stay just slightly ahead of their deadlines.

Freddie Phillips had by now taken up permanent residence in the makeup room, and Spock's ears had become the least of his worries. With the ears having been refined and perfected been during "The Cage," their application was now just a rather time-consuming science. For that reason, as the weeks passed and we started shooting, Leonard always had first call in the makeup chair.

By about six A.M., Leonard had already reported for work and could generally be found relaxing in Freddie's barber chair, stinking up the makeup room with his fried-egg sandwiches while Phillips proceeded to turn him into a Vulcan. First Freddie would shave off the tips of Leonard's eyebrows, leaving just the inner third on each side. Then he would whip out his trusty spool of rolled yak hair (yes, I did indeed say "yak hair") and glue the upswept edges of Spock's brows into place. The ears would go on next, followed by a quick dusting of pancake and a final once-over in the mirror. When the look had met with Leonard's approval, Freddie would move on to the rest of us.

Though it generally took about an hour to do Leonard's makeup, the rest of us actors could each be in and out of the chair in about ten minutes. This was of course due to the much more elaborate cosmetological processes behind creating Spock, and it's also due to the fact that Leonard was much uglier than the rest of us. However, at *this* early stage of

Six a.m., Leonard reports to the makeup room. (© 1993 Paramount Pictures)

the game, Phillips was still basically unpacking, as well as looking over our first few scripts and formulating some theories in regard to one of our earliest and most gruesome guest characters.

While skimming through an early draft of the script for "What Are Little Girls Made Of?" Freddie couldn't help but notice that one of the main characters was going to be a menacing, seven-foot-tall android. This intrigued Phillips, and when Ted Cassidy (who had just finished playing Lurch on *The Addams Family*) was cast in the role, Freddie called him, asking that he come in for some makeup tests.

Several days later, Cassidy sat down in Phillips' undersized makeup chair and allowed the artist to transform him from a smiling young actor into an evil, hulking monster. First Freddie covered Ted's head with a latex skinhead wig; then he applied a sort of grayish-green base coat over Cassidy's entire face. Once all that was done, Phillips darkened the area around each of the actor's eyes and employed a black grease pencil to sharpen the angles of Ted's cheekbones, forehead and chin. The end result was quite frightening and really served to drain all the humanity from Cassidy's face. In short, he looked like an android.

Phillips then ushered his newly created android over to Bill Theiss, who had the giant try on a possible costume. Once the transformation was complete and Cassidy was looming ominously about the wardrobe trailer in full regalia, the pair led the actor to Roddenberry's office hoping to attain Gene's approval on their work, or to at least just scare the hell out of him.

I was in Gene's office at the time, and while we were both a bit unnerved at first sight by this towering monster, Gene was nonetheless thrilled with his android. After offering up a couple of minor suggestions, he gave Phillips and Theiss the okay they wanted, and then talked all four of us into helping him play another one of his practical jokes.

Roddenberry explained that for weeks an extremely persistent local tailor had been making the rounds of the lot, trying to talk anyone who'd listen into buying one of his suits. I was familiar with this guy because he'd called *me* on several occasions, and he'd also been badgering a lot of the cast and crew. As it turns out, on this particular occasion he had finally succeeded in getting Gene to grant him a quick appointment. In fact, he was on his way up when Bill, Freddie and the hulking demonic android named Ted came knocking. That's when the light bulb blinked on over Gene's head, and he was struck with a wicked but brilliant idea.

Flash forward half a minute, and you'll find that Gene, Bill Theiss, Freddie, Bob Justman and I are all huddled outside the side door of Gene's office, giggling . . . literally giggling. The reason behind our silliness could be found just fifteen feet away, because there, with his feet up on Gene's desk and Gene's phone at his ear, sat this seven-foot-tall bald green creature that Bill and Freddie had created, and that Ted Cassidy was now bringing to life wonderfully, pretending that he was Roddenberry.

Cassidy was brilliant in the role, yammering machine-gun style into the phone and saying things like, "Babe, we need thirty K added to the special-effects budget or the Enterprise ain't gonna fly . . . comprende, compadre?"

Now, at precisely this moment the brave little tailor with the obnoxious little personality is nearing Gene's door. Dorothy Fontana intercoms the inner office and Cassidy, as Roddenberry, says, "Yeah, yeah, let him in." The doorknob turns, the door opens up and this suit-hawking salesman's come face-to-face with a monster. Cassidy now raises one finger at the guy and continues talking into the phone, milking this performance with everything he's got. "Is that gross or net?" he demands, adding, "Bounce the above-the-line by me one more time, will ya, babe?"

By now, of course, you'd expect that this tailor would have run screaming through the office walls, complete with full Bugs Bunny flourish. But that was not the case. Instead, having finally gotten his foot into the door, and with dreams of a "big and tall" (and green) sale rolling around in his head, the tailor was not about to be denied. And then, right in front of a hulking seven-foot-tall monster, he launches into, "My friend, I'd like to make you an offer that sounds too good to be true . . . one suit, two pair of pants . . . forty-nine dollars!"

Upon hearing that, Gene, Freddie, Bill, Bob and I explode in laughter, and we bound through the office door (I did a lot of hiding behind office doors, didn't I?) loudly yukking it up as we come stumbling, teary-eyed, into the room. The salesguy immediately figures out the joke, but instead of being embarrassed or angry, he remarkably, and without a moment's hesitation, starts trying to sell cheap suits to all six of us.

Guilt-ridden over the prank, Gene and I each bought some really ugly plaid pants.

By April 1966, the *Star Trek* crew had completely taken over most of Desilu's "Gower Street" lot (which had housed *I Love Lucy* years earlier) and taken up fairly permanent residence on its Stages 9 and 10. Stage 9 was crammed with the entire innards of the *Enterprise*, and 10 would ultimately house every alien planet we'd ever visit.

At the same time, the cast of the *Enterprise* was rapidly falling into place. Leonard and I were both set, and Roddenberry, along with Joe D'Agosta, who finally left his job at Fox to officially join the series as our casting director, was just about to fill the roles of some new and/or redesigned characters.

Their first priority was to find an actor to fill the role of Dr. Leonard "Bones" McCoy, third in a string of *Enterprise* doctors. John Hoyt, who played the doctor in the first pilot, got axed by the network, and Paul Fix, who took the job in "Where No Man Has Gone Before," was not invited back. I asked Dorothy Fontana to shed some light on the reasoning behind the cast and character changes.

Gene didn't like Paul Fix all that well, and he felt there was a certain vitality missing from the character. He also wanted to make the doctor a little bit younger, a little bit less of the "wise old man" counseling and talking down to the ship's captain. So the doctor became more of a contemporary.

At this point, De Kelley, having turned down the role of Spock in the first pilot, got embroiled in the long, strange series of events that would ultimately make him a doctor. Kelley explains:

Gene and I had worked together on *333 Montgomery*, but of course it failed. It did not sell. And time passed, and I started doing some more television stuff, but Gene and I stayed in touch. In fact, when he began work on the second *Star Trek* pilot, he offered me the role of the doctor, but the network had turned me down because, and it sounds funny in retrospect, they couldn't see me as a doctor. And one day, several weeks after I'd been dumped by the network, I came by Gene's office, and he gave me another script and said, "Read this, and see how you'd feel about playing the criminologist."

It was a pilot script, and it was called *Police Story*. This was not the anthology show, this predated that by fifteen years at least, and it was Gene's original concept. So I read it, liked it and I ended up playing this rather cranky, cantankerous criminologist.

We shot our pilot about a month after you guys had wrapped "Where No Man Has Gone Before," and after several more weeks had passed, I called Gene to see if he'd gotten any word about whether or not this thing might sell. Gene picked up the phone and I'd barely said hello when he started yelling "De! De! De! I'm so happy you called! The network just saw you in *Police Story* and now they want you for the *Star Trek* doctor." So I said "Well, wait, what about *Police Story*?" and he said, "They haven't decided yet." So I actually signed two contracts, one for *Police Story* and one for *Star Trek*. And if both had sold, Gene was going to let me do both of them at the same time. I was going to be the first person ever to appear in two television series at one time.

Jimmy Doohan and George Takei were next aboard. Both men had been in "Where No Man Has Gone Before" and they had both impressed Roddenberry to the extent that he expanded their respective characters, Scotty and Sulu. Nichelle Nichols also earned a spot in the *Enterprise* crew by impressing Roddenberry with a previous appearance. Hers, however, dated all the way back to *The Lieutenant*. Remembering Nichelle's particularly strong performance, Gene created Uhura with her in mind. In fact, over the next several weeks, they'd work together in fleshing out the character. Nichelle explains:

Gene's original dream was to have a cast of seven and tell their stories on a weekly basis. With that in mind, he and I would get together as often as possible to discuss the ins and outs of my character. I mean all through our first season, we'd sit for hours on end, talking about Uhura's life. I remember we came up with the idea that she'd come from a place called the United States of Africa, that her people had been of the Bantu nation and that her native tongue was Swahili. All of this really helped him in terms of writing for the character, and it certainly helped me to play her.

By late May, Roddenberry was still pounding away furiously at the type-writer, but with his cast and creative personnel in place, and with a sizable stack of scripts that were nearing completion, Gene approached our first days of shooting with a secure and confident feeling that the production was running quite smoothly, and that the most hectic period of his life would soon be behind him.

Boy, was he wrong.

ON THE SET
LIGHTS, CAMERA AND PLENTY OF ACTION

On May 24, 1966, we officially began filming our first episode, "The Corbomite Maneuver." This show began as an easy-shooting, uncomplicated script that found the Enterprise threatened with destruction by Balok, the ill-tempered (not to mention ugly) commander of a superior alien vessel called the Fesarius. The bulk of the show is then spent almost entirely on the Enterprise bridge as Kirk converses with Balok and attempts to bluff his way out of the situation. We couldn't have asked for an easier maiden voyage, and for that reason it was hoped that this simple, self-contained story would allow us a chance to ease ourselves into the rigors of weekly shooting. With no large action or on-location scenes to worry about and no major costume changes or unusual prop requirements, "The Corbomite Maneuver" allowed all of us a basic primer in shooting our weekly episodic epics.

In fact, this introductory episode was so simply produced that in shooting the famous scene in which an Enterprise landing party beams aboard the Fesarius and realizes that the superbeing Balok is in fact a harmless, childlike being, we didn't even bother building a Fesarius set. Instead, throughout the scene, as Kirk befriends the little green supergenius and partakes of Trania (which was actually disgusting, warm, food-colored apricot juice . . . a subpar

KIRK MEETS THE REAL BALOK. (© 1993 PARAMOUNT PICTURES) PRECEDING PAGE: PUBLICITY STILL, TAKEN JUST AS WE WERE BEGINNING PRODUCTION. (© 1993 PARAMOUNT PICTURES)

"Feinberger"), we were all just standing around the *Enterprise* briefing room, which had been emptied of props and draped with some shimmering blue cloth to suggest a completely different interior.

Thanks to the simplicity of this inaugural production, our first few days of shooting came off without a hitch—for most of us. Nichelle Nichols, however, had an *extremely* rough week, and her tale of woe begins on her first morning on the job. She arrives at the studio, gets made up and into wardrobe, then takes a quick walk around the set, where she's immediately approached by a large man in jodhpurs and a leather cap. The man says nothing as he saunters up to Nichelle; he then reaches out with his large left hand, gives her face several quick squeezes and says, "Oh . . . look at that beautiful skin, look at those beautiful eyes. I think I am going to do some *great* things with you!" Nichelle recalls:

He came swaggering over to me, staring at me, and I could feel his eyes upon me. Then, as he squeezed my face, he sat down next to me, getting very close, and looking into my eyes. So now I'm going to punch him in his rather considerable gut, but at the same time, I was worried that maybe he was one of the producers or something, so I figured it probably wouldn't be such a good idea to slug him.

Instead, when he said, "I'm going to do great things with you," I just made a face and said, "Yeah, you just try it." And the guy then sort of saunters on out. A couple of minutes go by, and now I notice that Joe Sargent, our, director, is huddled up with this face-squeezer, discussing something. Once they'd finished talking, this guy starts lighting the next scene.

He's saying, "Okay, give me a nice soft fill from the left," and "I'll need a bit more light over here." . . . And then it hits me. This guy who's been squeezing my face isn't a sleazeball after all . . . he's our cinematographer. And when he said, "I'm going to do great things with you," he wasn't speaking sexually, he just meant that he was going to make me look good on camera. My fear went away, and I just started laughing at myself.

The face-squeezer's name was Jerry Finnerman, and while he had worked as our camera operator on *Star Trek*'s first pilot, he'd now been promoted and was rapidly proving himself to be an absolutely brilliant cinematographer. He was responsible for the photographic and lighting techniques for almost all of the seventy-nine original *Star Treks*, and though he never squeezed *my* face, he did manage to "do great things" with the rest of us E*nterprise* crewpersons, too.

Nichelle had now survived day one, but she was just about to encounter the horrors of day two. She recalls:

At the time I was driving this old car, and on my second day on the job, I actually had an accident on the way to the studio. And I ended up with a big split lip, a busted knee and a bruised right ankle. At the scene of the accident, I had nŏ makeup on, and my hair was in curlers and falling all down into my face, I had blood coming out of my mouth, so that when the cops called the studio and told them that I'd been in an accident, I freaked. Not so much because I was embarrassed to have been in an accident, but because I was new on the job, insecure and embarrassed to be seen looking as unkempt as I appeared.

Now the studio tells the cops that they'll send someone out to get me, and I take the opportunity to hop into the back seat of my smashed car and pull myself together. There was no way I was going to miss the day's shooting. Luckily, I had planned on going out after work that evening. I had a dinner date, and so I had my big beautiful tan bag with me, which was filled with my makeup and hair stuff, and brushes and combs and perfume, you name it.

While Nichelle's in the back seat primping, the paramedics come racing in, with sirens blaring and red lights flashing. They then sprint

NICHELLE, HEAVILY MADE UP BUT STILL BEARING THE AFTEREFFECTS OF HER ACCIDENT. (© 1993 PARAMOUNT PICTURES)

out of their van yelling, "Where is she? WHERE IS SHE? Where is the injured party?" The policeman in charge of the accident scene now points over at Nichelle's rather crumpled car and says, "She's in the back seat, and she's bleeding out of her mouth." So now, while visions of massive internal injuries and severe hemorrhaging dance in their heads, the paramedics race toward what's left of this car thinking, "Oh, this poor woman, she MUST be dead." However, by the time they get over to Nichelle, she's finished making herself presentable, and in trying to appear capable of going back to work, she's now standing next to a crushed left fender and trying her best to smile.

"Hi, guys," I said to them, and they were like, "Not now, lady, there's a severely injured woman in the back of this car!" I literally had to convince them that I was the *severely injured woman* they were looking for.

Once that was done, they dragged me to the Santa Monica Hospital emergency room and patched me up. I can still remember the doctor. He was this cute little guy, and he's doing this whole comedy schtick for me while I bleed. He's going, "Ahhh, you're so lucky. You got a nice Jewish doctor, and I just got back from Mexico, so I'm calm, relaxed, and sharp as a tack. When I'm done with you you're not gonna feel *good*, you're gonna feel *great*! I'm gonna fix you up so good, you're going to be better than new."

So now while he's joking, he's stitching up my lip, he's giving me shots, he's fixing my knee and when he's finished, he says, "Now listen to me. Go home. Lie down. Go to bed, because when this stuff kicks in, you're really gonna feel it." And I of course said, "Okay, doctor, anything you say," but inside I was thinking, "Gee, with the shots and all, I actually don't feel all that bad. . . . I'm going to work."

So I had the runner that came over from the studio drive me back to the set, and I just told everybody that I was fine, and that my lip had swollen up because of a little bee sting. I was able to fool pretty much everybody with my story, so I got into costume, touched up my makeup and headed for the *Enterprise* bridge set, which is where we were shooting that day. And now Bill and Leonard and George all take their places and man their stations. And if you'll remember, Uhura's station is slightly above everyone else's, up a stair and behind a railing, and I'd just about settled into my station when I notice that my eyeballs are, quite involuntarily, starting to roll up into my head. My vision is starting to blur, I'm starting to slump over Uhura's equipment and I realize, "I'm fainting." And now I should explain that all my life I've fainted in slow motion, and by that I mean as I'm actually passing out, the things around me invariably appear to be moving in slow motion. So now, all around me, and appearing as if they're moving at a snail's pace, people are turning toward me, concerned and frightened by my obvious problem. And I can remember Bill yelling, "Oh my God, Nichelle!" and running toward me, in slow motion, of course. And now some production type yells out, "Bill, is she alright?" and Bill yells back, "She's okay, she didn't hurt herself." Then this idiot yells something like, "Oh, good, then we can move on." To which Bill replies, "What, are you kidding? To hell with moving on," and he literally picked me up, took me to my dressing room, got me dressed and then drove me home.

And at this point in time, Bill was driving this amazing Stingray. I had never seen it before, and I can remember that when I hobbled out to the parking lot with Bill and realized that this was *his* Stingray, and that I was going to be driven home in this car, I made some overmedicated comment like, "That is so-o-o-o-o-o fine. When I get to know you better I'm going to ask for a ride in this Stingray. It's BAD, you know."

So now I pour Nichelle into the car, seat-belt her in and it's obvious that she's *really* out of it, just barely aware of her life. I then drive over to her house, which was on the corner of Jefferson and La Brea, and park the car. Now, as I'm getting out of the car, I can see her fumbling around, trying to unbuckle her seat belt and open her door. So of course, I panic, because if she gets that belt undone and opens that door, she's going to just plop out headfirst onto the sidewalk, and it's going to be my fault.

"Nichelle!!" I holler, hoping she'll sit still. "Stay right where you are! Don't move, it's okay. I'll get you now! Don't try to get up by yourself!" And all the while I'm yelling, I'm running around to her side of the car. By the time I got to her, she'd gotten the door open, but luckily she was still too woozy to work her seat-belt buckle. So now I had to sort of reach inside the car and lift Nichelle out of her seat. I get her vertical, she throws her arms around my neck and I'm trying my best to hold her up as we wobble toward the front door. Nichelle recalls:

By now my neighbors have come out to stare, but at this point I'm just too stoned to be embarrassed. We make it to the top of my pathway, Bill carries me up the front steps, raps on the aluminum storm, and watches as my eight-year-old son yanks open the inner door, sees me in my condition and finds this strange man carrying me. My son then makes the meanest, nastiest face he can muster and yells at Bill, "What the HELL have you done to my MOTHER?!?!?!"

So now Bill's trying not to laugh, and he's fumphering around going, "No, no, you don't understand. She's gonna be okay, really, I haven't done anything to her. My name's Bill, I work with your mommy. She'll be just fine." And all through this, I'm still sort of out of it and hearing the conversation as if I'm far away, y'know? But through it all, I'm smiling, even laughing, because this was the beginning of a real relationship.

Ever the trooper, Nichelle was back at work the next morning, and as always, she was bright-eyed, beautiful and in complete control, delivering a splendid and thoroughly professional performance. I can remember being deeply impressed that she'd risen so far above and beyond the call of duty for the good of the show.

Actually, while we're on the subject of impressive devotion to duty, I should take a moment and introduce you to the finest film crew ever assembled, Star Trek's gang of forty. These guys were simply unbelievable, routinely working through our long, hard, sweaty hours of shooting with supreme competence and unshakable good humor. They seemed to be constantly in motion, dashing about our sets in all directions, consistently running two steps ahead of our breakneck shooting pace. Their efficiency seems all the more remarkable in that these guys were almost always dealing with untried, uncomfortable and unusual shooting situations. There was nothing standard about Star Trek's status quo.

Each of our directors had his own distinctive visual style, but no matter who was calling the shots, every Star Trek episode was prepared and shot in a similar fashion. By that I mean that the director of any given episode would be allowed one week's preproduction (preparation) and six days of shooting. No more, no less. With that in mind, during the preproduction week, our directors would come in cold, reading the script for the first time on Monday morning. Once they'd reached the big finish, it was time to get busy . . . really busy.

At the top of their "things to do" list was casting, and before the morning was over they'd have already come knocking on Joe D'Agosta's office door. With Roddenberry and Bob Justman at his side, the episode's director would throw out some thoughts on what he felt the week's guest characters should look like. The four men would then inevitably kick around some alternative ideas, argue a bit and ultimately come to some sort of collective conclusion as to the look of each new character.

As D'Agosta began contacting talent agencies, looking for suitable actors, the meeting would break up, and our director would spend the next several days knee-deep in preparations regarding the episode's sets, props, special effects and lighting requirements. While he was doing all of that, he'd also find time to meet with Bob Justman, breaking down the script (which by now he'd read at least twenty times) and putting together a shooting schedule designed to maximize efficiency and minimize delays.

Toward the end of the week, Roddenberry, Justman, D'Agosta and our

director would reassemble in D'Agosta's no-frills office. There they'd meet the hopeful actors. D'Agosta would generally bring in three or four contenders for each part, and after each had read, the four men would once again put their heads together, argue and ultimately come to a consensus. The lucky actors and actresses who'd landed roles would then immedi-

AN EARLY AND RATHER SILLY ROUND OF PUBLICITY STILLS, TAKEN JUST AS WE WERE BEGINNING PRODUCTION. (© 1993 PARAMOUNT PICTURES)

ately be sent over to Bill Theiss, who'd already roughed out their characters' basic costumes. He'd now take the actors' measurements and go to work, customizing each outfit to fit perfectly.

Our directors ran through all of this preproduction activity in working toward an ultimate goal of saving time on the Star Trek set, and the reasons behind this were obvious. I mean, when you're shooting an hour-long science fiction film in the ridiculously inadequate timespan of six days, every moment on the set is precious. There is no time to experiment, no time to try out new ideas, no time to waste. In fact, it was only through extremely efficient shooting practices and miserly allocation of time that our episodes ever got finished at all.

For those reasons, throughout the shooting of every Star Trek episode, it was made absolutely clear that time was a very precious commodity. In fact, in order for us to stay on schedule, we had to shoot anywhere from ten to an unheard-of thirteen pages of script per day. There was no room for error, and as a result our directors were often forced to cover the action of each scene in a minimum number of shots. With that in mind, our first take of any given scene was generally a "master" shot, wide enough to cover everyone and every action in the scene. Once we'd knocked that off, we'd move in for close-ups, and depending on the number of actors in the particular scene, this could become a really time-consuming piece of business. However, this was also an aspect of production where thorough directorial preparation could pay off rather handsomely.

As the close-ups were nearing completion, our director would invariably look at his watch. Most often he would grimace, grumble and order us on to our next scene, but should a smile appear, it was obvious that we were running ahead of schedule and could now spend a few additional moments shooting alternate takes of the scene we'd just covered. This time, however, our director would be after some more artistic, more creative filmmaking. As a result, if you're watching Star Trek and you notice an especially fancy camera move, zoom or even an unusually dramatic lighting effect, you can be sure that the director of that particular episode had done his homework well and was able to find time for creativity.

We actors would aid the cause of efficient production as well, in that we prided ourselves on a minimum of flubbed takes. Toward this end, we even set up a special table just off the set, and whenever our crew got busy lighting a scene, the actors could most likely be found huddled around this table rehearsing.

I'd never seen that sort of thing before, but with time being at such a premium on the set, in the writing of our scripts and in the production of our shows, rehearsal time was almost nonexistent. That lack of rehearsal time really shows up on screen, so every moment we could grab around the beat-up old table became precious. It really gave us a chance to kick the tires of our scenes and thrash out any rough spots that might be looming inside without ever having to waste time in front of the camera. As a result, by the time the crew was ready to roll, we actors were, too. All in all, it was an efficient and rather satisfying way of doing things.

Working most closely with our directors was face-squeezer/cinematographer extraordinaire Jerry Finnerman. Now the first question that's probably popped into your head is, "What exactly is a cinematographer?" The answer, in an extremely insufficient nutshell, is that a cinematographer creates the look, feel and depth of any scene through the subtle use of lighting and camera techniques. Got a spare couple of years? I'll tell you exactly how he did it. If not, it will have to suffice to say that Jerry used lights, lenses, angles and filters the way a painter would use color, texture, light and shade, manipulating them masterfully in creating mood, ambiance, character and depth.

As cinematographer, Finnerman worked closely with a guy named George Merhoff, the chief gaffer, who was in command of our lighting technicians, making sure that their work was done efficiently, safely and above all else quickly. He was amazing, and a bit unusual. In fact, this guy actually commanded his troops with a set of whistles. I mean, way up on the catwalks, high above our sets, there would always be this handful of lighting technicians hanging and focusing lights. Forty feet below them, way down on stage, you'd find George, and he'd stand there, hands in pockets, just whistling. Actually, I shouldn't say "just whistling," because he was really quite precise in his blowing, ordering his overhead guys around by utilizing a well-defined and extremely effective series of toots. Two low toots and a high tweet meant "Focus the key light a little to the left," and three tweets and a toot meant "Tilt up the backlights." He worked his technicians in exactly the same manner that those New Zealand sheepherders work their border collies.

However, even more unusual was the fact that in a business where film crews often tend toward the surly side, that was never the case on *Star Trek*. On our set, those guys generally ran around smiling, kidding each other, telling rotten jokes and sharing the workload with a good-natured sense of fun and camaraderie. In fact, I can even remember that one of our biggest, burliest electricians, a guy named George Hill, used to regularly celebrate his crew's accomplishments by rewarding these seasoned professionals with . . . candy.

I'm serious. Hill, this rather large, tough-looking, hairy-knuckled man, would almost never be found without his sewing box full of assorted, individually wrapped hard candies. Then, whenever the crew was able to complete a lighting configuration or set change ahead of schedule, he'd allow each of his cohorts to snag one treat out of his big goodie box. This guy always paid for the candy out of his own pocket, and it was great fun to witness the astounding results he was able to conjure up with this tiny bit of positive reinforcement.

In fact, our crew guys became so efficient, so quick and so gung-ho in their work that it became commonplace to find free cast members and production types just standing around the set watching them. One of the most frequent visitors was Dorothy Fontana, who had this to say about our crew:

> It was a point of pride that whenever we had to change sets or stages, they'd send the lighting crew down ahead of time, and by the time the camera crew and cast got there, everything would be up, lit and ready to go. Most other crews wouldn't or couldn't do that. In fact, it's almost unheard of. As a result, most times cast and crew have to sit around waiting for sets to be lit.

As you can see, positive attitudes and professional pride were indeed the norm on the *Star Trek* set, and it was not unusual to find our crew working with unbelievable attention to detail. The best example of this may well have been a man named George Rutter, who functioned in the official capacity of script supervisor. Basically, Rutter never moved; he simply sat still, in a tall director's chair, while staring at all of us actors eagle-eyed and taking copious notes in regard to our on-set activities. While this may sound rather psychotic, it was in fact essential to *Star Trek*'s production, because Rutter's obsession with our every move allowed him to accurately ensure that our performances were identical throughout each take of a given scene.

For example, let's pretend Leonard and I are performing a scene together. We set up for our wide master shot, and the director yells, "Action." Kirk now runs over to his trusty Vulcan pal asking, "Hey, Spock, is that your nose, or are you eating a banana?" Spock turns and gives his captain the old Vulcan evil eye, raising his left eyebrow accordingly. Throughout the scene, Rutter's sitting in the back, gawking at us, manhandling a stopwatch and scribbling furiously into a notebook.

The director yells, "Cut. Print it!" and of course he adds, "Bill, your performance was exquisite!" Now we move in for the close-ups, and Leonard's is first. Kirk again goes through his banana shpiel, and Spock again gives him the eyebrow treatment. "Cut," yells the director, "Print it! Bill, your performance was breathtaking. Let's move on." At this point, Rutter finally stirs, raising his hand and his voice to point out that Leonard raised his *left* eyebrow in the master shot, but his *right* eyebrow in the close-up. "Aw, geez, Leonard, you screwed up again," yells our director. "Why can't you be more like Bill?" We'll have to shoot the scene one more time, but a potential continuity disaster has been caught by George Rutter, man with a notebook.

I should point out that while Rutter indeed kept vigil to maintain the consistency of our performances, he also kept track of each scene's length, lighting setup, prop locations and photographic techniques. All of these observations were noted so that on the off-chance that we might have to reshoot a particular shot or even a whole scene (usually due to technical difficulties), we could accurately re-create the original.

Still, Rutter's pride in his work was matched all over our set by equally caring, concerned and talented crewmen. Our sound guys, for example, could often be found squatting on the floor with their eyes closed while grimacing and squeezing a pair of earphones tightly against their heads. Listening to me sing? No. Instead, they were usually just monitoring the audio playback of our previous scenes, ensuring that what they'd recorded was sharp, clear and free of background noise.

They did this for two reasons. First and foremost, they were checking their own work and genuinely trying to do the best job they possibly could. Second, due to the antique plumbing that ran throughout Desilu's studios, it was not at all uncommon for their highly sensitive microphones to pick up the audible, noticeable and rather unmistakable sounds of toilets flushing throughout the building. Quite obviously, these sounds would seem out of place aboard the *Enterprise* . . . where *did* we go to the bathroom, anyway?

On the visual side, Cliff Ralke also bears mention. Cliff was our dolly grip, which means he was responsible for moving the wheeled contraption upon which our camera and cameraman sat. On most sets, these heavy camera dollies are shoved around by big, ham-fisted guys who are hired more for their bulk than for their artistry, and as a result most filmed television shows keep their camera movements to a bare minimum. On the other hand, take a look at most *Star Trek* episodes and you'll notice that our camera moved about quite often in a seemingly effortless cruise around our sets. These unusually graceful visuals could be directly traced to our unusual dolly grip Cliff Ralke.

Cliff was by no means large, nor was he ham-fisted. In fact, he was quite the opposite in that he worked all day in a television studio, but the real *passion* in his life was music. Cliff was a talented musician, a talented composer, and I really think that his artistic nature somehow managed to translate itself into his graceful, delicate camera moves. Our directors noticed Cliff's unusual abilities almost immediately, and as a result they began to feature his unique talents more and more prevalently throughout their episodes.

As a footnote, Cliff's musical aspirations were realized when, shortly after *Star Trek*'s cancellation, he stood high atop an L.A. bridge, heaved his grip tools into the water below and began devoting his full attention to his musical career.

Last but certainly not least, I could not possibly forget to mention my pal Al Francis. Al ran our camera throughout *Star Trek*'s first two seasons, and ultimately became our cinematographer during season three. He was a wonderfully talented man, a good friend, and he was able to give me a real insider's take on what made *Star Trek*'s crew so great.

The thing that was so great about *Star Trek* was it never felt like work, it never felt like a show, it felt like a family. I had worked on features, big television shows, small television shows, and I'd never seen anything like it. Everybody felt genuinely friendly toward most everyone else. There were jokes, there was laughter, and you'd never come in to a morbid set. Even when there were problems, you'd find yourself smiling.

And all the actors were great, but we really thought the world of the three main guys. So Star Trek wasn't so much a series as it was an enjoyable gathering of friends who just happened to get together and make television shows twelve hours a day, five days a week. None of us were there for the money, we were there because we loved to shoot that particular show.

I could not hope to sum things up any better than that. What I can do, however, is take it a step further and explain that the feeling of camaraderie among our cast and crew was so great that even on our rare days off, we'd often get together. In fact, at about this time I was going through a divorce that I really didn't want and I missed my daughters terribly, and in an effort to keep me from crying all the time, my friend Al Francis actually took me under his wing. We began getting together almost every weekend, driving out to the desert to ride our dirt bikes. Most often we were joined by a handful of Star Trek's stuntmen, a technician or two and even the studio's insurance underwriter, who specifically wrote into my contract that I was not allowed to indulge in any potentially dangerous activities.

These guys were extremely talented cyclists who'd tear through the desert looking like a middle-aged pack of easy riders. On the other hand, I generally looked more like "queasy rider," trying desperately to keep up with these seasoned, two-wheeling motorpsychos while simultaneously hanging on to my handlebars for dear life. Mostly, however, I putted along at the rear end of the pack while I ate the leaders' dust . . . and of course a generous helping of the indigenous bugs.

Still, though I was far outclassed, I *had* made *some* progress since my first time out. I can still remember that I was so excited about this whole dirt-biking idea that I went out and bought myself a brand-new set of orange motorcycle-racing leathers. They were gorgeous, but the problem was I had no idea how to get into them, and Al's wife ended up having to zip me in. We then loaded our bikes onto Al's truck and drove nearly three hours to a place called California City, which was located smack in the middle of the desert and offered some of the best motorcycle trails in the state.

By the time we arrived, I was hot, uncomfortable and sweaty (an unforeseen and unwelcome side effect of my leather suit), but really anxious to hit the trails. We jumped out of the truck, hurriedly unloaded our bikes, and in my unbridled haste to get started, I ignored proper procedure and just kind of leaned my bike against Al's bumper . . . which put a hole in my bike's gas tank. So now we'd driven 125 miles into the desert for the sole purpose of riding motorcycles, and in less than three minutes, I'd screwed us completely. We were sunk before we'd even kick-started our bikes. Now gasoline was pouring out of my cycle, and Al was sighing and doing his best not to yell at me.

He offered to let me ride his bike, but I just couldn't bring myself to do it, for two reasons. First, I felt guilty, and second, I was afraid that with my lack of riding skills, I'd end up breaking his bike too. So there we stood, two supremely disappointed would-be bikers, miserably standing motionless amid the gorgeous desert scenery and jealously lusting after the far-off whines of high-speed, high-revving dirt bikes. Not wanting to give up without a fight, we drove to the nearest town (which was really just two stores and a gas station), bought a fiberglass patch kit and tried to fix the hole in my bike. It didn't work, because we could never get the patch to adhere to the broken tank. However, we did find that it stuck quite well to the unprotected skin of our fingers. Finally, when we were unable to deny our thorough and humiliating defeat any longer, we dejectedly reloaded our bikes onto Al's truck and headed for home. Somehow, however, the drive seemed much longer this time, and before it was over, I must have said the words "God, Al, I'm so sorry. I really am so sorry" approximately one thousand times.

But we kept at it, and over time my cycle-riding gradually improved until it actually became quite . . . mediocre. I can even remember that on one of my very best days, one of the networks had sent a crew to film us riding. And for the sake of the show, they asked that I lead our pack for a while. With that in mind, I went full-bore crazy and decided to really take on these trails as fast as I possibly could. The network guys mounted a camera onto the helmet of a cycle-riding cameraman, they rolled film and we were off. I threw caution to the wind, overcame my own fear of falling and roared off far faster than I'd ever previously dared, taking jumps that I'd normally have avoided at all costs and careening along the hard-scrabble floor of the desert at maximum velocity feeling very, very cool.

That lasted about thirty seconds, for when I was finally able to look up from my extraordinary feat, I saw that the network camera guy was ahead of me, riding nonchalantly, almost bored, while he shot back at me. Suddenly my feat seemed a lot less impressive. Still, in the end, none of that really mattered at all. I had no intentions of ever giving Evel Knievel a run for his money, and the actual riding of these mortorcycles was really just an excuse to be with my friends and enjoy the desert, the ride and most importantly the company. Inevitably however, Monday morning would rear its ugly head, and we'd all return to work sore, bruised up, sunburnt and very happy.

Still, though our first days of shooting were proceeding very well, things weren't running quite so smoothly on the creative front. By now John Black was gone, having regretfully bowed out of his *Star Trek* contract to write a movie at Universal. In his place was Steve Carabatsos, who was hired on a thirteen-week trial basis. He would not be rehired. I asked Dorothy Fontana to explain the situation. And she told me that "Steve just wasn't as enthusiastic as the rest of us. I don't think he was comfortable with it. He functioned well, but I don't think he had the spark that Gene wanted."

As a result, Roddenberry was now working harder than ever, and though our first several scripts, "Balance of Terror," "Dagger of the Mind," and "Miri" among them, were now almost ready to shoot, Gene couldn't help but combine his final creative control with an unshakably perfectionist nature, and he found himself slaving through an endless series of

last-minute rewrites and revisions. Often he would sit in his office rewriting entire scenes that were scheduled for filming the very next morning. Midnight would pass, then two, then four, and still Gene would be tweaking. When he finally deemed his nocturnal efforts complete, he'd sleepily hand his pages

WITH **K**IM **D**ARBY ON LOCATION FOR "**M**IRI." (© 1993 PARAMOUNT PICTURES)

over to the mimeo crew and crash on his office couch. Amazingly, he'd be back at work within a few short hours. Bob Justman describes it:

> Due to the fact that we were all working like madmen, Gene's creative ambitions almost always ended up being hampered by his own human fatigue. At this point, no one understood *Star Trek* as well as Roddenberry, and certainly no one could write the show as well as he could. As a result, "The Bird" ended up having to rewrite every one of our scripts himself, and this would invariably cause problems, because due to the exigencies of his time, he'd tend to peter out as he worked his way through any given script.
>
> Gene's first act rewrite would *always* be terrific, just brilliant. Beautiful writing, and all of a sudden the script's characters would become somehow more real, more alive. It had everything. The second act would be very good, too. Maybe a notch less brilliant than act one, but still really fine.
>
> Gene's third act would tend to be passable, and his fourth act would always be an abortion. That's simply because by the time he got to the fourth act, he'd been up for two nights straight rewriting the damn thing and he was zonked, zombified, out cold. He'd literally be stumbling around his office, baggy-eyed and heavy-lidded. We'd always have this rewrite sent to mimeo, but most times we were lucky enough that we wouldn't have to shoot the fourth act until later in the week, by which time Gene could get some sleep, come back in and fix the end of the show.

This went on for days, even weeks at a time, and as you can imagine, it began to cause a lot of confusion on the set. Last-minute script revisions absolutely demand on-the-fly changes to sets, props, staging, lighting and direction. All of this takes up precious time and, when it becomes commonplace, causes massive production delays. This of course necessitates overtime, which causes big budgetary problems, and *that* caused Bob Justman's blood to boil.

Finally, the situation got so bad that Bob employed some extreme guerrilla tactics aimed at hastening Gene's completion of scripts. Bob would simply walk into Gene's office unannounced, jog up to the desk, then hop up. At that point he'd simply stand there, feet upon Gene's desk blotter, refusing to budge until Roddenberry had completed whatever script revision was immediately at hand.

Frowning underneath the belly of his associate producer, Gene would now sit at his desk toiling away at whatever script lay before him. And, as staring up at Bob Justman's groin cannot possibly be in the least enjoyable, he'd work harder and faster than ever before, churning out his revisions with unparalleled speed. When he was satisfied with his work, (or perhaps just unable to stand Bob's impromptu visit any longer), Gene would raise his fistful of script up to Bob, who'd snatch it up like a hungry animal and jump off the desk with a polite "Thanks, boss."

This stand-up standoff occurred on a regular basis until Roddenberry finally came up with an effective defense. Calling on one of L.A.'s most advanced locksmiths, Gene had a new sort of high-tech lock installed on his office door. Run by the mere flip of an electronic toggle switch, Gene's new lock was unpickable, unbreakable and infallible at keeping badgering Bob Justman away. Justman quickly became obsessed with beating the new security device, but it seemed that no matter how quickly Bob might charge into Gene's outer office, hoping to get a leg up (literally) on the week's script, by the time he reached Gene's inner door, he'd find himself locked out and well aware of the fact that there was no way in hell Gene was gonna let him in. Over time Bob grew frustrated with the door, and was never quite able to figure out that Gene's fancy new electronic lock was not operated by Gene at all, but by Dorothy Fontana, still Gene's secretary at the time, who'd simply flip the switch at the first sign of a Justman attack.

It's also quite interesting to note that throughout this period, although Gene was working on Star Trek's scripts almost entirely on his own, he did receive some creative assistance from an unexpected, unofficial and uncredited source—Majel Barrett. In fact, it was Majel's close proximity to the earliest Star Trek scripts that would ultimately allow her to finally become a regular Enterprise crew member.

As the series was beginning to get organized, before we'd begun shooting, I was helping Gene in any way that I could, making the show a little better, helping Gene to write more realistic, more conversational dialogue, whatever. He'd work every night, and it was always until two, three, four or five in the morning.

There were even two or three episodes where he'd just work straight through, then walk the script up to the stage in the morning.

So of course during this period of time I got to look at all the scripts as they were coming along. One of the first dozen or so was called "What Are Little Girls Made Of?" and as I read it for the first time, I saw there was a character with a very French-sounding last name. She was a doctor, and she was going out into space to search for her fiancé. By the time I'd finished the script, I was thinking, "I can do this. I know how I can do this."

So I went home and immediately bleached my hair. Next morning, I came into Gene's outer office and sat there near where his secretary sat and waited for him. When he got in, he walked by me, sort of half-smiled, nodded at me and grunted a hello.

I of course thought he hadn't even noticed anything different about me, for God's sake, but when he took a second look at me, he said, "Majel?! Is that you?!" He had no idea it was me.

I said, "Look, Gene, if I can fool you, I can surely fool NBC." He said, "Yeah, you're right." And I told him about the "What Are Little Girls Made Of?" script, and we decided that Dr. Christine French-name could easily be switched to Nurse Christine Chapel. And then, so that there would be no problem with NBC, we took my name off of the original pilot's credits, and replaced it with M. Lee Hudec, which is my real name.

I know that sounds a bit like the plot from an old episode of I Love Lucy, with Lucy Ricardo trying to finagle her way into Ricky's show down at the Tropicana. However, the difference is that unlike most of Lucy's schemes, Majel's plan paid off. She'd gotten her foot in the door, and she was well on her way to becoming a regular cast member.

The Enterprise was now fully staffed.

A COUPLE OF CHARACTERS

Throughout our inaugural days of shooting, there was a very tangible feeling around our set that Star Trek was shaping up to become something unique, and a project of real quality. After several *weeks* had passed, this initial sentiment proved irrefutable. Our work was challenging, our crew magnificent, and each new script seemed even more impressive than the last. In fact, in his painstakingly rewritten teleplays Roddenberry had now begun defining and *refining* Star Trek's main characters, exploring and deepening them with every new draft.

At the same time, this kind of creative growth wasn't just taking place on stage or behind a typewriter, it was taking place within the actors as well. Gene's scripts and the passage of time had allowed us to grow more comfortable in our roles, and as a result, by the time we'd completed our first half-dozen shows, our *Enterprise* characters were nearly fully grown.

I should add here that, in terms of playing Captain Kirk, I had it easy. I had come to the conclusion very early on that acting in this particular television project was going to be so backbreaking and all-encompassing that to create an unfamiliar character, and then to sustain that character for what could be *years* on end, would be next to impossible. With that in mind, I always played the character of Jim Kirk fairly close to home.

Surely the captain's wisdom, sagacity, courage and heroic capabilities were all fictional, having been so remarkably scripted for the character, but at his core, Kirk was, for the most part, me. An idealized *version* of me, certainly, but one that nonetheless sprang rather readily from my own inner workings. In short, I operated almost totally on instinct.

Of course, I was playing a fairly straight role, and for that reason, no matter what the writers gave Kirk to do—fight, love, lead the men onward in battle—I was able to use my own experience to find the emotional core of any scene. I wasn't so much acting as I was *reacting*, using my own internal makeup as the spine upon which I was able to build the character of Jim Kirk. We were basically one and the same, although Jim was just about perfect, and, of course, I *am* perfect.

On the other hand, Leonard approached his role from a whole different angle, in that playing Spock demanded that he create an entirely foreign character, entirely from scratch. As a result, our acting techniques were almost diametrically opposed. I asked Leonard to describe how he went about fleshing out the rather complex character of Mr. Spock.

The best tool that I had in playing Spock was some theatrical training that taught me to look for the differences between any exotic character and yourself, and then celebrate them. Y'know, I would ask myself, "What's intrinsically different about this character? How can I get myself out of my own shoes and into this character's skewed point of view? How does he perceive any given event differently than I might?" I was also constantly on guard in making sure that my own everyday habits wouldn't creep in and water down the character. Speech patterns, stance, walk, posture, sense of humor, sense of curiosity, all these things were no longer just natural habits, they merited serious thought. More specifically, it's this kind of conscious study that was behind many of the characterizations that have become so inseparable from the character of Spock.

If you think about it, the mind meld, the splayed fingers in the Vulcan greeting, and the neck pinch are all hand-oriented, finger-oriented characteristics. And that's because it came to me at some point that the Vulcans, and particularly Spock, were all part of a very tactile culture. And I thought, "Wouldn't it be interesting if many of their customs are formulated around how they use their hands?" Y'know, I had decided that the Vulcans were a peculiar race, with peculiar powers, and that much of that emanated from their hands.

The neck pinch, for example, came about while we were filming "The Enemy Within," in which Kirk, on the first of many occasions, gets split in two. One half became the good-guy captain, the standard loyal, brave and true version, but the other half was essentially the malicious opposite of Kirk, possibly television's first evil twin. At any rate, written into the script was a scene in which the evil Kirk is about to kill the nice Kirk, and if he does, we'll never get Humpty Dumpty back together again. Leonard continues:

In reading this particular script, I noticed that Spock is supposed to knock out the evil Kirk by hitting him on the head with the butt of a gun. I read that, and in drawing upon my training, I thought, "How dull. That's not Spock, that's generic private-eye stuff for how to knock a guy out." You know, this just wasn't Spock in the twenty-third century. So I looked for the difference, and I asked myself, "How would Spock render a human unconscious?" Finally I was able to come up with an answer from within his hand-oriented character background. The answer, of course, was the neck pinch.

So I said to Leo Penn, who was directing this episode, "Leo, I think we should forget about the pistol whipping, and try something different than that."

"What do you mean?"

"Well," I said, "Spock is a graduate of the Vulcan Institute of Technology, where he took a number of courses in human anatomy. Now, the Vulcans have an energy that comes off of their fingertips, which if properly applied to the appropriate pressure points of the human anatomy will render any human unconscious."

So now Leo's looking at me with his mouth open, and he's obviously got NO IDEA what I'm talking about. But since I had already discussed my idea with Bill, and since Bill had understood exactly what I was talking about, we decided to demonstrate the technique to Mr. Penn. So I came up behind Bill, pinched his neck and HE really sold it, because he dropped like a rock to the studio floor.

A similar situation came up as we shot "Amok Time," which I thought was a very exciting episode. It was beautiful, very poetically written by

Theodore Sturgeon, and it also marked the first episode in which the words "Live long and prosper" were spoken. For the first time, we were going back to Spock's home planet of Vulcan, and I must tell you that Leonard couldn't wait to start shooting. He was really anxious to see what the writer, director and Matt Jefferies had come up with in the way of a look for Spock's home planet. Leonard continues:

was thrilled, and as we rehearsed, I was really touched by the story line, and by the dramatic power of the scene which immediately follows the fight wherein Spock appears to have killed Captain Kirk. Later, as we shot this scene, and T'Pau says to Spock, "Live long and prosper," I was almost overcome by the emotion of the scene. Spock was supposed to reply to T'Pau, "I shall do neither, I have killed my captain and my friend," but I could barely choke out those moving words. Then, as T'Pau and Spock exchange parting gestures, I was again able to call upon this very hand-oriented character background in coming up with the four-finger split-down-the-middle greeting. It is in reality a Jewish rabbinical blessing, but it seemed quite appropriate.

Leonard's theories on the basic customs and conventions of the Vulcan race played a major role in his portrayal of Spock, and in time he even managed to pass on a bit of Vulcan digital tradition to Mark Lenard, who'd come aboard to play Sarek, Spock's father. Leonard continues:

e had just begun shooting "Journey to Babel," and I was talking with Mark Lenard. We spoke a little bit about Vulcan culture and customs, and I mentioned to him this thing about the hands, and he used it, and actually expanded upon it as you can see in the episode's first shots, wherein he and Jane Wyatt appear as my mother and father. As they walk together, and he

OPPOSITE LEFT AND RIGHT: From "Amok Time." Fighting with Leonard, and his stunt double. (© 1993 Paramount Pictures)
ABOVE: Celia Lovsky as T'Pau. (© 1993 Paramount Pictures)

introduces her as his wife,
you'll notice that instead of
holding hands, as most couples
would do, they're very casually
holding the first two digits of
their hands in contact with one
another. It's a small thing,
almost a throwaway, but it
really helped in defining and
clearly illustrating the differ-
ences between cultures. The mind meld fits into this category, too,
because I was able to explore the facial contact thing, looking for
pressure points on the face with the fingers.

Still, in creating a character as unique as Spock, Leonard's efforts
weren't always met with such unconditional approval, and at times he
really had to fight to protect and strengthen the character of his pointy-
eared counterpart. One of the best illustrations of this situation came
about during the production of our seventh episode, "The Naked Time," as
Leonard and John D. F. Black locked horns over the budding personality of
Mr. Spock. Leonard explains:

Very early on in the series, there was a defining incident for me,
and it had to do with my confrontation with John D. F. Black
over his script for "The Naked Time." As you probably
remember, the story begins when an *Enterprise* research party
returns from a dead planet, bringing with them, unknowingly, a
virus that would ultimately be very quickly passed amongst the
crew. It was extremely contagious, and was passed by perspira-
tion, coupled with physical contact. Shake hands . . . you got it.

Anyway, this was a virus that caused one to lose their inhibitions and release their most repressed emotions. With that in
mind, there was an interesting potpourri of events that this virus
would unleash. Sulu, for example, had a whole swashbuckling,

swordfighting scenario which represented his ultimate fantasy. One of our red shirts experienced extreme self-doubts, and another began to fancy himself as an Irish king. Also in this draft was a moment where Spock cries.

As originally scripted, the scene would have begun with Spock walking down a corridor openly sobbing. At that point, we'd cut away and find that another infected crewman has begun frantically running around the ship, slapping grafitti paint jobs all over the walls of the *Enterprise*. In subsequent shots, we'd find several more crewmen beginning to lose their inhibitions, and just when the pandemonium is beginning to overwhelm the ship, we'd come back to Spock.

Spock is now riding in an elevator, crying. He gets to his floor, and when the doors open, the graffiti guy runs up and paints a big black mustache on Spock's face. At that point, Spock cries even louder. Leonard continues:

Now, that's very imaginative, very inventive, very theatrical and very funny, but I felt that it was not really significant or appropriate for Spock. I mean, Spock was crying . . . but so what? There was no context for it, no discernible root force, no underlying cause for what's going on. You know, in a strange way, this one-shot extra who's walking around doing the paint jobs all over the place is a lot more interesting than Spock, who's weeping. It seemed to me like we were wasting some really strong dramatic possibilities, all for the sake of an easy sight gag.

So I said all of this to John Black, and I also said that what I felt we really need to do here was a scene in which Spock's basic inner conflict, the human versus the Vulcan, rises to the surface and motivates his tears. I mean this draft of the script found Spock fighting through all this emotion in public, and I felt that would be a terrible thing for Spock, because he's a very private person.

So I said to John, "I think Spock would look for privacy when he feels the urge to cry. When he can no longer resist his tears, he would probably look for a private place in which to battle it out with himself."

And John's reaction was very negative. It was typical producer/writer-under-pressure kind of stuff. "C'mon, leave it alone because

I'm working on next week's script. Shoot it, just shoot it." This kind of thing. And he complained about "hurting the rhythm of the script."

I've got to break into Leonard's story here to explain that "it hurts the rhythm of the script" is a sort of basic, all-purpose producer's excuse that's fed all too often to actors seeking script changes. Good, bad, legitimate, frivolous, it doesn't matter. If a producer doesn't want to deal with your suggestions, he'll probably just tell you that what you're suggesting "hurts the rhythm of the script." It's the TV producer's equivalent of "the dog ate my homework," or "the check is in the mail." It's just an easy, somewhat plausible excuse that generally has no basis in reality. With that in mind, Leonard's determination and fiercely protective nature in regard to Spock drove him over Black's head to Roddenberry.

I called Gene about it, and I told him just what I'd told John. In talking to Gene, I was very careful to be politically supportive of his producer but about an hour and a half later, here comes John Black out to the set. So now I'm feeling, "Ahh, this is great!" I'm feeling that someone's actually listening to me.

And Black was funny, he came onto the set and said, "Let's go talk someplace." We went to my dressing room, and he said, "Okay, tell me your idea again. Daddy says I have to listen to you." And I had already formulated a basic concept of the scene, so I said, "Look, John, just get me into a room, and write me a half-page, a quarter-page, where you see Spock walk down a corridor and slip inside a door. As the doors close behind him, he'll burst into this emotional struggle." And John asked, "Well, what's this struggle all about?" And I said, "It's about love and vulnerability and caring and loss and regret, versus $C=\pi r^2$ and $E=mC^2$. Spock is a scientist, he is logical, and he feels this can't be happening to him. It's that kind of struggle. It's logic versus emotion. It's rational control versus uncontrollable urge. With that in mind, going behind closed doors will speak to the basic privacy of the character."

So John wrote that and some other stuff, six or eight lines maybe, and it was exactly what I needed. Spock was now able to slip inside a door, close it behind him, struggle for a moment, then cry. At this point, he would start babbling, and the cause of his internal struggling would become obvious. Problem was, when it came time to shoot this stuff, a whole new set of obstacles had to be overcome.

Marc Daniels, who was directing this particular episode, came up and asked, "What do you have in mind for this scene?" So, playing director, I said, "Just put the camera here, behind the desk. I'll come in the door, I'll walk toward you, I'll come around, I'll sit in the chair, and I'll start to have this babbling conversation with myself, and I'll cry. Now, if you'll dolly around getting closer and closer, we can meet at the end of the scene. We can see Spock's entire breakdown in one long dramatic shot."

Okay, now it's five-thirty, I got out to get my ears and makeup touched up, and the time is important because we're on a very rigid schedule. With overtime being so ridiculously and prohibitively expensive, we'd have to wrap each evening at exactly six-eighteen. Didn't matter if you were in the middle of a sentence, come six-eighteen, we wrapped.

So now Jerry Finnerman starts to light the scene and it's obvious that this will be our last shot of the day. I'm in the makeup chair, getting touched up, and now in comes Cliff Ralke, our dolly grip, who was always a very supportive person, and he says, "Excuse, me Leonard, but you'd better get out there, because they're changing the shot you guys just talked about."

So now Leonard comes out to the set, and the director has indeed changed the shot they'd just agreed upon. It's important to note, however, that the reasoning *behind* this change, though not particularly sensitive to Leonard's needs, was rational and perfectly valid. You see, as previously discussed, this shot would have entailed a one-hundred-and-eighty-degree camera move starting on one side of the set, then slowly dollying completely around to the opposite end. This caused problems because the long, involved shot required a lot of lights and a time-consuming, involved setup that Jerry Finnerman didn't think could be accomplished without going into overtime. Finnerman discussed this situation with Daniels, and together they decided that the most efficient way to shoot this scene would be in a series of brief cuts, each of which could be lit quickly and with relative ease.

They were going to have Leonard enter in a wide shot, then cut. Next, in a slightly tighter framing, they'd follow him as he crossed the set and sat down. Cut. An even tighter frame would catch the beginning of his speech, and they planned to cut once more, zooming to a close-up as Spock began weeping. This made sense in terms of production efficiency, but Leonard felt this shooting sequence would really damage the dramatic impact of the scene. He continues:

> said, "You're going to lose the continuity and fluidity of the scene if you shoot it this way. I will not be able to do it as well, and I think the end result will just seem choppy and phony."

By now it's five forty-five, and with no time to debate the situation, they got hold of Gregg Peters, our first A.D., who was the equivalent of the hatchet man. He was the guy who'd always call the six-eighteen wrap, and we all discussed the situation. Finally, Marc Daniels said, "Let's go for it. Let's try to get it done."

Now the lighting crew ran around setting up the shot, and I think it was about six-fifteen when they finally said, "We're ready."

Marc had me walk through it once, and by now production types were standing around behind the camera, looking at their watches and saying, "He won't make it. He'll never do it." So the tension was really mounting.

So basically I know this has got to be a flawless, one-take thing. Y'know, I've got one crack at it before they shut us down for the night. If I were to screw up, we'd almost certainly have gone right back to the cut-and-chop scenario come morning. Anyway, this was the scene that I'd asked for and fought for, and now the logistics of the situation were such that there was absolutely no room for error. There was a lot riding on this, and I wouldn't have been so adamant in my battling if I hadn't felt that this scene was extremely important. I felt like it merited my efforts, in that it truly defined, for the very first time, what the Spock character was all about.

Now the lights go on, the cameras roll and we nail it. They get the pan, get the one-hundred-and-eighty-degree dolly shot and the scene ultimately worked really well in illustrating Spock's inherent inner conflict. This went directly to the heart of what Gene and I had originally spoken about in regard to the character of Spock. It was an opportunity that I absolutely did not want to miss, and an opportunity to plant a seed in defining a certain edge of the character.

I should explain that when it comes to defining and protecting a character, television actors often fight a constant battle to be heard. With that in mind, it sometimes becomes necessary to make waves, to speak up and to take a stand, saying things like, "Wait a minute, my character wouldn't say this," or "do this" or "act like this." It's an often-inevitable and always unpleasant situation, and it can easily strain working relationships. Bob Justman explains:

Bill always wanted the script to be as good as he could get it, but at the same time he understood the process of getting a teleplay up to even "shootable" status, much less to "quality." And as long as he had lots of stuff to do and could play the captain well, acting heroic and fooling around with the numerous assorted babes, he was fine. He was willing, enthusiastic, gave the show everything he had without causing many problems, and I think Gene was pleased by that.

On the other hand, Gene had a problem with Leonard. Leonard was always very demanding in regard to his character, and he was always fighting to protect him, fighting to make sure Spock didn't just become the equivalent of Uhura, saying, "Hailing frequencies open, Captain." Leonard wanted the character of Spock to be important, and to be pivotal, and to have *raison d'être*.

All of that is perfectly legitimate, but it became troublesome in that Gene was under such a tremendous amount of pressure just to get the scripts out. Y'know, Gene's already overloaded, and he's getting calls fom Leonard saying, "You've got to do something about this script, my part is written incorrectly," and "Why do you need a character like me, if I'm not going to be utilized properly?" Leonard got in Gene's face at a time when Gene was just desperately trying to get these scripts out.

But Leonard came to find that he could seek me out and express his misgivings about any script we were about to shoot. I was happy to listen to him, because in my mind I figured that if Leonard's character is improved, the show is improved. If the show is improved, we're all better off, and if it costs us some time and a few sleepless nights, so be it. What counts is what ends up on the screen.

So I'd listen to Leonard's complaints, and if I thought they had merit, and they almost always did, I would go to Gene and say, "I agree with Leonard, we need to fix this." Then Gene would be more likely to make the change. He'd do it grudgingly, because he had no idea where he'd find the time to make the changes in question, but he'd do it nonetheless. The air would grow less tense, and Leonard would be mollified . . . never entirely mollified, but that's Leonard.

On the other side of the coin, there are many occasions when an actor's enthusiasm toward exploring and expanding a character will result in circumstances that are far more humorous than confrontational. For example, as Leonard mentioned, one of the scripted subplots of "The Naked Time" found Mr. Sulu acting out his fantasy of becoming a Three Musketeers–style swordsman. This, I must tell you, made George Takei ecstatic . . . as it turned out, too ecstatic. You see, in real life George had always fancied himself as a daring, dashing swordsman, and though he'd never picked up a saber in his life, he was absolutely thrilled at this opportunity to jab his way through the bowels of the *Enterprise*.

However, what none of us expected was that once George actually got hold of his sword, he went crazy, absolutely nuts, literally bounding around our sets all day, slashing and jabbing at whoever dared cross his path. I mean, Takei gets this dangerous weapon in his hand and he completely loses control, darting around the studio, swatting our crew guys and poking at big Teamster butts.

THE MANIC MUSKETEER. (© 1993 PARAMOUNT PICTURES)

This is not a good idea! A couple of these guys even went so far as to threaten George's life. "Ha-HAAAAAAA!!!!" he'd gleefully exclaim, "You are powerless against my mighty sword."

One guy gave him a dirty look, another gave him the finger.

As you might have guessed, George's talent for swordplay was in direct opposition to his gusto. You've heard the expression "loose cannon"? George was more of an "unhinged épée." I'd be unfortunate enough to learn this firsthand in shooting a scene in which Kirk and Sulu had to fight one another on the *Enterprise* bridge. Even worse, though Sulu would be flailing away with his sword, Kirk, as scripted, was unarmed. I really began to wonder if perhaps Gene was out to kill me.

We'd choreographed this fight sequence very simply, hoping that the sheer simplicity of our moves would prevent this raging samurai D'Artagnan from lopping off one of my ears . . . or worse. Anyway, we

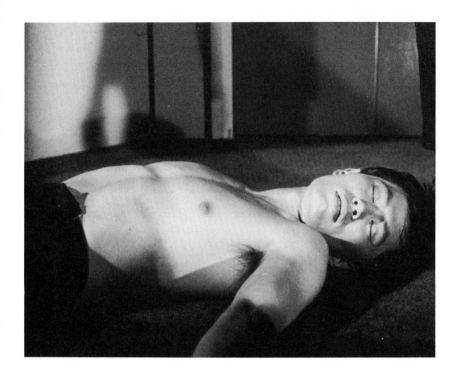

rehearsed the scene a couple of times, and every single time we went through our appointed paces, George would go gung-ho and clobber me. Meanwhile, Leonard's watching all this and he's cracking up every time I scream out in pain. I was *not* happy.

Then when we started shooting, George's adrenaline level shot up even higher, and he got a gleam in his eye that just about assured my impending death. "Roll 'em," I hear from behind the camera, "Action." George thrusts. I dodge. George whips his sword through the air with a wild unscripted flourish, and I dive to the deck in a very uncaptainly display of fear. Leonard's now on the floor, laughing out loud as George tells me, "Hey, don't worry, I know what I'm doing." Somehow I was not reassured.

"Roll 'em, take two." George thrusts. I dodge. George stabs me. Pokes me right through my velour top, puncturing my left nipple. I get Band-Aided, and while I'm grimacing I hatch a plan.

Back on the set for take three, I say to our director, "Look, Marc, I've got a great idea about how to end this thing. Let me give it a shot." Now the cameras roll again, and even before George has gotten his sword up from his hip, I run into the frame, grab him by the neck and choke this demented Zorro wannabe to the ground. Daniels yells, "Cut! Print it!" and falls out of his director's chair laughing. Leonard and I follow suit, and even George manage to smile, although I really do think that some small part of him was upset that he didn't get to run me through. Next time you happen across "The Naked Time," look closely at this scene, and you can't help but notice Captain Kirk's rather convincing look of terror. This may seem like good acting, but as you now know, it was actually just me quaking in my boots.

THE GRIN

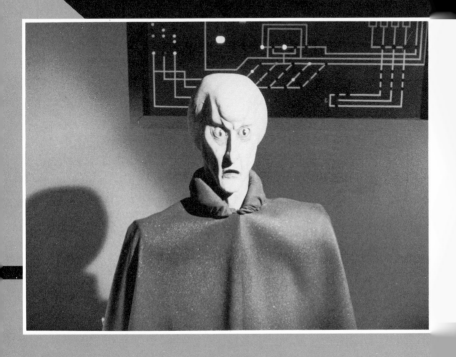

y now we were filming at full speed and churning out a new episode every six days. Our workload was mountainous, the pace was hectic, and the entire situation proved truly exhausting for cast, crew and creatives alike. Add to that the mounting pressures of a rapidly approaching premiere date, and you'll understand how everyone on our set began growing increasingly tense. In fact, by late August the stress levels had increased to such overwhelming magnitude that people began to crack.

The first situation arose just ten days before Star Trek's premiere episode, and it centered around our photographic effects. This was the aspect of production that basically allowed the Enterprise to fly, through the use of specialized visual and optical techniques. It was also a recurrent source of frustration throughout our first season, with extensive delays and cost overruns nearly grounding the starship for good.

Early on, a man named Bill Heath had been selected by Desilu to function as Star Trek's postproduction executive, supervising the scheduling and budgetary facets of the series' numerous photographic effects. Heath was essentially a bean counter who was brought in by the studio to keep Star Trek's specialized optical artists functioning in a cost-efficient manner. As it would turn out, Heath's penny-pinching would cause far more problems than they'd solve.

Heath, a loyal and rather driven Desilu employee, was out to save money wherever possible. As a result, when it came time to begin creating the series' opening credit sequence and visual effects, he simply called in the Anderson Company, the effects house that had worked on our two pilots. That sounds fairly logical, until you realize that the Anderson Company was a young and rather small shop that even at first glance must have seemed ill-equipped to handle the massive needs of a weekly Star Trek series. Still, in an effort to cut costs, Heath decided they could do it alone. This was a decision that would soon be exposed as completely invalid.

Several months passed, and Roddenberry began to grow increasingly uneasy over the fact that he hadn't received any new footage of the *Enterprise* in space. He'd also seen nothing in regard to the show's opening credit sequence. Needless to say, as August wore on, Gene's "uneasiness" soon graduated into full blown-panic. He'd call Bill Heath repeatedly, only to be told time and again, "Don't worry, babe, we'll be just fine."

Finally, as push was rapidly becoming shove and Heath's platitudes were becoming less and less credible, Gene demanded to see for himself just what kind of effects mess *Star Trek* was in. First, he and Bob Justman got together and called Bill Heath, reading him the riot act, courtesy of Ma Bell. Justman remembers the phone call like this:

> "It's September, Bill, and we haven't seen anything. We don't have any shots of the fucking *Enterprise* other than what's in the pilot!"
>
> "Don't worry," says Heath.
>
> "That's it, we're not gonna wait anymore. You've got to show it to us. I don't care what kind of shape it's in, just show us what you've got."

Twenty minutes later, a disgruntled Roddenberry stormed into the Anderson Company with Bob Justman in tow. They confronted Daryl Anderson, the head of the company, and demanded that he show them anything and everything that had been created for the new series. Anderson then gathered up the firm's *Star Trek* footage, took Gene and Bob to a screening room and scurried back up to the projection booth. The lights went out, the projector started and the pair went slack-jawed as they witnessed three minutes' worth of footage, more than half of which was blurry, choppy, phony-looking or otherwise unusable. They were up shit creek without a paddle.

"Daryl, what is this?! It's almost September, and in a few days we go on the air! Where the hell is our footage?!" screamed Justman. Anderson, who was sweating profusely, started to shake. He then began jumping up and down in the middle of the projection room screaming, "Oh My GOD! You'll never make your first airdate!!!" At this point he burst into tears and ran from the room. Justman gave chase.

nderson was a sweet, nice man, and by the time I caught up with him in the studio, he was weeping uncontrollably. He was jumping all over the place and screaming. He was crying so violently that I finally just grabbed hold of him, and hugged him to me. I said, "That's okay, Daryl, that'll be okay. That's okay, Daryl." And they ended up shipping the poor guy off to Palm Springs.

Anderson was heading off to some R&R, but Roddenberry and Justman were nowhere near as lucky. They now had to somehow find a way out of this massive, Bill Heath–inspired jam. Sitting silently in the darkness of Anderson's screening room, they brooded about this monstrous problem until Gene finally drew a deep breath, looked over toward Justman and said, "Come with me."

The pair now rounded up every shot of the *Enterprise* that had been created for the show's two pilots and added them to their pitiful pile of new stuff. Next, Gene commandeered an editing room, where the two men performed a small miracle, working through the night, cutting together *Star Trek*'s now-legendary opening sequence. Justman recalls:

e really put that main title together from nothing, literally from garbage, trims and rejects. We got lucky, and we kind of disproved the old notion that you can't make a silk purse from a sow's ear. Still, this near-disaster left Gene with a real hard-on against Bill Heath. He was really angry because not only had Heath procrastinated in getting the effects done, he also wouldn't allow Anderson to hire enough people to do them. He was functioning solely in the interest of saving the studio some money, and he was working against the good of the show. On top of all that, he had lied to us.

It was so bad that even Gene, who was a notoriously gentle man, wanted to go down and separate Bill Heath from his head. He wanted to kill him.

Daryl Anderson may have been the first to crack, but by now *everyone* was running on empty. We had all worked so intensely and under so much pressure for such a long period of time that the situation proved to be truly unhealthy, and with the show's premiere looming ever more ominously on the horizon, something had to give. It finally got to the point where Bob Justman suffered a nervous collapse. He explains:

was getting to the studio at five in the morning, and I would leave at about eight-thirty or nine P.M., at which point I would go home, eat a quick dinner and work some more. Reading scripts, reading stories and dictating memos until I fell asleep. Throughout that first season, I averaged about four hours of sleep per night. I was working this hard because I was just so imbued with Gene's attempt to create something worthwhile, to do something of value. Still, I was beside myself I was so tired.

Then one night I came home from the set at my usual time, which was about nine or nine-thirty, at which point my wife, Jackie, made me dinner. I ate quickly and when I'd finished, I stood up to take my plate to the sink, and I set it down, and then it hit me: utter despair and exhaustion, coupled with the feeling that I just couldn't face another day. All of a sudden I found myself without the strength to carry on. Everything hit me at once, and I grabbed hold of the kitchen counter.

My own inability to function more than twenty hours a day just kind of slammed into me. I was despondent that I couldn't go on and I just started to cry. I was weeping. At the same time, I was trying my best not to make any noise, because I was embarrassed and ashamed of myself for being so weak as to give in to my emotion.

And then my wife came in and she caught me there, still leaning over the counter. She sat me down, poured a double Scotch into me, then proceeded to pick up the phone, call Roddenberry's office and read Gene the riot act. She said, "I don't care what happens to the show, I'm taking Bob away, no matter what you say. He needs a rest desperately, and what you've been putting him through is truly unfair. We're going to Hawaii."

Now Gene, poor Gene, he's stuck on the phone, getting yelled at by my wife, and he's just as surprised by all this as I was. It was coming totally out of the blue. So he says, "Of course. Go to Hawaii. Bob needs it. I know he's been working way too hard. I can tell, because lately he's been even more irritable than he usually is." The next day I went to the airport and got on a plane bound for Hawaii. I was still really worried that Gene might hunt down Bill Heath and do something terrible to him, but I got on the plane.

But now Gene, in trying to make me feel better and to have some fun with me, has decided to play some games. They started as soon as we got to the airport.

Jackie and I are walking along, heading for our gate, when I notice out of the corner of my eye a guy named Rick who was a runner in Gene's office. And he's following Jackie and me, hiding and trying to avoid being seen, and he's sorta peeking at us from behind potted plants. It was obvious that something was very definitely up.

Meanwhile, we're now just about ready to board the plane, and I notice that all of the airline personnel are watching me. And I notice that these two stewardesses on the plane are staring at me, looking completely pissed off, sighing and acting as if I've somehow interfered with their whole way of doing things.

So we get on the plane, and I get to my aisle, and there's three seats across. Jackie's seat is on the aisle, I've got the window, and in the middle seat is Balok, the giant, cadaverous clay monster head from "The Corbomite Maneuver," our first episode. Gene was definitely behind the joke, and he'd evidently worked it out with the airline and gotten them to okay bringing this disgusting thing aboard for a gag.

So now everybody's waiting for me to react to this thing, but there was no way I was gonna give 'em the satisfaction. I just walked in, sat down next to the monster, read a magazine and pretended that there was nothing out of the ordinary.

Meantime, in the seat behind me is a guy who's had way too much to drink. He is just out of control, and he thinks this is the funniest thing he's ever seen. And he's laughing, "HA-HAAAAAA!!! HAAAAAA!!" and he's slapping the back of my chair, and carrying on and wheezing his drunken breath all over me. Finally Rick just came back on the plane and took the monster out.

So now Bob and his wife jet off to Hawaii. They land in Honolulu, run down to the other end of the airport, board a prop plane for Kauai, fly to Kauai, get into a cab and drive off to a place called Hanalei, where they will stay in an absolutely beautiful cottage on a bluff overlooking one of the most lush and gorgeous views in all of Hawaii.

They check in just in time for the monsoon. Even as they're unpacking, sheets of rain begin to fall, and it will continue pouring throughout the vacation. Still, Bob makes the most of the situation by sacking out and trying to catch up on his rest. For the first time in months, he actually begins to relax, and that's when another one of Gene's practical jokes kicks in.

Bob's out bodysurfing in the rain when a bellboy comes running down the beach to give him a telegram. Bob sloshes out of the surf and reads the now-soggy missive. "Ignore Bill Heath's phone call," it says. "Will explain the incident later."

So now, of course, Bob panics, and he runs up to the hotel, still in his swim trunks, making a barefoot dash through the lobby toward the nearest pay phone. With visions of bloodshed, Bob places a long-distance call to Gene's office, and his worries intensify when Dorothy Fontana tells him that the boss isn't in.

Bob now wanders back down to the beach with his stomach churning even more violently than the sea. He sits stewing in the hotel room, certain that Gene's done serious bodily harm to Heath. An hour passes and there's a knock at the door. It's another bellboy bearing another telegram.

Bob's *agita* doubles as he opens the envelope and reads, "I know it sounds bad, but don't worry about this whole thing with Bill Heath. Will explain in my next letter." Again Bob runs off to the hotel lobby, flip-flops flapping at a sprinter's pace, and again Dorothy suppresses a laugh and lies that "The boss is out." Nauseated, Bob goes back to his room to obsess. This goes on all day, with a telegram arriving every hour, each one bearing a message like "Ignore Bill Heath's legal threats" or "Don't worry, I'm told I have a really good defense."

By the end of the day, after countless phone attempts to locate Roddenberry have proven unsuccessful, Bob's an absolute wreck. Finally, just as the gray, drizzly day is turning to a black, rainy night, Bob gets yet another telegram. Turning white with apprehension, Bob's hands tremble as he begins to read.

"Don't worry," it says, "Your secretary now admits you're not the father." At this point Bob knows he's been royally had, and though he'd been able to suppress his laughter in regard to the Balok head, this time he lets loose, guffawing mightily all the way back to his cottage.

When the week was over, Justman arrived home fairly refreshed and almost immediately went back to work. Soon after his arrival, however, he found Roddenberry suffering the earliest symptoms of a very similar collapse. Gene had been pulling double duty while Bob was away, attending to an even more mind-numbing array of details than usual, and as a result he was now absolutely fried, and obviously sinking fast. Within hours, Bob was back at the airport, but this time he was bidding "bon voyage" to Rodden-berry . . . and Balok, who just happened to be occupying the adjoining seat.

THE
UNSUNG
HERO

At this point in the story, entering from stage right is a man who was directly responsible for the lion's share of the creative contributions that served toward making Roddenberry's *good* science fiction show into a frequently *great* one. His name was Gene Coon.

Coon, who'd grown up in Nebraska, escaped courtesy of the United States Marine Corps and spent four years serving in Japan and China. Upon his discharge, he settled in Los Angeles, working as a freelance writer and eventually getting work on such shows as *Dragnet*, *Peter Gunn*, *Bonanza*, *Rawhide*, *Wagon Train*, and a whole laundry list more. Oddly enough, Gene was also one of the few writers able to bounce back and forth between writing dramatic TV fare and comedy. In fact, Coon was responsible for reshaping a failed one-hour World War II drama pilot into the successful half-hour sitcom *McHale's Navy*, and he also co-created *The Munsters*. This sort of intergenre hopscotch is almost unheard of in Hollywood, and it really serves as the perfect evidence of Coon's remarkable and unique talents. I asked Bob Justman about Coon's earliest association with *Star Trek*.

Our first thirteen scripts were just about complete, and by the time Gene came back from Hawaii, he had decided to kick himself upstairs and become executive producer. He told me, "I'm bringing in a new producer/writer to work very closely with you, and I'd like you to meet him. He's been working on *The Wild, Wild West* and he's the one that's responsible for all the really interesting concepts on that show. He's coming tomorrow."

I had never watched *The Wild, Wild West*, and so I had no idea what Gene was talking about. Still, I thought this was great. Roddenberry really needed help, he really needed to rest, and I figured that if Gene felt that this guy was *good*, he was probably terrific. So the next day arrives, Coon comes in and I meet him, and I looked at this guy, and to me he looked like a banker, or a Methodist preacher ... a cold dispassionate type of guy. He had close-cropped hair, a funny midwestern accent and his flesh looked kind of white and puffy. He didn't look like a writer.

He looked more like my concept of the cold, cruel banker who forecloses on the widow's mortgage. For those silly reasons, my first gut instinct was to dislike him. But as soon as we talked a little bit, I realized that I was wrong, and that this guy was a real gentleman. Then, when I first saw what he could write, I practically fell in love with the guy. He was just great. He could write the premise and the teleplay. He could do it all. He'd just sit down, smoking and smiling, while he came up with these absolutely mind-bending ideas and the teleplays to flesh them out. He was just perfect for *Star Trek*, exactly what we needed, and absolutely brilliant.

Over the years Gene Coon would write many of our very best episodes, and he'd produce even more. With Coon at the producer's post, *Star Trek* really began to click, and throughout his association with the show he produced the majority of our most successful outings. One of Coon's most important contributions to *Star Trek* can be found in the humor that he infused into every script. Coon's comic interludes were met with immediate viewer enthusiasm and very quickly became an important element of the series. Leonard recalls *his* own involvement in the lighter side of *Star Trek*.

It became very clear the fans really loved the "Bickersons" relationship that found Captain Kirk regularly caught in the middle of the battles between Spock and McCoy. You know, DeForest would be squared off on one side, full of this crotchety sort of ebullience, and he'd be needling Spock, probing for feelings and humanity.

On the other side, Spock would always be playing it straight, but underneath he was having a great time in sending McCoy up the wall by insisting that his arguments just didn't make any sense. You know, he'd be saying, "I don't understand what you're talking about, you cranky old doctor."

ABOVE: **M**IXING IT UP WITH THE "CRANKY OLD DOCTOR" AND A POINTY-EARED
GEORGE BURNS. (© 1993 PARAMOUNT PICTURES)
BOTTOM LEFT: KIRK, SPOCK AND THE FLIVVER, FROM "A PIECE OF THE ACTION."
(© 1993 PARAMOUNT PICTURES)
BOTTOM RIGHT: ON THE SPOT IN "THE CITY ON THE EDGE OF FOREVER."
(© 1993 PARAMOUNT PICTURES)

And I always tried to play these scenes very dry, perhaps raising an eyebrow, but never more than that. In fact, in all these arguments, I always modeled Spock after George Burns and his cigar. George's rather bemused, unflustered acceptance of Gracie's ramblings really influenced Spock's interaction with McCoy.

Coon's brand of humor always grew organically from within the characters. Captain Kirk never slipped on a banana peel for a laugh, we never put Spock in drag, and that's because while those things automatically draw knee-jerk laughs, they would have worked to the detriment of our characters. Instead, Coon felt that *Star Trek*'s humorous moments could be used not only to solicit laughter but also (as with the Bones/Spock bickering) to deepen our characters and the relationships between them. I asked Dorothy Fontana how this all came about.

The show was pretty straightforward in the beginning, but then we realized that any time we'd give the characters something humorous to play with, the show really sparked. So of course we said, "Hey, let's do some more of that." And we began to see the opportunities for humor in a lot of the interpersonal reactions and interchanges between characters, you know, for example, this is probably just about the time where Bones starts bickering with Spock. Humor is such an important part of any person, and these characters were no exception. I mean if Kirk had just remained lantern-jawed all the time, he would have been a good character, but he wouldn't have been nearly as fully dimensional as he became. He wouldn't have been as well-rounded. You know, you had to like the fact that he had a sense of humor and that he was able to laugh at his own mistakes as well as at funny situations or at what other characters might do. So humor became a major component of the personal interchange scenes that we put in.

Toward this end it was Gene Coon who decided that Kirk and Spock should awkwardly attempt to drive a twenties "flivver" automobile in "A Piece of the Action," and that Kirk, when put on the spot by the cop in "The City on the Edge of Forever," would come up with this pathetic explanation for Spock's rather strange appearance:

Kirk

Ah, you're a police officer . . . I recognize the traditional accoutrements. My friend is obviously . . . Chinese. I see you've noticed the ears. They're actually easy to explain.

Spock

Perhaps the unfortunate accident I had as a child . . .

Kirk

. . . yes, the unfortunate accident he had as a child. He caught his head in a mechanical . . . uh . . . rice-picker. But fortunately there was an American . . . um . . . missionary living close by who was actually a . . . uh . . . skilled plastic surgeon in civilian life . . .

During Coon's tenure on the show, the good-naturedly argumentative relationship between Bones and Spock became wonderfully real, as did the friendship between Kirk and Spock and the "complaining miracle worker" characterization of Scotty. With that in mind, although the Star Trek characters were conceived and created by Roddenberry, they really came to life, fully formed and recognizably human, under the direction of Gene Coon. Coon took Roddenberry's characters and made them people, made them a family.

I should also point out that Gene Coon created many of the basic conceptual points upon which he'd ultimately construct some of our best episodes. The Klingons, the Organian Peace Treaty and the Prime Directive were all conceived by Coon, and once they were in place, Star Trek's mission became even more believable. With Coon's inventions, Kirk, Spock, Bones and the rest had specific goals, specific orders, rules to follow and some terrific bad guys to fight.

In the past, many of these specific contributions have generally been assumed to be Roddenberry's, and that's simply not true. Coon, having died in 1973, was never able to give interviews, work the conventions or do the talk shows, and as a result his name and,

JEFFERIES' IMAGINATION FORTIFIES A COON CREATION WITH THIS EARLY SKETCH OF THE KLINGON BIRD-OF-PREY. (COURTESY WALTER M. JEFFERIES)

more important, his creative contributions were lost in the shuffle. Quite simply, Roddenberry created *Star Trek*, and Coon made it fly.

It's also interesting to note that Coon's writing techniques were as unusual as his stories. His widow, Jackie, explains:

Gene Coon loved writing. I've known a lot of writers, and while I think they're interesting people, they usually have a real depressed sort of heaviness about them. Gene wasn't like that at all. He never complained about having to write, he actually liked the process. He'd be thinking through his *Star Trek* scripts, and whenever he got stuck on a certain point or story angle he'd just go to sleep, knowing that the problem would have worked itself out within his head by morning. I have no idea how he could do that, all I know is that he'd jump up out of bed at five or six in the morning, feeling like a million bucks, run to his typewriter and the stories would just spill out, fully formed, from his fingertips. He'd write like a demon on fire till noon or one, then he'd pack it in for the day. I asked him about it one time, about why he wrote the frenetic way he did, and he told me, "I have to write this way. I have so much in my mind that I can't get it on the typewriter fast enough." So that's how he worked. He felt sensational, loved his work and then we'd go off and play for the rest of the day.

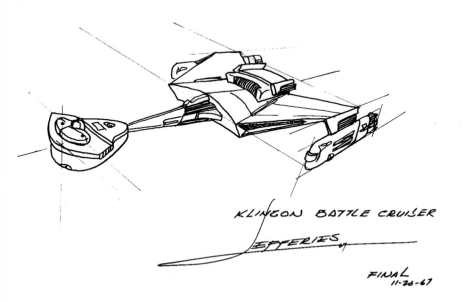

KLINGON BATTLE CRUISER

JEFFERIES

FINAL
11-20-67

Coon's prolific fingers quickly earned him the moniker of "Fastest Typewriter in the West," but unlike most speedy writers, his work was

never sloppy or hastily hacked together. Instead, it was always exciting and full of unexpected twists and turns. For example, "The Devil in the Dark" stands as a prime example of prime Coon.

It all started with a blob of rubber. You see, a guy named Janos Prohaska, who spent his career designing, building and acting as half the creatures, monsters and apes in Hollywood, worked with us quite often on *Star Trek*. Over the course of our three seasons, he'd create the Mugatu for "A Private Little War" (actually, what he created was the Gumatu; it was only when De Kelley kept repeatedly blowing his lines and saying "Mugatu" that we changed it), and the rock-man Yarnek who forces Kirk to fight alongside Abraham Lincoln in "The Savage Curtain." However, on this particular occasion Janos had shown up on the lot all excited about this enormous rather nondescript rubbery blob that he'd invented. I took a look, and I have to admit, I came away less than impressed. To me, this thing just looked like a lumpy piece of indoor/outdoor carpet. But Janos was obviously excited, and he wanted to show us what this creature could do. So now he takes a chicken, a dead store-bought chicken, and he just kinda throws it into the dirt. Then he smiles at us. None of us have a clue *why* he's smiling, but he's smiling nonetheless. He then gets under this blobbish creation and kind of wiggles up over the top of the chicken, all the while grunting, roaring and trying his best to sell the idea that this thing is alive. Now he lurches forward once more, and out of the back of this "monster" comes a complete chicken skeleton. We all immediately begin laughing, and Coon, who's got tears in his eyes, is yelling, "That's GREAT!!! I LOVE that!! We HAVE to use that!!!"

And that's exactly what he did. He went off and wrote "The Devil in the Dark," a story in which a "monster" would ultimately turn out to be a hero. In the story, Federation "pergium" miners have been digging away on the planet of Janus VI, and lately they've begun dropping like flies, swatted by this big blob of rubber, now known as the Horta. When the *Enterprise* crew is called in to exterminate the big pest, Spock ends up mind-melding with the creature, and he realizes that in killing the miners, the Horta has simply been attempting to protect its eggs, which the miners have been routinely destroying as a result of their digging. Suddenly this nondescript killer has become a sympathetic creature, valiantly fighting to save its children. This unique brand of unusual, intelligent and highly compelling storytelling stands as a perfect example of Coon's remarkable and very special talents.

At the same time, I've got to tell you that Gene Coon's real life was every bit as romantic and exciting as his fiction; in fact, he lived through one of the most profound and incredible love stories I've ever encountered. It begins rather humbly as Coon, upon his discharge from the

Marines, takes advantage of the G.I. Bill and enrolls in the Columbia School of Broadcasting, hoping to get in on the ground floor of the brand-new medium that experts swear will soon be sweeping the country. The class was tiny and consisted of eight discharged G.I.s, and two women, both of whom were still in their teens.

In time, Coon developed a real fondness for one of the girls. Her name was Jackie, and she seemed to return his feelings. However, Gene's own awkward shyness kept him from ever acting upon his deeply romantic feelings for the girl, and instead, he privately wrote her a long eloquent letter, expressing his love and asking her to marry him. Sadly, Coon was never quite able to muster up the courage to give his note to Jackie, and over time she misconstrued his shyness for lack of interest and began seeing another class member. Several months later, she became that man's wife.

Coon was devastated by his wasted opportunity, but eventually he began dating Joy Hankins, the other female class member. Within a year, they too would be married. Still, though happy with Joy, Coon never quite got over Jackie, and she never forgot about him. Over the course of the next decade, both couples would move to Virginia, where they'd remain friendly and get together often. However, as their careers progressed, they'd each relocate, ultimately losing contact with each other.

Lapse dissolve and it's 1968. Coon's working on *Star Trek*, and his marriage to Joy has grown rather unhappy. At the same time, a series of incredible coincidences is conspiring to reunite him with his first love. Jackie had by now begun acting and modeling, and she'd become rather successful, most recently appearing in the film version of *Sweet Charity*. As a result, her 8" × 10" head shot had now garnered a place of honor in (of all places) the Universal Studio commisary.

Enter coincidence number one. Lunching with a friend on the Universal lot one day, Coon sits down, begins eating and chatting with his friend, then stops in midsentence, astounded to see Jackie's face staring back at him from the cafeteria wall. Thrilled with his discovery, Coon hires a private detective to track down the whereabouts of his first love.

Enter coincidence number two. Even before this private eye's earned his first week's pay, Coon's driving to the studio one morning when he notices a huge new billboard being unveiled over Sunset Boulevard. At dead center is the smiling, beautiful face of . . . Jackie. Coon narrowly avoids careening into a city bus, regains his composure and continues on toward work, smiling. At the office, he immediately asks his secretary, Andie Richardson, to find out which ad agency had put together the Sunset billboard and ask that they have their model contact him.

Enter coincidence number three. Shortly after Coon's near-collision, Richardson comes running into his office, waving a newspaper and explaining that she's just read in the society pages that Jackie is in the midst of a divorce. "Find her," says Coon, "Get her on the phone." Richardson does some research, makes a few calls and within the hour the pair has reunited, at least by telephone. Jackie remembers:

> I remember clearly that the first thing I asked him was, "Are you happy?" and he just broke down and cried. It was overwhelming. We made a lunch date for the next day. I had never stopped loving Gene. You don't get over a first love, you move forward, but it remains a treasure in your heart. We got together the next day, and the feelings between us were still so strong that I said to him, "I never want you to leave again."
>
> After lunch, we talked some more in the car, and Gene told me that he'd become so unhappy in his marriage that he'd recently bought himself a gun, planning to kill himself. That would have been his way out. So when he found me again, he just threw all caution to the wind, and by six o'clock, we'd decided to get married. At that point, Gene summoned up all of his courage and divorced Joy. Actually, he felt so incredibly guilty about leaving Joy that he just left her with everything, absolutely everything.

One of Coon's best friends at the time was Bill Campbell, familiar to virtually everyone reading this book as *Star Trek*'s villainous "Squire of Gothos." He tells the story of a party attended that very evening by, among others, Roddenberry, Majel, Gene Coon, and Joy. Campbell continues:

> Roddenberry and Coon are standing together at this party, which was probably some kind of *Star Trek* thing, when Roddenberry says, "Boy, Joy looks great tonight, and she seems in really fine spirits." At which point Coon says, "Well, yes, but I don't know how she's going to react after tonight."
>
> "What do you mean by that?" Roddenberry asks, to which Coon replies, "I'm leaving her tomorrow." But then they went home after

the party, and Gene backed off on telling her. She couldn't help but notice that something was bothering Gene terribly, and in the end she just asked him, "What's happening here? Did I say something wrong? Did I do something wrong? What is it?" At that point, he told her everything, they cried together through the night and in the morning, he just put his papers into a briefcase and left.

Jackie became Coon's wife soon after, and in the remaining five years of Gene's life, their days were filled with happiness, passion and a love that even the most imaginative romance novelist could not possibly have concocted.

Still, even when you're supremely talented and lucky in love, you won't *always* encounter smooth sailing. For example, at the time Coon was just setting up his office space, Roddenberry was nearing his breakdown. So of course it fell upon Coon to become initiated into the show with a sort of "out of the frying pan and into the fire" approach. Normally this wouldn't be too tough, but as circumstances would have it, Coon was going to have to completely rewrite a script that had come in from one of our most talented and most frequent contributors, Theodore Sturgeon.

Gene had worked on the script and gotten it to the point where he felt it was ready to shoot. NBC, however, had other plans. The script in question was called "Shore Leave," and as originally written it was extremely fantastic and bizarre. The network read this script and immediately voiced some objections. They worried that viewers were still unsure of what *Star Trek* was actually all about, and that to send the *Enterprise* crew off on a very abstract sort of adventure so early on in the life of the series might just confuse these viewers into changing the channel . . . perhaps for good. As a result of their fears, they sent Roddenberry a memo asking (i.e., demanding) that this script be reworked and rewritten to the point where it would become crystal clear that this was not standard operating procedure for the crew of the *Enterprise*.

Literally moments before he was shuttled off to the airport for his well-deserved and much-needed week of rest, Roddenberry typed out a memo to Coon describing the rewrite that needed to be done and specifying exactly what NBC had requested. However, in the haste that accompanies the start of most vacations, the memo never made it off Roddenberry's desk.

Coon then got hold of Sturgeon's script, looked it over and, having no knowledge of NBC's edict, came up with some dramatic twists and changes to the story line that made it much more exciting. Unfortunately, they also made the episode even more absurd. Days passed quickly, the script was sent to mimeo, production schedules were written up, preliminary shot lists were prepared and on the eve of shooting, Roddenberry came home.

Tanned and healthy, he was able to return to the office with a lei still dangling about his neck and his psyche still basking in the afterglow of Hawaiian sunshine. This calm, relaxed state of mind lasted about three minutes, as one of the first things Roddenberry did was to pick up Coon's revised script for "Shore Leave."

As Roddenberry began to read, he nearly gagged on his souvenir bottle of macadamia nuts. In front of him lay a terrific but completely unusable script. Adding to his homecoming headaches was the fact that this script was to begin filming ... tomorrow morning. Coon was already busy rewriting three new scripts, so, thanks to a misrouted memo, Roddenberry had no choice but to get back to work twelve hours early with an unscheduled all-nighter. However, in this case even the genius of Roddenberry was no match for the extreme lack of time. Dawn broke over the Hollywood hills, and Star Trek's production crew was already en route to the wildlife ranch that would serve as "Shore Leave's" main location. By six-thirty A.M. Gene had pounded through a first rough draft of the teleplay's early scenes, but he was nowhere near finished and had absolutely no idea of how to end the show. I can still remember him roaring up to our production vehicles in a cloud of dust, handing his first new pages over to Bob Justman, then immediately planting himself in the shade. Sitting on the ground with a yellow legal pad, Roddenberry began work on the second half of the show.

Gene's overnight script got us through the first day's shooting and was actually quite good: Tight, exciting and stamped all over with Roddenberry's trademark style. Still, we actors were forced to fill in some of the dialogue holes Gene left unattended, and as a result, this particular episode is full of ad-libs. The day wore on, and as we were wrapping at the end of the shoot, Gene was still at a loss in coming up with an ending for

the show. Finally, over a long, long dinner with cast and crew members, Roddenberry was able to work up one of *Star Trek*'s most spectaular "Big Finishes" and add into the script samurai warriors, a World War II bomber, even some of the many animals that lived year-round at this wildlife park.

One, a tiger, is featured throughout the story line, and at one point, riding on a swell of insane ad-lib fever, I came up with the idea that Captain Kirk should have a fight scene with this striped carnivorous monster.

Now, the words "stuntman" and "phony tiger" are probably already buzzing about your cerebellum, but I can assure you that, strangely enough, I wasn't the least bit interested in such precautions. Even stranger, I can remember being really excited about the whole thing. I mean here I was, this middle-aged actor, caught up in the adrenaline of the moment, and I stood there, like a dope, actually contemplating hopping on top of Shere Khan. Roddenberry, who really

OPPOSITE: SHOOTING "A PRIVATE LITTLE WAR" ON LOCATION AT L.A.'S VASQUEZ ROCKS. (© 1993 PARAMOUNT PICTURES)

ABOVE: LEONARD AND I CONFER WITH DIRECTOR MARC DANIELS WHILE WE SMILE AND TRY NOT TO SWEAT. (© 1993 PARAMOUNT PICTURES)

LEFT MIDDLE: BETWEEN SHOTS, THE CAMERA CREW GETS SET AND THE LIGHTING GUYS READJUST THE ROW OF MIRRORED REFLECTORS THAT SUBSTITUTE FOR OUR STUDIO LIGHTING. I CONTINUE SWEATING. (© 1993 PARAMOUNT PICTURES)

LEFT BOTTOM: LEONARD'S NOW SUCCUMBED TO THE HEAT, AND I'VE CHEERFULLY OFFERED TO SHOOT HIM. (© 1993 PARAMOUNT PICTURES) had about a hundred thousand other things to worry about, came over and tried to talk me out of this unarguably stupid idea, but I was, for some unfathomable reason, determined to go through with it.

Then Roddenberry did something brilliant. With his arm around my shoulder, we strolled through the park as he tried to convince me that I was far too important to the show to risk wrestling the man-eater. He really wasn't getting far, but then, and in retrospect I'm sure it was premeditated, we "stumbled" upon the tigers' habitat at precisely feeding time. There sat the tiger I would be battling: enormous, majestic and gnawing away at a bone full of red meat.

Immediately my testicles rose up into my Adam's apple, and the ignorant machismo that had been pulsing so heartily through my veins was now replaced by sheer abject terror. I stood there trying not to look too horrified as I now gracefully backed down, "for the good of the show." "Sure," I said, "I'll forget about fighting with this little kitty . . . if you really think it's best." At which point Nimoy wanders over and wickedly says, "Y'know, Gene, I *could* just give him the old Vulcan pinch."

In retrospect, it's easy to surmise that the most basic, underlying reasons behind *Star Trek*'s predilection toward greatness can easily be traced back to its Genes.

SHOTS
I
DA

A fter getting burned by Bill Heath and the Anderson Company, Gene Roddenberry and Bob Justman had conspired to make sure that they'd never again get so far behind the optical eight ball. For that reason, they hired a man named Eddie Milkis. Eddie had worked with Gene as an editor on *The Lieutenant* and had impressed him to the point that Roddenberry went out of his way to specifically recruit Eddie into overseeing all of *Star Trek*'s postproduction. Milkis remembers:

I first met Gene in 1964, when he was producing *The Lieutenant* and I was a film editor. In those days every one-hour series hired three editors, but they'd run into trouble on *The Lieutenant* because Gene always gave the editors so much trouble about getting things exactly right. As a result, they'd fallen behind schedule. Anyway, they brought me in as a fourth editor, and almost immediately something really began to click between Gene and me. By the end of the season, we had formed a great relationship.

By the time *The Lieutenant* folded I'd become a little bit disenchanted with the business, and I hated having a hiatus that forced me to be unemployed for three months each year. As a result, I'd gotten a real estate license, and I ended up joining my brother-in-law in the real estate development business.

Then, in 1965, Gene called me and said, "I'm doing a pilot, for *Star Trek* . . . you know, the show we used to talk about. Would you come and edit it for me?" I said, "No, I can't, Gene. I'm in a different business now." I got another call from him about a year later, and he asked me about editing the second pilot. Again, I said no.

After that, he'd call me every once in a while, and we'd talk about how things were going, and then, in August of 1966, he called me one evening at about six. I can remember the call so precisely, because it really changed my life.

I was sitting in the real estate office, and the business had become really rocky. Things were falling apart, and I knew it. Gene tells me, "I'm in trouble. We've shot some episodes, and the people they have here doing the postproduction tell me there's no way we can make our airdates." "How can that be?" I asked him. "That just can't happen."

He then asked me to come by the office and discuss the situation. I said, "Fine, I'll come over first thing in the morning," and Gene says, "Oh, no, no. I don't have time for that. Can you get over here now?" I said "Alright, I'll swing by on my way home."

So I went in and I met with Gene and Bob Justman and Herb Solow, Desilu's "executive in charge of production," and they laid it all out for me. They were using Desilu's postproduction department and things were in total disarray. Then Gene said, "I'd like you to come in and run the postproduction department for us." I said, "Gene, I don't know how to do that, I'm just a film editor. I don't know anything about bossing people, or organizing a department . . ." And Gene stopped me by smiling and saying, "Ahhh, sure you do." I laughed, and by the time that conversation was over, I'd been hired. I started working there the next morning.

The first thing Milkis noticed was that with the Enterprise constantly cruising about the outer reaches of space, there were a huge number of special effects shots in each of our episodes. He also noticed that this enormous workload was simply too much for the Anderson Company to deal with. As a result, our special effects just weren't getting done, and Star Trek's postproduction work was rapidly falling further and further behind schedule. With that in mind, one of the first things he did was to consult with Bob Justman, then hire four additional special effects houses, so that Star Trek's effects could be worked on simultaneously in several different locations.

While that began solving one of Star Trek's postproduction problems, there were plenty more that needed attention. Music, sound effects, shooting the Enterprise miniatures and the editing of each episode were all responsibilities that soon found themselves squarely perched on Eddie's shoulders.

The editing of each Star Trek episode, although an extremely time-consuming process, actually presented Mr. Milkis with a relatively low number of headaches. In fact, in supervising *Star Trek*'s handful of extremely talented film editors, Eddie simply kept an eye on the proceedings, offering creative suggestions or comments aimed at strengthening the timing or look of any given scene. This marked Milkis's favorite aspect of *Star Trek*'s postproduction because, having been an editor, he dearly loved the process. Milkis explains:

> What I really loved about the editing was being able to approach the job from a storytelling standpoint. I think editors who work this way can do wonders. I really loved taking the pieces of any given scene and making something good out of them. I mean even when your ideas didn't work very well, you could simply take the whole scene apart again, shot by shot, then reconstruct it in a whole new way. If you were lucky, you then got to say, "Oh my God! That works! What a difference!" It's a very creative and satisfying process.

Once a rough cut was made of each episode and approved by Justman and Roddenberry, Eddie was able to . . . get right back to work. That's because although the show had *begun* to resemble its final form, it was still lacking music, sound effects, visual effects and any specific shots of the *Enterprise* miniatures that might be demanded by the individual script.

Supervising the production of *Star Trek*'s photographic effects was far and away the most time-consuming of Milkis' responsibilities, and it wasn't at all unusual for the work to run far behind schedule. With that in mind, I asked Eddie the obvious question: "What the hell took so long?" He answers:

> The guys at the Anderson Company and in fact all of the guys who created our special effects were good, but at the same time, you have to remember that this was 1966, and we just didn't have the technology that exists today. Nothing was easy or computerized, and the technology that we were working with would now be considered absolutely antique. In fact, in creating most of *Star Trek*'s visual effects, we were really relying on guesswork.
>
> Y'know, we'd come up with some way to do a certain visual effect, and then we'd test it. We actually made up ninety percent of the effects as we went along. We'd just take a stab at it, based on what we thought would work. But then a lot of the time the

effect wouldn't come out the way we thought it would. We'd work it through and it'd come out *facacta*. So we'd have to redo it, and most of the time, it'd take us three or four tries to get it right.

Of course, until you've redone and perfected one shot you can't really go on to the next. That's how things got so backed up.

Throughout this period, Milkis was beginning each day with a five-thirty A.M. meeting with Bob Justman. They'd discuss how things were progressing on the postproduction front, then look ahead at future episodes, making early plans for *their* needs as well. The reason behind the extremely early meeting was simply that both men would always be far too busy to meet at any other point in the day. Milkis, in fact, spent the better part of most days keeping tabs on the effects labs, and the better part of each *evening* supervising the shooting of *Star Trek*'s miniatures. He recalls:

I was working from about five-thirty in the morning until midnight, or sometimes even later. That's because throughout the first season, we were desperately short on traveling shots of the *Enterprise*. Y'know, we needed generic shots of the ship flying across the screen, or toward camera, and we also had to shoot a lot of script-specific stuff as well.

And as you know, we really worked with two different miniatures. One was about three feet long, and we'd use that whenever we needed a pod to blow out or to launch a shuttlecraft or whatever. Basically, whenever we needed to customize or damage the model, we'd use the small guy. We'd never do that kind of stuff to the big one; we needed to preserve her.

Actually, the big model had lights running all around the saucer area and was loaded with detail. It was really intricate. It was also eleven feet two inches long, and impossible to shoot. It was just too big. Anyway, after a full day of running from lab to lab and spending some time in the editing room, I'd have to go over to a place called Film Effects, where we had a guy named Linwood Dunn shooting our miniatures.

They had a big stage there, and the first thing we did was to paint the whole thing blue. That's because we knew we'd be doing "blue-screen" effects, which basically allowed us to shoot the ship, then remove this blue-paint background and add in an outer-space panorama.

TWO VIEWS OF THE THREE-FOOT ENTERPRISE: (ABOVE) MOUNTED FOR
SHOOTING, AND (RIGHT) IN MY HANDS FOR A PUBLICITY STILL. (© 1993
PARAMOUNT PICTURES)
BELOW: SHOOTING THE ELEVEN-FOOT MODEL AGAINST THE "BLUE SCREEN"
BACKGROUND. (© 1993 PARAMOUNT PICTURES)

Anyway, we generally hung the ship about four feet off the floor, and then ran dolly tracks for the camera across right underneath it. Then we'd shoot, and if the ship was supposed to look like it was flying toward camera, we'd just dolly in toward the front, then pan away at the last possible second. When we got back to the lab, took out the blue, added a background and processed that shot, it'd look like the ship was "flying" right into camera. We'd do the same kind of thing whenever the ship was supposed to fly across the screen. If we shot film and dollied left, the ship appeared to move to the right, and vice versa.

This wasn't really a new process, it was just hard to do, because you could either do it perfectly or not at all. If the color of the ship wasn't precisely right or if your lighting was slightly off, the shot wouldn't work. You'd end up not being able to remove the original blue background. You were either perfect or dead. One screwup, and the whole night's work would be wasted.

Speaking of screwups, throughout the first season of Star Trek, a good number of Eddie's most nagging headaches were caused by us actors, ably assisted in our incompetence by the "director of the week." You see, in creating Star Trek's recurring visual effects, there were specific procedural guidelines that needed to be followed to the letter, and it actually took us quite a while to figure that out.

As an example, for any member of the Enterprise crew to beam off the ship, it was absolutely necessary for us to walk over to the transporter and quickly get in position for beaming. Then, as the huge lighting device underneath the station kicked on, we had to stand perfectly still for about fifteen seconds. At that point we were to exit, briskly and without flourish, as the cameras continued rolling, shooting the empty set.

Following this procedure, the boys in the lab could then take this footage, watch us come into frame and prepare for beaming, then chop out the section where we exited. Then they'd splice on the footage of the empty set, throwing in a fancy dissolve and shimmery glitter effect for good measure. Once that was done, another Enterprise crewman was gone.

That's how it was *supposed* to work, but throughout most of the first season, none of us really understood the procedure, and as a result we were constantly entering incorrectly, moving around or even delivering lines while we were in the midst of beaming. Needless to say, this drove Eddie Milkis nuts.

In the beginning we were always looking at footage and saying, "Well, they fucked it up again." Y'know, the actors would walk around while they were supposed to be beaming, or a director would end the shot without filming the empty transporter room. There was a lot of confusion in those early days, because nobody really knew how the special effects were constructed.

The phasers were always troublesome, too. You guys needed to hold your hand perfectly still while you shot, so that we could add in the line of fire back at the lab. But because nobody could ever manage to perform that simple task, we'd end up with a jiggling hand that shot this steady stream of phaser fire. This immediately exposed the trick, and we were sunk. We'd reshoot sometimes, but usually we had to make do with what we got.

On the other side of the coin and on the other side of town, Eddie was working with Bob Justman and a guy named Doug Grindstaff in creating all of *Star Trek*'s sound effects. Here, too, *Star Trek*'s unusual settings and dramatic situations took a normally routine aspect of filmmaking and complicated it immeasurably. For example, most standard television shows create all of their sound effects by simply making use of a tape library, and everything from gunshots to screams to moose mating calls can be found quite easily at any good sound shop in Hollywood.

However, since *Star Trek* was constantly dealing with unknown life forms that moved and breathed and spoke unlike any before seen on television, these preexisting sounds were of little use. With that in mind, Milkis, Justman and Grindstaff had to create their own. I asked Eddie how they did this.

We'd usually start with something really ordinary. For example, if we needed a strange metallic sound, we might take a bell and just kind of bop it with a hammer or tap our feet on top of it. Then we'd say something like, "Okay, let's take that sound and run it through an echo chamber." We'd do that, listen to it and play some more. We might add some high end, or some low end, maybe some reverb or a wind effect, and finally it would sound right. Other times we might just hit the leg of a chair and use that.

As all of these aspects began coming together, they'd be shipped off to the editing house, where guys like Fabian Tjordmann, Bob Swanson and Frank Keller would create a small miracle by taking the episode's original rough cut, adding in all of the above elements and putting together a version of the show that was almost complete. Roddenberry would inevitably suggest a change or two, and when the editors had reemerged from the darkness of their work areas and satisfied Gene's requests, the episode had officially reached "final cut" status.

However, "final" did not mean "finished." The episode still had no music. For that, a print of the actual film was sent to a selected composer, who'd watch it and then write the music that would accompany every

scene. Once that rather large task was complete, an entire orchestra full of musicians would be shoehorned into a sound recording studio, where they'd play the composer's work while actually screening the particular episode. This allowed the composer to make sure his musical charts were in perfect synch with the on-screen action. If a salt vampire's sneaking up behind Bones, you want to make sure that the suspenseful musical buildup comes to a head at exactly the moment the good doctor gets grabbed. To be even slightly off on the timing of the crescendo's climax would be to completely destroy the scene's dramatic tension.

Once the orchestra had gone home, this episode's dialogue, sound effects and brand-new musical score were all mixed together into a final soundtrack. These elements were then added into the mix as the finished episode was constructed from the episode's original negatives. The resulting hour-long product was then screened by the perpetually pooped Milkis, dubbed and shipped out to the network.

At last this episode of *Star Trek* was complete, and Eddie Milkis could breathe a sigh of relief . . . then immediately get started on next week's show.

OPENING NIGHTS

s the summer of 1966 was ending and *Star Trek* was nearing its premiere date, we all had a pretty clear sense that it was really shaping up to be something special. However, we were also beginning to suffer the inevitable assault of stomach butterflies, which would soon transform themselves into opening-night jitters.

Roddenberry was no exception; in fact, he was probably the most nervous person on the lot. Pacing endlessly about his office, Gene looked not unlike the polar bears at the San Diego Zoo. Actually, if those bears chain-smoked and wore plaid cardigan sweaters, there'd be no telling 'em apart.

Finally, when the stress of the upcoming premiere became magnified by Gene's neverending parade of production headaches, he decided to put himself out of his own misery. During Labor Day weekend, Gene tucked sixteen-millimeter prints of both *Star Trek* pilots under one arm, threw a representative sample of *Star Trek*'s most impressive costumes over the opposite shoulder, got on a Cleveland-bound plane and paid a last-minute call on the world's largest science fiction convention.

Called Tricon, this particular event stands as irrefutable proof that the science fiction convention did *not* start with *Star Trek*. In fact, even in 1966 this annual gathering was more than twenty-five years old. It had begun in the early forties, and throughout the ensuing years it had grown into the largest and most prestigious gathering of science fiction enthusiasts any-where.

For that reason, Gene decided to fly to Cleveland, hoping to bounce his new show off a real and quite knowledgeable audience. On the Friday morning of this long weekend, he called the Tricon organizers, offering to attend the event and allow the attendees an exclusive sneak preview of his new NBC science fiction series. The promoters jumped at his offer and asked that he bring those few costumes along, as the convention was planning a "futuristic fashion show."

In Cleveland, the woman in charge of this fashion show is having a terrible day. She's driven to Cleveland from *Los Angeles*, and is, as you might expect, a bit groggy from the trip. Doubling her stress level is the fact that she is unexpectedly coordinating this event alone, due to the sudden appendicitis of her partner. Now, although she is trying her best to tackle the myriad details involved in putting together such a spectacle, she is becoming increasingly plagued by logistic and scheduling problems, and increasingly annoyed. Her name is Bjo Trimble, and though she'll go on to become perhaps the single most important fan in the history of *Star Trek*, her first involvement with the show and Gene Roddenberry was somewhat less than cordial. Bjo explains:

This "futuristic fashion show" was by no means a simple costume contest; it was much more organized, structured and involved. And the folks in charge of the Tricon convention had been less than cooperative throughout. They'd say, "You have exactly one hour for your show, no more, no less. It starts at exactly seven and ends at exactly eight. Not a second long, not a second short."

So I had twenty costumes to include in this thing, and as I worked through the logistics of the show, I realized that if my timing was perfect, I could pull this thing off, right on schedule. Thirty seconds later, one of the Tricon organizers comes up to me and says, "We forgot to tell you, but we have this Hollywood producer here, and he's brought with him three costumes that he would love to put in your show."

By now I was in no mood to be accommodating, so I just said, "Forget it. No way! Beat it!"

This guy then says, "Well, we already promised him that you'd include them."

I said, "I don't care! It's my show, go away!"

So now he says, "Look, the guy's standing right over there, and he brought this stuff just so you'd put it on display."

I rolled my eyes up into my head and said, "Well, who is he?"

"Gene Roddenberry," the guy tells me.

"Gene WHO?!" I said back to him. "I've never even heard of him. Forget it."

Next thing I know, this great big bear of a man with a cherubic Irish face walks up to me and says, "Hi, I'm Gene Roddenberry.

Can I take you for a 'cup of coffee?" So I said, rather grumpily, "Yeah, fine . . . whatever."

I really didn't want to give in, but Gene was persistent, charming and at one point he even showed me his costumes by having three local models parade them in front of me. I can still remember that one of these costumes was the one that Sherry Jackson wore in "What Are Little Girls Made Of?" and that the model who wore it actually had to spend most of her evening beating men off with a stick. Even Harlan Ellison, who was there as an honored guest, was trying his best to move in on her.

By the time they'd finished their coffee, Bjo had not only agreed to include the Star Trek fashions in the show, but she'd also okayed making special mention of Star Trek and its upcoming premiere. "There's a special kind of Irish charm that they say can drive the birds out of the trees, and Gene was loaded with that."

Once the fashion show had ended, Gene was able to screen a copy of "Where No Man Has Gone Before" for the attendees. Standing just behind the last row of seats in the jammed auditorium, Roddenberry was understandably nervous as the house lights dimmed and his film began to unreel upon the silver screen. At this point, he can't help but notice a rather large man who's conversing loudly, holding court with the half-dozen audience members who've gathered around him. He's telling stories, laughing and paying absolutely no attention to Gene's film. Annoyed, Roddenberry strides purposefully toward the distracting center of attention, taps him on the shoulder and says, "Hey! For Christ's sake, be QUIET! That's my pilot on the screen."

Once confronted, the offending audience member sheepishly pipes down. However, even as Gene is returning to his back-row vantage point, he is cornered by a convention official who sarcastically intones, "Congratulations, you just insulted Isaac Asimov." As you might expect, Roddenberry was mortified.

Now, throughout the screening of the film, Gene's sweating profusely, wringing his hands as he apprehensively awaits the pilot's ending and the reaction of this audience. Legend has it that as the pilot was nearing its dramatic conclusion, Gene closed his eyes, unable to bear the suspense of the upcoming moment of truth. As the episode drew to a close and the end credits began to unreel, Roddenberry drew a deep breath, awaiting the audience reaction, and was stunned, nearly into sickness, when no sound at all rose from the auditorium seats. Opening his eyes in horror, Gene was sure that this group, at best, was entirely indifferent to his offering.

However, what Gene didn't understand was that instead of disliking "Where No Man Has Gone Before," this group was thrilled by it. In fact, they'd been so thoroughly impressed that they now sat silently reading the credits and taking mental notes, recording the names of the people responsible for such a fine science fiction outing. Once the credits had finished flickering, the audience rose as one, applauding thunderously, stomping their feet and hollering for more. The conventioneers' overwhelming response prompted Gene into screening "The Cage" as an extra added attraction.

When "The Cage" was met with equally earsplitting approval, Isaac Asimov suddenly appeared at Gene's side. He went out of his way to apologize for his earlier rude behavior and to thoroughly praise what he'd just seen. A friendship was formed, and Roddenberry drew a deep and satisfied breath. He could now relax, secure in the knowledge that his feelings about Star Trek were not the least bit idiosyncratic. It was indeed a great show. Then, with the memory of Star Trek's overwhelming acclaim still fresh in his mind, Gene wired the following telegram to Desilu's head of television production, Herb Solow.

756P PDT SEP 3 66 LB367 CTA271 CT CLB506 NL PD
CLEVELAND OHIO 3 HERB SOLOW, VP TV, DESILU
STAR TREK HIT OF THE CONVENTION, VOTED BEST
EVER. RECEIVED STANDING OVATION. GENE R.

September 8, 1966: Hot on the heels of Gene's incredible success in Cleveland, Star Trek arrives on the air with a resounding . . . thud. The network had looked at all of the episodes we'd filmed (among them such classics as "Mudd's Women," "Charlie X," and "The Naked Time"), and from them they chose our absolute worst, "The Man Trap," as the premiere. As you probably know, this particular episode revolved around a salt-sucking vampire for whom Bones has a Jones. It was a dreadful show, one of our worst ever, but at the time the network felt it could "best introduce the audience to the basic concepts inherent within the framework of the program."

Gene argued against the choice, but nevertheless "The Man Trap" aired, we cringed, and by the time the next day arrived, we found that our ratings were at best mediocre, and that most of our reviews could best be described as lousy. For example, *Variety* commented:

> "Star Trek" obviously solicits an all-out suspension of disbelief, but it won't work. Even within its sci-fi frame of reference it was a ... dreary mess of confusion ... trudg[ing] on for a long hour with hardly any relief from violence, killings, hypnotic stuff and a distasteful, ugly monster ...
>
> By a generous stretch of the imagination, it could lure a small coterie of the smallfry ...
>
> The performers are in there pitching, but the odds are against them in all departments—script, direction and overall production. William Shatner ... appears wooden ...

Wait a minute. Hold on here. Me? Wooden? Wooden?!! Mr. "SCOTTY! SPOCK!! I NEED WARP DRIVE IN THREE MINUTES OR WE'RE ALL DEAD!!!"? Me? The "Ham-osauras"? Wooden?

> ... same goes for Leonard Nimoy, costarred as Mr. Spock, so-called chief science officer whose bizarre hairdo (etc.) is a dilly ...

Okay, at least *that* portion of the review makes sense, as I've often seen Leonard as a bit of a "dilly." Still, the review concludes as follows:

> ... The biggest guessing game is figuring how this lower-case fantasia broke into the sked.

It seems ironic that just as the battle to get *Star Trek* on the air had been won, another fight was brewing. This time the crew of the starship *Enterprise* would be struggling to avoid cancellation, and the odds were stacked against us.

BIGG
THIN

reeted with bad reviews and bad ratings, Gene returns to the office, where he completely ignores these negatives and continues plugging away, swimming against this tide of negativity, thinking surely his luck will change for the better. He was wrong. In fact, he's barely even settled back into his desk when his secretary, Dorothy Fontana, quits. This leaves Gene without his right hand or his first line of defense against the unceasing onslaught of the Justmans, Coons, prospective writers and evil network suits.

Actually, Dorothy didn't just quit her job; she took on a whole new career, leaving her secretarial duties behind so that she could pursue writing full-time. I asked Dorothy about taking that giant step.

had done the teleplay on "Charlie X" and I was in the middle of writing another for the episode "Tomorrow Is Yesterday," and I came to the conclusion that I just didn't want to be a secretary anymore. And I said to myself, "I think I'll give it a try. I've got some money in the bank, and even if I don't sell *anything*, I'll be okay, and at least I'll have tried." Actually, I was kind of hoping that Gene might let me write some more *Star Treks*.

So I gave my three weeks' notice and I said, "Gene, I love working with you, but I really want to write. You know I've been working toward this all of my life, and now that I've got some credits under my belt and a little bit of money in the bank, I have to give it my best shot." And Gene could appreciate that ambition because at one point he had to face a very similar decision in regard to leaving the police force. So he survived, but he did hate losing a good secretary.

So now, a bit nervous and more than a bit anxious, Dorothy goes home, works on her script for "Tomorrow Is Yesterday," and waits by the phone, hoping for more. Surprisingly, her "big break" comes less than two weeks later with a call from Gene.

ene called me and said, "I've got a script by Jerry Sohl that's called 'The Way of the Spores' and it's just not working. So I'll tell you what. Steve Carabatsos is just finishing up his contract, and I'm going to need a story editor. If you can rewrite this script in a short period of time, write it quickly and write it well, please the network and please the studio, I will back you as my new story editor, and I will tell the studio that I want you and *only* you."

So of course I said, "Okay, it's a challenge and I accept it." I got to work on "The Way of the Spores," and I turned it into "This Side of Paradise," the Spock love story. Now in the original draft, the love story was between Sulu and the girl, and these spores are off in a cave somewhere, so the script was weighed down by the fact that our characters kept having to blunder into this cave to become infected. The solution to that problem was "Don't go near the cave" . . . simple enough. So I went into Gene's office and I told him, "I think I've solved the problem. Instead of the pods being only in this one cave, let's put them all over the planet. They'll be growing like weeds so that no matter what you do or where you go, you can't escape them. They will infect you no matter what." Gene thought about all that for a moment and said, "That's very interesting. Okay, go write it."

I realize that may sound unusual, but Gene was like that. If you hit him with an interesting idea or an intriguing take on something, he'd say, "Go work it out." In short, he trusted the opinions of his co-workers and loved watching them come up with creative solutions. And of course, on a much less noble front, fostering the encouragement of independent problem-solving couldn't help but make Gene's job a little bit easier. Dorothy continues:

hen Gene told me to "work it out," that's exactly what I did. I sat down and thought about the story and I said, "What doesn't work here? Why is this not as exciting as it should be?" One of the big problems was this love story, because there was just something about it that didn't seem important enough. Not to say that the character of Sulu wasn't important, but it would be more important and there would be more at stake if the romance involved Spock. Spock would finally be able to feel love and experience its joys, breaking through the walls of his Vulcan training, which wouldn't allow him to feel. So this seemed like it would be a great character thing, and we could get away with Spock behaving this way because he'd be under this alien influence, taking him out of himself. His normal walls of reserve were gone, and he was free to feel. It was really unique.

I mean in "Naked Time" Spock experienced some feelings, but they were grief and sadness, so he hadn't yet experienced joy, and it would become a major character thing. At the same time, Kirk would be fighting against *his* feelings, against the effects of the spores, and experiencing a different sort of grief in that he did not want to leave his love, which was of course the *Enterprise*. So you had a situation of one character finding a love and finally being able to feel, played against another who was fighting against having to give up a love, which was his ship.

And I got the script in on time and the reaction to it was terrific, so I got the job.

Dorothy came on board in early December, and her job entailed working closely with Roddenberry and Coon, doing rewrites as assigned and quite often working directly with our freelance writers, making suggestions on how their scripts could best suit the needs of *Star Trek* and offering them creative notes from the pair of Genes. By the time she had officially begun fulfilling her lifelong dream, a fellow *Star Trek* employee was also meeting with unexpected on-the-job success. His name was Leonard Nimoy.

Within weeks of our premiere, it became obvious that Leonard and the character of Spock were becoming something of a national phenomenon. Spock fan clubs had begun to spring up, the press made him a favorite target and even the network had come full circle, at one point going so far as to send Gene a uniquely twisted memo demanding an answer as to why he hadn't been featuring Spock in every story. These same network executives who'd previously demanded Spock's removal from the *Enterprise* were now doing their best to take full credit for the popular Vulcan's success.

My character of Kirk was also becoming quite popular, but the swelling interest in Spock was growing by leaps and bounds, and to be perfectly honest, this really began to bother me. I mean, I had spent the better part of my career performing as a leading man on stage, in films and on televi-

sion, and by the time *Star Trek* came along, I'd become quite accustomed to carrying the vehicles I appeared in. However, once the show had been on the air for a couple of

months, although Captain Kirk was still the lead character, all of a sudden Spock's popularity began increasing exponentially with the passing of each new week. I was now faced with no longer being the only star of this show. And to be unflatteringly frank, it bugged me. I wasn't proud of these feelings, but they were simply the natural human reaction.

All of this was truly odd for me because I'd never felt this sort of jealousy before. I was always for "the team," and "the peace" and "the play's the thing," so these new feelings caught me totally off guard, and I had absolutely no clue about how I should go about dealing with them. I can even remember that I finally went so far as to bring my problem into Roddenberry's office, where he said to me the wisest thing he could possibly have uttered. He said, "Don't ever fear having good and popular people around you, because they can only enhance your own performance. The more you can play to these people," and by that he meant Leonard and DeForest and everybody else, "the better the show." And he was absolutely right. It suddenly made perfect sense.

I can clearly remember listening to Gene, and how his words sank straight into my soul. Still, in retrospect, I've got to wonder if Gene was being sincerely supportive or just using a very effective technique in handling a jealous, agitated actor. Either way, it worked, and whatever the reason, it was exactly the right thing to say.

Strangely enough, however, just before Spock began to get famous, there was a period of time where a series of events conspired to make Leonard wonder if anybody would ever know his name. The first took place at the dentist's office. Leonard recalls:

One time, early on in the series, I remember I had a very severe tooth problem. And I had been seeing a particular dentist about it, but one day on the set I was in a lot of pain, and it was so bad that I knew I had to get off the soundstage and into my dentist's office. So I called him, and I told his secretary that I was having a lot of pain in the tooth he'd been working on.

"Well, the doctor is on vacation," she tells me, "but there's another dentist in the office who's covering his patients. If you want to come into the office, he'll see you." So I said "Okay," and I walked off the stage as Spock, and I got into my car as Spock, drove all the way down Sunset Boulevard as Spock. And then I parked the car down the street from the office, got out of the car and walked across the street, up to the office, and nobody blinked an eye.

Now I walked into the building and stepped into an elevator full of people, and the elevator got very quiet. I get off at my floor and I walk into the office, where there's a lady, writing at her desk. And I walked in, and I stood there in front of her, and she looked up, then looked right back down at what she was writing.

"Can I help you?" she asks in a sort of bored nasal monotone. "Yes," I said, "I'm Leonard Nimoy, and I'm here to see the doctor about my tooth." "The doctor will be with you in a few moments," she says. So now I sit down in the waiting room, looking like a Vulcan, and I read *Newsweek*.

Not a word was spoken until maybe twenty minutes later, when the secretary comes in and says, "The doctor will see you now."

She now walks me in, and I meet this dentist. "Hello," he says, "I'm Doctor So-and-So." I say, "How do you do, I'm Leonard," and he says, "Please sit down and tell me what the problem is."

So I sit down, he works on me for a half hour, at the end of which he says, "Okay, you're all done, if you have any more trouble, your regular doctor will be back on Monday."

They never said a word to me about "What is this? Who are you? Are you crazy? Are you sane? Is it safe for me to put my fingers into your mouth?" Can you imagine the conversation that took place after I'd gone?

Several weeks later, I had the pleasure of riding with Leonard in a convertible down Hollywood Boulevard as part of the annual Christmas parade. They have this parade every year with celebrities riding in open-air cars down Hollywood Boulevard. It's a big community event; thousands of people line the sidewalks. Along the way, they have people with microphones announcing who's coming up. "And now here's the star of *Bonanza*, Lorne Greene," and "Say hello to Gilligan himself, Mr. Bob Denver!" That kind of stuff. And of course the crowd goes, "Yay, hooray, hooray."

Anyway, as Leonard and I were coming down the street we were sitting side by side, and when we get to the guy with the microphone he says, "Here they are, the stars of *Star Trek*, William Shatner and Mr. Leonard NIMSY!" Leonard just kind of sighed, rolling his eyes, as I told him two things. First, I said, "You're never gonna forget that," which has proven true over the years, mainly because I keep teasing him with this story. And second, I said, "You're so good on our show that any day now everybody everywhere will know your name. In fact, you won't be able to go *anywhere* without people pointing at you and saying, 'Hey, there goes Lionel Nimoy!'"

With that, Leonard punched me in the arm. However, within a few weeks, my predictions about Leonard's popularity were undeniably coming true, and the events of his first personal appearance really drove the point home. Leonard recalls:

My very first personal appearance was in Medford, Oregon, and it was around the end of January, so we'd only been on the air four or five months. It was also the only time I ever did what I did there. I went to Medford, Oregon to be the grand marshal of a parade, which they have every year, and I went as Spock in character, and I was supposed to ride in an open-air car down the main street in Medford. We never made it.

They got me out of the hotel and into the car, and I remember we were supposed to drive about a mile down the main street in town and into a public square, but after we'd driven about a block, the people began to come off the sidewalks and rush the car. They surrounded it, and it was all they could do to get me out of there. It was just a mob scene.

And I really didn't know what I was getting into. I really didn't know what it was all about. I wanted to explore the Spock character and find out what it would be like to be among the people on the streets of an American city as Mr. Spock. I wanted to see how people would react to the character. I thought I might learn something, and I thought it might be nice for the people to see Spock, but it turned out to be pretty bizarre. They didn't know whether or not to touch me, and they didn't know quite how I'd react, and I didn't quite know how to react. And I guess deep down, I thought, "They know me as Spock, and if I don't come as Spock, they won't have any way of relating to me." You know, I guess I thought they'd stand on the curb going, "Who's that guy? We came to see Spock."

Over the years, Leonard has finally come to understand that his fans generally flock to see him because they really love his work. They aren't showing up to meet Mr. Spock. Instead, they're hoping to get a little bit closer to someone far more interesting, the man, the actor, Mr. Leonard Nimsy.

MY
FAVORITE
EPISODE

PRECEDING PAGE: **M**IND-MELDING WITH
THE **H**ORTA. (© 1993 **P**ARAMOUNT
PICTURES)

or almost thirty years now, I've been asked time and again, "What's
your favorite episode?" and for almost thirty years I've replied to
that question with a sort of stock gag answer. "My favorite episodes," I'll
say, "are the ones wherein I got to play dual roles. They were challenging, different and had twice as much of *me* in them. I mean, how
could they not be just great?"

That's the answer I've always given, but the *real* answer to the question of my favorite episode is "The Devil in the Dark," which was a terrific
story. Exciting, thought-provoking and intelligent, it contained all of the
ingredients that made up our very best *Star Treks*. However, none of that
stuff qualifies it as my favorite.

We shot this particular episode, our twenty-sixth, during the first half of
March 1967. By this time we'd spent the better part of a year churning out
a season's worth of shows. We'd come through the fire, and by this time
we'd all gotten to know each other pretty well, we'd felt our way through
forming relationships, both personally and professionally, and we'd actually become quite comfortable with each other.

Now, early on the second day of shooting this episode, I got a phone
call that told me that my father had died. And it's many years ago, so my
memory of my beloved father now is one of joy and purity and I remember
him wonderfully. The grief is long since gone, and just the joy of having
known him and loved him and of knowing that he loved me remains. But
at that moment in time, the pain was awful. My father had died.

He died in Miami, in the early morning, and as my flight arrangements
dictated, I was going to have to fly there in the early evening. No matter
how we juggled flights, there was just no way for me to avoid having to
wait about five hours before I could get to Miami out of the Los Angeles
airport. It was almost lunchtime by the time my travel arrangements were
finally firming up, and as I was just getting off the phone, I can remember
hearing Gregg Peters, an A.D., saying, "We're gonna break for lunch, then
shut down for the rest of the day. Everybody go home, we'll not shoot

today. Bill is leaving." And I said to Gregg, "Please don't do that, my plane doesn't leave until six, and I don't know what I'll do with myself for these remaining hours if I'm not here. Please, let's continue to shoot."

An hour later, after we'd broken for lunch and after the tears and the anguish, we started shooting what we'd been rehearsing all morning. And all through the scene, I kept having trouble with a particular line. My emotion was getting in the way, making me forget. And even though I really can't remember most of the day's details anymore, the one thing that I recall perfectly and that I'll never forget is the closeness that my friend Leonard had toward me. Not *just* emotionally, but physically as well. I mean I've seen film of elephants that support the sick and the dying with their bodies, and Leonard somehow always seemed physically close to me.

Our cinematographer, Jerry Finnerman, whose father had also recently passed away, stayed close, too. And together, they kind of herded around me, assuring me that there were people close by in case I wanted to talk or just needed a friend. Between Leonard and Jerry, we were able to make it through that awful afternoon, and I was able to fly out that evening to my father, warmed by their love and affection.

That's what makes this episode my favorite.

As I flew off to my dad's services, the crew went ahead and shot the scene where Spock mind melds with the Horta. Now, as you know, the Horta is the creature that's the mother of the eggs that are being destroyed in the episode, and because of this, it's in great pain. So of course as Spock taps into its mind, he too experiences the creature's anguish. With that in mind, he gets very emotional and yells out something like, "Pain, PAIN!!!" Still, by the time I got back to the set, this was all in the can, and I had no chance to see it.

At the same time, I was desperate to show the cast and crew that even though I'd just buried my father, I was okay, that I was still me, that I was physically and emotionally ready to really give it my best. Toward that end, I was joking around on overdrive. It was a nervous reaction to my own tension, grief and anxiety, but it was nonetheless quite effective in making my point. First up, we had to shoot my reaction shots to Leonard's Horta mind meld. And those pieces of film would then be edited together with the shots of Leonard. So while they were setting up the camera for this shot, Leonard started to walk me through the scene, and he said, "Well,

Bill, I was kinda over there and I said something like, 'Pain, pain,'" and I could tell he was a little embarrassed about it, so I said, "Wait a minute. Wait a minute." I went to Joe Pevney, who was directing, and said, "I wish Leonard would do the scene for me, so I could really see what I'm supposed to be reacting to." And now Leonard's hemming and hawing and he says, "Oh, it was really nothing, I was just kinda standing around going, you know, 'Pain, pain' or something."

But I kept pleading with Leonard until he finally gave in to my request, went over to the Horta costume and got ready to run the scene for me. At which point I said to him, "Now Leonard, do this thing full out for me, will ya? Don't just say, 'Pain, pain,' let me really hear it! Do it for me!!" So now Leonard sighed, took a moment to prepare and then launched into a full-bore mind meld.

"PA-A-A-A-A-A-IN!!!" he howled, "Oh, PAIN, PAAAAAAAAIN!!!"

At which point I yelled, "Jesus Christ! Get that Vulcan an aspirin!!"

The crew broke up laughing, Leonard shook his head at me in disgust and all at once I felt a whole lot better.

DYSFUNCTION
FAM

urprisingly, throughout the period of time when Spock was becoming something of a national phenomenon, Leonard's relationships with the studio and Gene were growing increasingly distant. This made no sense to Leonard, who felt betrayed, since his efforts had benefited the show and the studio much more fully than anyone could have imagined. He hadn't been praised or congratulated; instead, the folks running the show seemed to go out of their way to create a distance. Leonard explains:

ctors are always looking for a home, and when *Star Trek* came along, that's precisely what I thought I'd found. I'd spent fifteen years, from about 1950 to 1965, feeling like a visiting distant cousin who'd come and work on other people's sets for two or three days, and then be told, "Okay, you're done, please leave." I'd find myself envying the regular casts and crews of these shows and feeling like they led a really blessed life. Y'know, this steady working relationship of running characters, running crew members, writers and producers could really be seen as a sort of family.

As a guest on these shows, you're allowed to visit for a day or two, share a couple of meals and play a couple of scenes, but then you're gone and someone else fills that guest spot. You might find a haven for a moment, but you never find a home.

I was in desperate need of that home, and for the stability and familiarity that this sort of family could provide. So when *Star Trek* came along and we started working, I thought, "Wow! A new family's being created here, and I'm a valid member! I'm not a guest anymore!" We were forming a group of people who'd be working together and learning together, going through similar experiences, creating together. I thought it was terrific.

Gone were the days where they'd write your name on the dressing-room door with chalk and just wipe it off three days later, or sit you down on a canvas chair that's got a piece of masking tape stuck on it with your name attached. One of the things that made me feel good about Star Trek early on was that they painted my name onto my own personal parking space. I know that sounds funny, but to me it really signified that this working relationship was going to be at least semipermanent. It would take a bit of effort to remove that paint.

In this family construct, I felt like Bill and I were brothers, that Roddenberry was a sort of father figure, as were the studio heads at Desilu. Weeks went by, we'd gotten on the air and when the Spock character really started to take off, I was very proud, and in a way I felt as though I were pleasing Daddy; it was like pleasing your parents at report-card time. You know you've done a good job, and you hope and even assume that your parents will say, "Well done, son," and give you a nice pat on the back. I guess that's what I was expecting.

Instead, the father figures on Star Trek took on an attitude that I'd never anticipated, becoming suddenly and irrationally para-noid. They kept saying, "That son of a bitch is gonna want more money. He's going to start dictating to us about where and how and when he will do a scene." They saw Spock's growing popu-larity as somehow threatening to them, and I had a really tough time with that. It sent me to therapy.

I had a big investment going here in that after fifteen years of struggling, looking for a home, I'd finally found one, and even though I was doing my best to please, I found myself being told, "You're a problem for us." In effect, "We don't like you here."

I could not understand that. I mean, I came to work every day, knowing my lines and hitting my marks, and in terms of audience reaction, I was really bringing something to this party. I was expecting love, kindness and support, but what I got instead were hostility and avarice.

"Hostility and avarice" are words perfectly chosen in that they really do describe the "father figures'" shift in attitude toward Leonard. However, rather than try to describe how these feelings became manifest around the increasingly popular actor, it would be much more meaningful to illus-trate them. Any number of examples exist, but two, in particular, bear retelling.

The first example comes over Leonard's simple request for a telephone in his dressing room, and before I go any further, I've got to explain that throughout the run of Star Trek, our main stage had ONE phone line. As a result, it became almost impossible to get calls in or out. This frustrated everyone, and after a particularly aggravating series of missed messages and waiting for the phone, Leonard made his request:

We were all stuck in a situation that found forty people trying to survive all day with one telephone and none of us had phones in our dressing rooms. Finally, when it was getting really hectic for me, I said to one of the production people, "I need a phone in my dressing room, and I'll pay for it."

"Sure, no problem," they said, but as the days passed, nothing happened. And I kept asking about this phone and being told, "We're working on it." Several more days went by, a week, and another, and by now I was getting really angry.

"Where the hell is the telephone?!" I yelled.

"Uh . . . well . . . uh, Mr. Solow wants to talk to you about that."

So now Herb Solow, Desilu's "executive in charge of production," comes down to the stage, and we sat in my dressing room having this ridiculous conversation in which I said, "I need a phone, I can't handle my business on that stage phone."

"You can't have it, it's not in your contract."

"I know that, I'm not asking you to give it to me, I'll pay for it myself. I'll pay for the installation and the bill."

"Nope, can't do it."

"Why?"

"Because then all the other actors will want one."

"And . . . ?"

"And they'll think I'm paying for yours."

"I'll tell them that I'm paying for it myself."

"They won't believe you. The answer is still no."

Certainly this was an irrational argument on Solow's part, but it serves to perfectly illustrate the studio's paranoid unwillingness to deal with the growing popularity of Spock and the man who played him. There was even a point where the studio went so far as to send Leonard a memo that officially denied him access to the studio's pencil and pen supply. Leonard had requested some writing utensils so that he could answer a bit of his fan mail, and was told that such items were not part of his contract. One would assume Solow was riding Leonard in this especially nasty manner in the hopes of keeping him under control should his popularity continue to grow. You know the attitude: "Give him a phone and he'll want a car."

Finally, with all the problems Leonard faced in getting the studio to provide him with such simple things as pencils, paper clips and a phone, you can imagine the kind of economy-sized headaches he suffered through in attempting to secure an air conditioner for his sweltering office. You see, between Star Trek's first and second seasons, Leonard was able to renegotiate his contract, get a raise and a couple of perks as well. One of these was a converted dressing room that he could use as an office.

At about the same time, Leonard had hired a lovely young woman named Theresa Victor to coordinate his fan mail, travel arrangements and personal engagements. She'd work in the new office space all day while Leonard was out shooting. Between set-ups, Leonard would check in with Theresa, sign a few pictures and attend to personal business whenever he got the chance. This seemed like a perfect working situation, but it quickly became apparent that there was a problem. That's because while the studio had indeed fulfilled its part of the bargain by furnishing Leonard with an office, it was a strictly no-frills situation. The office was small and shabbily furnished, but what really drove Leonard crazy was the fact that this tiny office, which bore only two tiny windows and no breeze, always became stiflingly, unbearably hot long before lunchtime. This obviously rendered the place virtually unusable for the better part of each workday.

With that in mind, Leonard sweatily and repeatedly complained to the front office about the situation, and after being stalled for several days, he was once again met with hostility instead of humanity. Told that "your contract calls for office space, but makes no specific provisions for air conditioning," Leonard's request was denied. Now steaming both literally and figuratively, Leonard was not the least bit mollified when the studio offered a compromise, opening up its miserly purse strings wide enough to equip Leonard's office digs with a tiny, used and completely inefficient window-mounted exhaust fan.

Two days later, Los Angeles gets hit with a mid-July heat wave, and as the mercury stretches for 105 degrees, Leonard finally cracks. Then, with a gleam in his eye, he hatches a plan. "Lie down on the floor," he tells Theresa, and with a puzzled look, she obliges. "Okay," he continues, "now whatever you do, don't move." Leonard then gets on the phone, calls the studio's medical personnel and in a frantic voice pleads, "Help, I just got back to my office, and my secretary's been overcome by the heat! She's passed out and we need your help! Come quick!" Leonard hangs up and Theresa cracks up, but by the time the medics arrive the pair has composed themselves sufficiently to convincingly portray heat prostration. The medical types immediately begin applying cold compresses to Theresa's head, and while she begins "reviving," Leonard runs around the office saying things like "Thank God I got here in time, or this could have been a lot worse." News of this "near disaster" quickly rises upstairs to the studio heads, and in no time, a large, shiny new air conditioner arrives at Leonard's office door, and it's installed and humming, happily puffing large, freon-chilled breezes throughout Leonard and Theresa's office. Leonard's guerrilla tactics had won the battle, although his relationship with the studio had deteriorated even further.

At the same time, another cast member's relationship with *Star Trek* was falling completely apart, and this time the end result brought about much more drastic, far more permanent consequences. Grace Lee Whitney had come aboard on our first episode, playing Yeoman Rand, and as you probably know, she disappeared from the *Enterprise* after just thirteen episodes. It's always been said that she was written out of the show because her character's crush on Captain Kirk prevented him from becoming engaged in any episode romances. However, while that statement does bear a bit of credibility, it is by no means the *real* reason behind her departure. The true story was nowhere near that pleasant, and in fact it's quite sad, quite painful.

Adopted as a child, Grace had grown up troubled by a nagging and cruel self-image of worthlessness, of inadequacy and of being an outsider. In time, these insecurities and internal doubts grew larger and pushed Grace toward a lifestyle of prolonged and heavy substance abuse. She was also, by her own admission, a sex addict.

All of this was in place long before Grace ever auditioned for Star Trek, but with an addict's ability to mask her own addictions, she was hired to play Yeoman Rand without anyone even suspecting she had a problem. However, what she *couldn't* hide was the fact that alcohol and an unhealthy diet had conspired to make her noticeably overweight.

Asked by Bill Theiss to lose about twenty pounds so that her miniskirted uniforms would look more appropriate, Grace immediately began taking large amounts of diet pills, hoping to lose her extra weight quickly. She was successful in her dieting, but as an unwelcome side effect, she developed an addiction to the pills. Over the next several weeks, Grace was constantly battling to stay thin, she continued abusing the diet pills and her dependence on the drugs grew to the point where she was taking them almost constantly. At the same time, to mask the nervousness that came along with the amphetamine-based drugs, she began drinking rather heavily.

Even during our first few weeks of production, Grace had become noticeably distracted, visibly ill, and as a result her performances suffered terribly. By the time we were filming our tenth episode, Grace's condition had worsened to the point where her scenes were consciously being given to other characters or completely written out of episodes. For example, Grace was to have co-starred with Captain Kirk in our eleventh episode, "Dagger of the Mind," but her deterioration forced Roddenberry and Justman into a decision to rewrite the episode, adding the guest character of Dr. Helen Noel and entirely deleting Yeoman Rand. Further, in Grace's final episode, "The Conscience of the King," her performance consisted solely of walking onto the bridge in the background of the scene, taking a quick look at a particular piece of equipment, then exiting. She was let go the following day.

Grace also states that her tenure on Star Trek was made especially painful due to two sexual assaults, both of them triggered during intoxicated meetings with co-workers. The first, at the hands of an extremely inebriated network executive, turned violent upon the man's inability to perform. The second came at the hands of a much closer co-worker from within the ranks of Star Trek and was equally repulsive. Grace had a hard time talking about these incidents and asked that I not reveal any of the names or details of the attacks. With that in mind I will respect her wishes and simply state that the untarnished, perfect veneer of *Star Trek* is not without its cracks, not without its dark side.

At any rate, Grace's firing once again triggered her own deeply ingrained feelings of abandonment and worthlessness, and it marked the beginning of a personal slide that would become so deep and so horrendous as to ultimately include a harsh, skid-row existence and prostitution.

Thankfully, in the mid-eighties Grace got help, got sober and got her life back on track. She pulled herself up by the bootstraps and now lives happily with her family in a small Northern California town. Her story, which could so very easily have been entirely tragic, now has a happy ending. Today Grace continues recovering with the help of a twelve-step program, and even helps fellow substance abusers by lecturing at prisons, colleges and even *Star Trek* conventions. Her own goodwill and good intentions have triumphed over her troubled past, and her future looks brighter than ever.

She is a remarkable woman.

TO STAY OR NOT TO STAY

Although Leonard and Gene were beginning to lock horns, one of our supporting cast members was actually ready to quit the show. As you might expect, this actor was unhappy in regard to the size and importance of her role, but as you probably *wouldn't* expect, we're talking about Nichelle Nichols. She explains:

It got really frustrating, because I would always read my original script and then I'd read each subsequent rewrite, which on *Star Trek* often totaled three or four, and there was a week-to-week consistent pattern being formed. You know, I'd get the first draft, the white pages, and see what Uhura had to do this week, and maybe it was a halfway-decent scene or two, sometimes more, and then invariably the next draft would come in on blue pages and I'd find that Uhura's presence in the show had been cut way down. The pink pages came next and she'd suffer some more cuts, then the yellow, more cuts, and it finally got to the point where I had really had it. I mean I just decided that I don't even need to read the FUCKING SCRIPT! I mean I know how to say, "Hailing frequencies open," and Uhura's participation in the final version of any given script was rarely more taxing than that.

It got to the point where I felt like somebody must be going through the scripts and just slashing every time they see the name "Uhura" above a line of dialogue. Finally, after a particularly brutal series of cuts and an episode where a guest actress was brought in to visit a planet while Uhura stayed at her post doing nothing for an hour, I went to Gene and complained.

"Why is this happening?" I ask him. And Gene does his best to explain his point of view, and he's talking about staying true to the show, but by now I'm really angry and it actually gets to the point where I say to him, "That's it, I quit. I'm leaving."

And now Gene looks at me across the desk and says, "Don't do this."

"I have to," I tell him.

Now this whole confrontation went down on a Friday evening just after we'd finished shooting for the day. And as it turned out, Nichelle was scheduled to attend an NAACP fund-raiser that night. Although extremely upset, she went home, changed and attended the fund-raiser. That's when an amazing thing happened.

was sitting at my table and I was chatting and saying hello to people when all of a sudden a man comes up to me and says, "Miss Nichols, I'm sorry to bother you, but there's someone over here who would really like to meet you." And I said, "Well . . . uh, I guess that's okay," at which point he leads me across the floor and up to a table that's surrounded by a lot of people, and he says to me, "I must tell you, the man that wants to meet you is a big fan, a really great fan."

And now I'm thinking to myself, "Well, that's nice," and suddenly the man that's led me through the crowd sort of squeezes in through the people around the table, and the next thing I know, the crowd sort of parts down the middle, and sitting there smiling at me is Dr. Martin Luther King.

So now I'm immediately thrilled. I mean, Dr. King is a fan? Of MINE? And we exchanged greetings, and he told me how much he enjoyed Star Trek, and about how happy he was that I was part of the cast.

And so I told him about what had been happening in regard to our scripts, and about my meeting with Gene, and that I had actually decided to leave the series.

And he looked at me and said, "Don't do this. Nichelle, you can't do this. Don't you know that the world, for the first time, is beginning to see us as equals? Your character has gone into space on a five-year mission. She's intelligent, strong, capable and a wonderful role model, not just for black people, but for all people. What you're doing is very, very important, and I'd hate to see you just walk away from such a noble task."

That just floored me, and I realized that there was a real responsibility attached to what I represented each week. So I came back into Gene's office Monday morning, told him the whole story about me and Dr. King and I told him that I was absolutely, positively staying. And from that point on, Uhura's importance became a little more clearly defined, and the scripts featured her a little more prominently . . . not always, but at least on a more consistent basis.

As a result, the *Enterprise* has ultimately been graced by the presence of Nichelle Nichols and Uhura throughout our every incarnation, and one can only imagine the vast amount of inspiration that's been provided over the years as a direct result of this one great man's advice.

EPISODE ON THE EDGE

As the weeks of production turned into months, we began to put out some very good shows. Gene Coon's hand was being felt in every script now, and the results are quite noticeable as you scan a list of the shows we put out toward the latter half of our first season. "Space Seed" (which introduced the world to Khan), "This Side of Paradise," "The Devil in the Dark" and "Errand of Mercy" were all terrific episodes, each somehow seeming to move and breathe with a little more zest than we had previously attained. In fact, it's during this period of time that we produced an episode that is almost unanimously hailed as *Star Trek*'s finest ever, "The City on the Edge of Forever." However, the story behind this terrific episode is long, tangled and truly weird. I asked Bob Justman to help clear it up.

Very early on in this first season, before we began shooting and before our first episode, Gene was looking to find well-respected and highly talented science fiction writers so that he could hire them to script episodes of *Star Trek*. One of the most prestigious names on his list was Harlan Ellison. Gene met with Ellison and immediately signed him to a contract, at which point Harlan went off to write us a ten-page story treatment.

Weeks passed before Harlan actually got his story to us, but I can still remember reading it and thinking to myself, "This is brilliant." Harlan just made a couple of minor revisions, NBC approved the script and Gene said, "Okay, Harlan, go ahead and write us a teleplay, and remember, we need it as soon as possible."

Lapse dissolve, and it's six months later. We're in full production and rapidly running out of usable scripts, and we still hadn't

seen anything from Ellison. Now I was rather friendly with Harlan at the time, because I'd worked with him in the past on *The Outer Limits*, and I knew that he was a real procrastinator when it came to actually writing his scripts. He has trouble getting started, because, let's face it, writing is an excruciating process. Still, he hadn't delivered yet, and we really needed his script. So I kept the pressure on him, calling him and saying, "Harlan, we need your teleplay. . . . Is it done yet?"

And of course it never was. It finally got to the point where I invited Harlan up to my office and proceeded to lock him in there overnight so he'd finish writing the script. "Harlan," I said, "I'm not going to let you out of there. You've got to finish the fucking script."

Harlan trusted Bob and knew that we really needed his script because we were in deep trouble in terms of our schedule. With that in mind, he went along with Justman's rather drastic plan and allowed himself to be locked up in Bob's office. Ellison proceeded to work in there all evening, even through the night; he finally ended up sleeping on Justman's couch. However, he did manage to finish his script, and in the morning he turned it in.

Harlan finished the script, but to get even with me for locking him in my office, he actually ate the houseplant on my secretary Sylvia's desk. I swear to God. It was a nice-sized leafy green thing, but Harlan chewed it up, right down to the stems.

In the morning, I've got a script, I'm smiling and I go off to my office to give it a quick read. I stop smiling. Harlan's script is brilliantly written, but completely unusable. At first glance, I can tell it's going to be hugely expensive, and at the same time, his *Enterprise* characters are speaking incorrectly and more importantly, behaving incorrectly. You know, these noble people who work aboard this great starship all of a sudden weren't acting so noble. Not very noble at all, dealing drugs to one another and the like. It was long, and there was just too much script for us to handle, the elements were far too expensive. For example, at one point in an early draft of this script, Harlan had a script

ABOVE: **R**ICARDO **M**ONTALBAN AS **K**IRK'S MOST FORMIDABLE ENEMY, THE GENETICALLY ENGINEERED SUPERMAN **K**HAN **N**OONIAN **S**INGH. (© 1993 **P**ARAMOUNT **P**ICTURES)

direction that read something like "a thousand people chase after our main character." So I said, "Harlan, you know we can't afford a thousand extras, we just can't afford them. We can afford seven extras. That's it, no more."

Now Harlan's next draft comes in, and he's changed that direction to "a large crowd of people chase after our main character." It was exquisite, extraordinarily well written, but for our purposes, useless.

Gene tried to reason with Harlan, so did I, but we both struck out. Harlan knew he'd written a terrific teleplay. He'd given us the required two drafts, and now there was no way anyone was going to talk him into changing it again. Harlan was angry now, and rather unapproachable.

Finally, when it got to the point where Justman and Roddenberry felt they were going to have to give up on the script, Gene sent me up to Harlan's house, hoping that I might be able to reason with him, and I have to admit, I failed miserably. At the time I was rather friendly with Harlan, and I'm sure that Gene felt like maybe he'd listen to me if I went up there and told him *why* his script wasn't usable. And I can remember driving up to Harlan's house on my motorcycle, getting inside the house and being yelled at throughout my visit. Harlan was very irate and within a rather short period of time he'd thrown me off his property, insane with anger at Justman, Roddenberry and Coon. I was just the messenger, but he was out to kill me, too. Justman recalls:

At this point, rather than give up on the script entirely, Gene went in and extensively rewrote Harlan's teleplay, completely revising the script and making it conform to the necessities of his high-tech but low-budget television show.

Actually, I should break in here for a moment to make it clear that there remains a great deal of confusion over whether Ellison's script was actually rewritten by Roddenberry or Gene Coon. I watched it again recently to see if I could hazard a guess, and in listening to the way the characters speak with one another throughout the show, joking, speaking colloquially and with a carefully constructed casual tone, I'd guess, and this is *only* a guess, that in reality "The City on the Edge of Forever" was probably *supervised* by Roddenberry, but actually rewritten by Gene Coon. Either way,

the resulting episode was, in my mind and in many others', the very best *Star Trek* of them all. Justman continues:

Harlan never forgave us for rewriting him, and out of spite he submitted his original script to the Writers Guild, and he end-edup winning an award for this script that's never been produced. Coon, Roddenberry and I were all in attendance at the awards dinner, and as Ellison walked away from the podium with his award in one hand and his script in the other, he shook them at us, smirking, as if to say, "There, that'll show you."

I looked at Gene, he looked at me and shrugged and said, "Well, that's show biz." So we just laughed it off. I mean, if the show hadn't been rewritten, the episode would never have been produced.

Believe it or not, Harlan Ellison, who had become so thoroughly disenchanted with Gene Roddenberry and his *Star Trek* creation, can actually be held directly responsible for saving the show when it appeared headed for cancellation at the end of our first season. Several weeks prior to his first skirmishes with Roddenberry and Justman, Ellison had just begun working on his script for "The City on the Edge of Forever" when rumors began circulating throughout the offices at Desilu that there was a good chance *Star Trek* would not be renewed. Ellison, who'd come in to meet with Gene about the script (remember, they hadn't yet locked horns), heard the gossip and, fearing the loss of this quality science fiction showpiece (and potential meal ticket), he contacted many of his fellow scribes, asking for their support in saving the show. The word spread quickly, and NBC began receiving thousands of letters and angry phone calls demanding that the show stay on the air. Demonstrations in support of the show rose up at Cal Tech and MIT, led almost entirely by students who were rabid science fiction fans and who'd

KIRK FORCING HIMSELF TO LET EDITH DIE. (© 1993 PARAMOUNT PICTURES)

heard of the show's precarious situation through Ellison or one of his personally recruited fellow believers.

Over the course of the ensuing years, this particular outpouring of support for the show would get lost, being eclipsed by the enormous public phenomenon that assured *Star Trek*'s survival into a *third* season. However, it is truly one of the show's greatest ironies that *Star Trek* may have owed its continued existence in large part to Harlan Ellison, a man who would shortly become one of the show's greatest detractors.

SEASO
TW

I never felt Star Trek was silly, I felt I was silly. Swallows kept trying to nest in the wig they gave me.

—WALTER KOENIG

ou've heard this story, I'm sure: In early 1967, the Soviet newspaper *Pravda* writes a long, angry editorial, complaining that even though the USSR was first in space, there is no Russian aboard the U.S.S. *Enterprise*. Gene Roddenberry gets hold of the scathing condemnation of his xenophobic American television show, reads it over several times and finally comes to the conclusion that the paper's arguments are well founded. With that in mind, he goes back to his office and immediately creates the character of Ensign Pavel Chekov.

That's the story. Here's the truth: This long-established, widely believed bit of *Star Trek* history is entirely false, and was simply the product of an overzealous public relations department. In reality, the true motivating factor behind *Star Trek*'s second-season cast addition wasn't the Russian press, it was the Monkees.

You see, at exactly the same time *Star Trek* was beginning to amass its small but rather loyal following, the Monkees were exploding onto television sets all over the country. These imitation Beatles quickly became something of a national phenomenon, and fans of the Prefab Four were generally quite young, quite vocal and extremely enthusiastic. As a result, followers mobbed the band at every personal appearance, group merchandise began rapidly flying off shelves all over the country, and the Monkees' TV show was a sensational and consistent ratings winner. For all of those reasons, Gene zeroed in on the lucrative bubblegum crowd and conjured up the character of Pavel Chekov as a consciously designed, rather close approximation of Mon-

PRECEDING PAGE: **ME IN TROUBLE WITH SOME TRIBBLES. (© 1993 PARAMOUNT PICTURES)**

TOP RIGHT: **WALTER KOENIG, TAKING THE LAST STARSHIP TO CLARKSVILLE. (© 1993 PARAMOUNT PICTURES)**

kees front man Davy Jones. Sure, Gene slapped a Soviet accent onto our new ensign, but one look at Chekov's first couple of episodes, and the rather bushy toupee he was forced to wear, will illustrate the Monkee mimicry point beyond a shadow of a doubt.

Still, despite the rather silly coiffure, Walter eased his way onto the *Enterprise* bridge with a minimum of difficulty, and his performances were immediately full of life, energy and a remarkable sense of fun. I asked Walter to tell me about his initial involvement in the show.

I was lucky in that Joe D'Agosta had cast me in an episode of a series called *Mr. Novak*, where I played a Russian student who wants to defect to the United States. I'd also worked for our director Joe Pevney on an episode of *Alfred Hitchcock Presents* and I'd done a guest lead for Gene Roddenberry on *The Lieutenant*. These were three of the four guys involved in casting Chekov. Gene Coon was the other. He brought in someone *he* knew, so it was really just between the two of us.

We both read, and afterward I didn't even get to go home. I just sat around for forty minutes, and then Bill Theiss came in and

said, "Follow me." He then took me to wardrobe where he got out one of those cloth measuring tapes, and he started measuring me from my crotch to my cuff. I said, "What are you doing?" and he said, "I've got to make you a uniform. You just got hired." I swear, that's how I found out I had the part. No congratulations, no ceremony, just this guy with a tape measure between my legs. It certainly did not hint at the significance *Star Trek* would ultimately have in my life.

Actually, when I finally got the details of the job, I was told that this was gonna be a one-shot deal, with just a possibility of becoming a recurring character. But at about this time George Takei was off somewhere shooting *The Green Berets* with John Wayne, and he ended up being delayed in coming back to the show. When that happened, I just kept getting called back, because they really wanted a regular character to be manning the *Enterprise* consoles. This went on for like twelve or thirteen episodes, and by that time the mail that was coming in for me had become overwhelming, and they found that I really *was* appealing to the eight- to fourteen-year-olds. I was getting six or seven hundred letters a week. Can you believe it? It was such a novel experience that I actually tried to read them all. It was great fun for a while.

While the rookie Koenig was getting accustomed to his duties on the bridge, we veterans were returning to our roles, confident about our characters and now comfortable with all of *Star Trek*'s hardware and terminology. This self-assurance transferred rather noticeably onto the screen. For example, watch any first-season episode (especially the earlier ones) and you'll find Leonard and me treating the *Enterprise* equipment with kid gloves, carefully and rather tentatively working our communicators, stepping into the transporter almost reverently and practically barking ship's commands at one another. Watch any episode from season *two*, and you'll find that this sort of technological reverence has given way to more mundane, matter-of-fact manhandling.

You see, we'd come to the conclusion that even the highest-tech trappings of the *Enterprise* would most likely seem rather mundane and ordinary to the crewmen who used them every day. With that in mind, from this point on you're liable to see Captain Kirk just sort of flipping his communicator open, wallet style, as he speaks. On the bridge, console buttons began getting swatted rather than lovingly pressed, and if you look closely, you'll notice that Kirk's phaser is often just tucked into the waistband of his pants.

However, this newfound credibility and confidence weren't always time-efficient. I can still remember Irving Feinberg and De Kelley going at it over the purpose and proper use of each one of McCoy's medical instruments. I can also remember an exasperated Jimmy Doohan trying in vain to teach a new and rather dull-witted "red shirt" the technical and procedural differences between beaming crew members up and beaming them down. Even George Takei, the sweetest guy on the planet, once had a fight with one of our directors, arguing strongly with him about which buttons needed to be pushed in order to fire the *Enterprise* phasers.

This director had set up a shot that he liked, and it demanded that George push a series of specific console buttons in firing the ship's phasers. George refused, arguing that to do the shot this director's way would be to undermine the underlying technological specifications that had been laid out during the show's first season. The pair argued about it back and forth, but with George steadfastly refusing to budge and the clock ticking relentlessly, George got his way and fired the *Enterprise* guns in the proper manner.

Meanwhile, on the other side of the lot, the working relationship between Roddenberry and Coon was growing stronger, more efficient and more creative each day. Sadly, since I was always on the set, I never got to see their creative sparks flying. Even sadder is the fact that neither of these creative geniuses is still around to talk about their working relationship. However, Bob Justman, who worked hand-in-hand with both, is always more than happy to give the play-by-play in regard to Roddenberry and Coon.

By the time we'd gotten into our second season, these guys were really cooking. Coon and Roddenberry would still get together and have preliminary writers' meetings, but because we'd been on the air for a while now, it was a much easier process. The prospective writers knew what the show was all about. They'd seen it on TV by now, or if not, we could have them watch a couple of episodes.

And basically, what each writer would do was to come in and throw story ideas at you. You know, premises, springboards, basic thumbnail sketches. And since our guidelines were by now so well defined, Roddenberry and Coon would sit there listening to these guys lob ideas, and they'd just go, "No, no, no, yes, no, no." If there was an idea which got a yes, the two Genes would then sit there with the writer, working with him to hammer out and shape the story. Once they'd done that, they'd say good-bye and the guy would go off and write us an outline.

As always, the outlines came back in about two weeks and were immediately revised by Coon, Roddenberry and Justman. However, by season two, another pair of cooks had elbowed their way into *Star Trek*'s creative kitchen. First, NBC's programming executives would read over each script, making sure that the story was "acceptable" and offering their own uniquely nonproductive comments. For example, these guys once read one of Gene's own scripts, in which a tire iron was being used to hold down a stack of newspapers, and asked him to "please change the tire-iron to a brick, in that said tire iron could possibly prove offensive to automotive sponsors, since it might conceivably be construed to imply the failure of one of their products."

Next in line would be the network's Broadcast Standards people . . . the censors. "Please delete McCoy's expletive 'Oh my Lord,'" they'd write, aghast at Roddenberry's blasphemy, "Please ensure that the Mugatu's appearance is not grotesque or shocking to the viewer," "Please avoid at all costs the open-mouthed kiss." This was real useful stuff, real progressive, real helpful.

Once those annoying hurdles had been cleared, the writer got back to work, penning two drafts of his teleplay. Just as before, the script would still be far from perfect, and it would now be revised extensively by a member of the *Star Trek* staff. However, as our second season rolled around, Roddenberry was delegating most of these rather time-consuming chores to Gene Coon. Bob Justman describes it:

> Gene Coon had come in and by our second season, he'd really picked up a lot of the slack. Coon, who was the fastest typewriter in the West, would do almost all of the rewriting and fixing. Once he was finished, the scripts would then pass through Roddenberry's office, and he would usually just do a little cleaning up, a couple of minor changes here and there.

Roddenberry was still working hard, supervising casting sessions, watching dailies, sitting in on story conferences and keeping an eye on our editing sessions, but his life had once again become "his" life. He no longer had to kill himself with work, writing and rewriting till dawn for weeks on end, personally working with all of our writers and fighting through every postproduction nightmare. *Those* duties had now been officially split up between three people. Gene Coon took charge of the endless series of writers' meetings, directors' meetings and production headaches. Eddie Milkis was now at full speed, and he had *Star Trek*'s special effects coming in at least a bit faster than they had been. And Dorothy Fontana had been promoted to script consultant, writing original scripts for the show and also rewriting others.

Take a look at the shows produced during this time period, and you'll find that they were some of *Star Trek*'s very finest: "Mirror, Mirror," "The

Trouble with Tribbles," "I, Mudd," "The Doomsday Machine," "Wolf in the Fold" and a good half-dozen others will prove that statement true. The *Star Trek* characters seemed really alive, and our stories were sharp, exciting, intelligent and frequently quite funny. I asked Dorothy Fontana about the creative process that went on behind the scenes at *Star Trek* and about how our scripts were written with such clarity, power and excellence of execution. She explains:

t's funny, but with the *Star Trek* scripts I was able to write from intuition and my own sense of logic. Remember, I had been with Gene through the whole process of creating these characters, and I had to watch all the dailies and the rough cuts, and I had come down and watched you all on the set, so I had a good feeling by this time of exactly who these characters were, and about how they should interact with one another and also about the kind of character the actors were trying to build into them. Everyone was contributing. Bill came up with the karate thing for the captain, because it was physical and it seemed appropriate that Kirk would be into that. Leonard came up with the neck-pinch thing because it was nonviolent, and right in line with Vulcan philosophy and the nature of Spock. And all of this was great, because when you're privileged enough to know the characters this well, you can be intuitive about them. When you know so much about the characters, you can solve most script problems without having to bring in an outside element or some convoluted plot twist. The answer springs from the knowledge that you're carrying around in your head.

Another aspect of *Star Trek* that heated up during this second season was our practical jokes. In fact, it is at precisely this point in our tale that Leonard becomes the target of my biggest and most prolonged practical joke ever: "the great bicycle heist." When I told Leonard that I planned to write about this incident, he immediately insisted that I print his side of the story, too. With that in mind, Leonard's comments will appear throughout this particular tale. His first blast follows:

Bill's mean, he's really mean, I've been telling people this for years, and I want you to believe me. I'm not kidding. He's mean. He's a mean person. He stole my bicycle. He hurt me . . . badly. I want you to know this. I want it written. I want it on public record.

Now, of course I wouldn't hurt Leonard for the world, but the problem was that every time we'd break for lunch, Leonard would run to his bike, hop up on the little seat, pedal off to the commissary and run up to the front of the lunch line.

It was the logical thing to do! Bill's right, I did have a bicycle. It had my name on it, too. That's right, said it right up front. Leonard Nimoy. Spelled it correctly, too . . . N-i-m-o-y. And I had to get on the bike because I only had an hour in which to get from the stage to the commissary for lunch, then back to the makeup department to have my ears touched up, then back to the stage and back to work, so I used a bicycle.

Now, one day they called lunch, and I went to get my bicycle and it was gone. So I came running back into the stage, and I was kind of upset, and I yelled, "WHO TOOK MY BICYCLE?!?! C'mon, guys, will ya?" And then they all sort of chuckled amongst themselves and gave me back my bike. But the next day my old pal Bill, my friend, got hold of my bicycle again, and he had the grips tie it to a rope and hoist it all the way up to the ceiling of our soundstage. Tied it right up into the rafters on a pulley. So now they called lunch, I ran outside, again my bicycle was gone and again I came running into the stage yelling, "Alright! Where's my bicycle?! C'mon now, this has gone far enough!" And as I'm yelling, the grips and gaffers and various assorted crew types are laughing and looking up just over the top of my head. So I look up to find that these guys have now lowered my bicycle down from the ceiling to the point where it's hanging just over my head, and just out of my reach. And of course THEY think this is a scream. So they're all standing around going, "Ha ha-a ha-a" . . . I mean, is this funny? Is it funny to hide a guy's bicycle?

Alright, I have to break in here to tell you that Leonard is indeed telling the truth, but he's only telling you half the story. Let me tell you the rest. When Leonard first got the bike, every time we'd call lunch, he'd pedal away like crazy, cut to the front of the lunch line, get his food and then smirk at us walkers, because while he was eating, we'd still be standing in line like a bunch of shmos, starving. I mean this is LUNCH! This is IMPORTANT! So to teach Leonard a lesson, and also because I just loved to drive the guy crazy, I went out the next day and bought one of those locks that stays locked even when you shoot it, and I bought some really heavy chain at the same time. Then, while Leonard was off doing his last scene before lunch, I snuck up behind his bicycle and locked it to a fire hydrant.

Fifteen minutes later, he comes sprinting out of the studio ready to pedal off toward the commissary, but of course he finds his bike chained up to a fireplug. And now he looks around, smacks his forehead and in a display of emotion that would shame any self-respecting Vulcan, he starts yelling, "WHO DID THIS?!"

"Who did what?" I asked him, screwing on my most angelic false face.

"Some idiot locked my bike to this fire hydrant," said my good friend/unsuspecting victim.

"Oh boy," I replied, "Some people. Y'know, that's not funny, it's sick." By now I was biting the insides of my mouth to keep from laughing. "C'mon, I'll walk with you down to the commissary."

The next day Leonard shows up with bolt-cutters, and while we're off shooting, he's out there trying to chop through about twelve feet of stainless-steel chain. Finally, with a lot of sweat and swearing, he hacks it loose and puts it away once more.

Forty-five minutes later . . . I steal it again. And before I go any further, I have to tell you that I breed Dobermans and horses. Now Dobermans are great dogs, beautiful, smart and very protective of their masters, very territorial.

Bill's dogs are meaner than he is, and that's not easy.

Anyway, as soon as I saw that Leonard's bike was unchained and that just anybody could have come along and taken it, I walked over and rolled the bike off to my dressing room for safekeeping. In fact, to make absolutely sure it would be safe, I left it with one of my most . . . uh . . . *territorial* dogs. Now, when Leonard once again finds that his bike is gone, and I must tell you that by now he's really beginning to suspect that I'm the guy who's been stealing it, he comes running over to me on the set saying, "Alright, where is it?!"

"Where is what?" I ask.

"You know what," he replies. "My bike, my bike."

"Ohhhhhhhhh," I say, "your bike. Well, y'know, Leonard, you left your bike right out in the open where it could easily be stolen again, so I did you a favor. I put it in my dressing room where it'd be safe." And then I went off to lunch.

Leonard joined me at lunch about twenty minutes later . . . walking . . . a bit mussed . . . and very upset . . . just because my Doberman had gone for his throat. So I told him that if he wanted to stop a charging Doberman, it was really very simple. All he had to do was to wait until the dog leapt toward him, and "while it's in midair, you just reach into its mouth, grab hold of its tongue and give it the Vulcan pinch."

The next day arrives, and by now I knew that to protect my bicycle I was going to have to resort to some fairly extreme measures. Now, at the time I was driving a big Buick land yacht, and I used to park it next to the soundstage every day. So to protect my bicycle, instead of leaving it anywhere on the lot, I simply put it into the back seat of the Buick, drove the car right up next to the soundstage, parked the car and locked it up for the day. I was taking no chances. Guess who had my car towed away.

It was actually one of those Radio Flyer bicycles, and I still have it. They're worth a lot of money today. Strangely enough, though, all this talk about lunch reminds me of a very funny story that happened at just about the same time.

We always started shooting in June and then we'd just keep cranking right through the summer. And one of the first things we learned was that you had to eat a light lunch. If you ate anything heavy and then went back out into the heat for the rest of the day, you'd end up really drowsy. And I remember there was one time we were shooting a scene in which Leonard and I are jumped by a few bad guys. We have a fight with them and it's "Bam!" "Smash!" "Kapow!" and Leonard pinches a guy, and I hit another couple of these monsters, and after we've knocked everybody out, Leonard and I are supposed to exchange about three minutes' worth of dialogue. Something like:

"What are we going to do, Captain?"

"I don't know, what do you think, Spock?"

"Well, Captain, there are some interesting possibilities that we should discuss . . ."

At this point, Spock and Kirk blah blah blah at one another for a while, and the scene ends with Kirk saying, "I've got an idea, you go this way, I'll go that way, and we'll meet up later."

Then Leonard and I are supposed to exit the set, and the scene's over. Piece of cake. Now, we rehearse, we roll cameras and we enter. Leonard pinches his guy, I hit my guy and then I hit another guy, and I kick a guy, and I tackle a guy, and I hit all the guys and Leonard stands there smiling at me. It goes off perfectly. So now the stuntmen have flopped to the floor just as we'd rehearsed, and Kirk and Spock begin their dialogue.

And it goes along fine, except that somewhere between "What are we going to do, Captain" and "I've got an idea," I can hear from the floor, "SNNNNNNXXXXXXXX!"

Now for those of you not familiar with the unconscious cartoon balloons of Dagwood Bumstead, I'll have to explain that "SNNNNN-NNXXXXXXXX!" is the official Webster-approved spelling for the sounds made by a really loud snorer. That's right—as you've probably figured out by now, one of our stuntmen had forgotten to go easy on the hot lunch and was now paying the price. He's asleep, sound asleep, under the table, snoring . . . louder than any human should be able to snore.

We both heard it, we both knew what it was and by the look in my eye, Leonard knew that I knew what it was, and by the twitch in Leonard's ears, I knew that *he* knew what it was.

So now Leonard and I are struggling through our dialogue and pinching ourselves trying not to break up on camera. Believe it or not, we actually got through to "you go this way, I'll go that way," and that's exactly what we did. However, the second we both fell out of camera range, I swear to you a chorus of guffaws rose up out of that set that literally shook the rafters. And as a topper, this loud laughter actually woke up our Sleeping Beauty, and he was in a foul mood for days thereafter.

Bouncing back across the lot, although Gene Roddenberry had by now begun to remove himself from the day-to-day headaches of actually producing *Star Trek*, he was indeed still firing on all cylinders, rewriting feverishly and channeling most of his energies into *Star Trek*'s scripts. Having spent the better part of the past four years burning the candle at both ends, not to mention the middle, Gene was beginning to burn out. However, because of *Star Trek*'s network commitment and his own sense of responsibility for the quality of the show, Gene was still functioning at full speed, and it is a credit to his genius that he was often able to overcome his own numbing fatigue and dredge up frequent and absolutely brilliant bursts of creativity. Dorothy Fontana provides an example:

We were working on the episode entitled "By Any Other Name" and written by Jerry Bixby. Gene and Gene were not entirely happy with the script, and so they asked me to do a rewrite. And generally, whenever I had a script to rewrite, the main thing it required was that I bring our regular characters into it more heavily, and tweak the relationships between them so that their behaviors were appropriate. Once that was done, I would start to analyze and revise the episode's story line, but this time I couldn't get past the premise that a half-dozen people were going to take over the *Enterprise*. I mean the *Enterprise* is carrying four hundred crewmen, so how are these six going to take over? And we wanted to avoid using any sort of easy way out like giving them godlike powers, so Gene Coon and I sat there and we said, "What if these half-dozen people hold Kirk, Spock and the rest of the command crew hostage down on the planet and insist that the rest of the crew beam down?"

Well, we decided that was no good, because frankly, even though Kirk, and Spock and the others are our heroes and the

Enterprise command group, they're not on the bridge all the time. Other crewmen *do* relieve them when they sleep or eat or whatever, and they can adequately run the spaceship. So if these half-dozen hijackers were going to try this hard-nosed exchange tactic, Kirk's first instinct would be to say, "Absolutely not." At which point he'd order the *Enterprise* to leave orbit, stranding himself, the hostages and the command crew on the planet together. The very character of Captain Kirk would not allow him to negotiate, nor would it allow him to waffle in his beliefs or place his own safety above that of his starship. The inner workings of the character were quite clear, and for that reason, this "exchange of hostages" idea was no good.

So now Gene Coon and I were back to square one, and we tried and tried but we just couldn't crack this thing. Finally we walked into Roddenberry's office and said, "Gene, we've got a real problem. How do six aliens take over the four hundred and some-odd crewmen aboard the *Enterprise?*" And Gene thought about it for a few minutes while we sat there, and while he was thinking he started to look at, then play with a souvenir that I'd found for him during a weekend trip to Tijuana. It was a simple little piece of Mexican black onyx that had been carved into an octagonal shape.

So now Gene's pushing this thing around with his finger, and he says, "Suppose the aliens have a weapon. And suppose they can point this weapon at anyone and reduce that person down to the very essence of their being, which we'll portray

RODDENBERRY'S SOLUTION PLAYED OUT IN "BY ANY OTHER NAME." (© 1993 PARAMOUNT PICTURES)

as just this kind of shape?" So by a leap of imagination, in a totally science fiction capacity, Gene solved our unsolvable problem. Took him maybe five minutes.

And as the episode evolved, we demonstrated the power of this weapon in the first act, and then we just took the command group and the aliens aboard the *Enterprise* where we had little bundles of these shapes scattered all over the decks, implying of course that aliens had gone through the entire ship, reducing anyone and everyone down to the very essence of their being. Reversing the ray would bring everyone back, and that gave the aliens real bargaining power. It worked beautifully in terms of drama, and of course, on a purely budgetary level, it allowed us to let all the extras off that week and replace them with a bunch of these cubes.

Still, although *Star Trek* was now rolling along quite well, by the middle of our second season the same enormous script responsibilities and workload that had driven Roddenberry toward a breakdown twelve months earlier were now beginning to affect Gene Coon. Bob Justman explains:

As you know, I used to write a memo in regard to every story outline and script draft that crossed my desk. They tended to be very detailed and a bit voluminous, in that they touched on everything I felt needed correcting in each script. I'd point out what I didn't feel we could afford, character inconsistencies, lapses of logic, whatever I could think of that might make the script better.

So now, once upon a time, this writer turns in a first-draft story that's about eight pages long, and REALLY bad. Muddled, inappropriate for *Star Trek*, a bit dull and almost totally unusable. In fact, this particular story outline was so far off the mark that my memo pointing out its flaws was over twenty pages long . . . single-spaced.

Now, my memos tended to be acerbic, a bit caustic, and the understanding that I had with Gene Coon and with Gene Roddenberry was that they'd never show my notes to the writers. That's because if they did, I'd then have to be very careful in what I said and in how I said it, so as not to hurt anyone's feelings. It would have really hampered me to work that way, in that I would have had to spend a lot of time considering what I had to say and structuring it in such a manner that I wouldn't offend anyone. This would have been very time-consuming, and in the end I wouldn't have been communicating very effectively.

However, in regard to this one story, Gene Coon had read my thoughts and he'd agreed with me almost competely. For that reason, when he finally met with the writer who'd come up with the story, Coon made the mistake of showing him my memo. I guess Gene felt that it would simply be easier to let my memo do the talking than to have to sit with this guy going point-by-point through the problems with his story.

So Gene says, "Here, read this," and even before this writer's gotten halfway through my memo, he's wadded up his own story, thrown it at Gene and said, "Stuff this up your ass!" at which point he storms out of the room.

I walked into Coon's office shortly after the writer left. I found him sitting at his desk with his head in his hands, and he was weeping, for two reasons. First, because this writer had come into Coon's office as a friend, and the memo really hurt him. By the time he left, this writer's feelings had been hurt, his psyche had been bruised, his confidence had been crushed and he was by no means any longer a friend. Gene was a very sensitive man, so that was really tough on him.

Second, once that writer stormed out of the office, Coon realized that there was now no way to develop that story into a workable script in any sort of timely manner, short of just starting from scratch and doing it himself. This meant more work, more sleepless nights and an even more unmanageable work schedule. Coon was already extremely tired, and this was almost the last straw. . . . He was ready to give up.

By the time we'd gotten through Thanksgiving, Gene Coon had indeed "given up." He was gone, and that was a shame. In the twenty-five years that have passed since Coon's departure from Star Trek, the specific reasons behind his quitting have become rather hazy, although it seems most probable that the incredible amount of work involved in producing the show must have worn him out, just as it had Justman and Roddenberry twelve months earlier.

However, though Majel Barrett has asked me to emphasize that Gene Roddenberry had the utmost regard for Gene Coon's skills as a writer, and

that she does not recall any serious controversy between them, rumors have surfaced from time to time that Coon and Roddenberry had begun to fight over control of the show, with Coon pushing for more humor, more action and fewer "message shows." Roddenberry, on the other hand, is said to have been pushing for drier, issue-oriented, more dramatic programs. The story also implies that when push came to shove and these two creatives couldn't reach an acceptable compromise, Coon was asked by Roddenberry to resign. This certainly *could* have been the case, as Roddenberry and Coon had by now begun growing rather competitive. Bill Campbell illustrates how the situation had even crossed over into their personal lives.

My wife and I would often get together with Roddenberry and Majel and Gene Coon and Jackie, just to play cards and chat, and I found that Roddenberry and Coon had become very competitive in almost everything they did.

I remember one evening when we were playing cards, penny ante, and these guys were really going at it. I mean, this was supposed to be a two-cent game, and all of a sudden everybody's dropping out of each hand except Gene and Gene, and we've got a

PRODUCTION STILLS FROM *STAR TREK*'S BARBED TELEVISION SATIRE "BREAD
AND CIRCUSES." COON AND RODDENBERRY BOTH WROTE DRAFTS OF THE
SCRIPT FOR THIS EPISODE, AND THEY FOUGHT CONSTANTLY OVER ITS TONE.
THIS *MAY* HAVE HELPED MOTIVATE COON'S DEPARTURE. (© 1993
PARAMOUNT PICTURES)

few hundred dollars in the pot. This really disturbed Majel and
Jackie, but they just kept anteing, raising each other, and the bidding was aggressive. They weren't kidding around anymore.
Y'know, Coon was self-effacing, and Roddenberry always hid
behind this mask of affability, but there was more between them
than met the eye.

Still, although the men would often go head to head, Coon's widow,
Jackie, also tends to dismiss these rumors, and she's got a theory of her
own behind Coon's departure from the show.

ene [Coon] never talked about *Star Trek*, never even watched it,
didn't say much about what was going on at the studio, and he
never said anything to me about a falling-out with Gene Roddenberry. If it *did* happen, it was a private thing, because my husband never said a negative word about Roddenberry.

Actually, I'd sincerely doubt that they were ever *really* at odds.
I'm sure they fought over scripts, that's part of the business, but
they remained very good friends right up until the time my husband died. We were over at each other's homes every single week,

and the two Genes would be out swimming or shooting pool, playing cards, all kinds of things. So I can't imagine there was ever any real blowup between them. Instead, I just think it was a combination of fatigue, burnout, wanting to write something besides *Star Trek* and sickness. There's no way to prove this, but I think Gene had cancer even before he left *Star Trek*. I think it had really begun to drain him. He lived another five years, but I really think the cancer was present early on.

Coon was followed as producer by a man named John Meredyth Lucas, and the possibility that Coon's departure was partly due to illness is reinforced by Lucas's recounting of getting the job on *Star Trek*.

I had written a couple of *Star Trek* scripts ("Patterns of Force," "The Changeling"), and I had gone on to direct a bunch of *Mannix* episodes. *Mannix* was shot on the same lot as *Star Trek*, and my parking space just so happened to be directly underneath Coon's office window. Now every once in a while, Coon would see me getting out of my car, and he'd lean out his office window and we'd talk about how things were going on the show. And then one day he told me he was going to leave, and he said, "Why the hell don't you take over? You produced *The Fugitive* and *Ben Casey* and that shit." And I of course jumped at the chance, because I've always loved science fiction. I asked Coon why he was leaving, but he never really explained it. He said he was "tired," but I got the impression he wasn't terribly well.

Still, no matter what the reason, Coon was leaving and Lucas was coming in. I asked Lucas about how the show was running as he came in.

The biggest fight we were having was with the network. And that's because they were really trying to turn *Star Trek* into a *Lost in Space* kind of thing. They wanted a giant green monster from space to show up and try to eat the ship each week. So it was a constant battle to try and keep our smarter, more personal stories going.

Gene Coon had done a great deal of that, and Rodenberry had too, but most of the time, when any sort of edict came down from the network, we just ignored it. But it was great to work on *Star Trek*, because working in the science fiction genre gave us free rein to touch on any number of subjects. We could do our anti-Vietnam stories, our civil rights stories, you know? Set the story in outer space, in the future, and all of a sudden you can get away with just about anything, because you're protected by the argument that "Hey, we're not talking about the problems of today, we're dealing with a mythical time and place in the future." We were lying, of course, but that's how we got these stories by the network types.

"Patterns of Force," the Nazi episode, was kind of like that. I mean, it was fun to write a well-meaning Nazi, a guy who for the right cause completely fucked everything up. Y'know, we started with the question, "How the hell did Nazism get past the shits and the street gangs and take root among the basically decent people? How did sane, reasonable adults come to buy into this bullshit?"

The answer seemed to be because it was efficient and because, in a society beset by all kinds of problems, it may have seemed like a feasible necessity. So it becomes feasible, and the

OPPOSITE PAGE AND LEFT: **L**UCAS'S **"NOMAD" FROM "THE CHANGELING,"** A CO-CREATION BUILT BY JIM RUGG AND SECOND-SEASON SET DECORATOR JOHN DWYER. (© 1993 PARAMOUNT PICTURES)

people take that leap. It was kind of like voting for Perot in the '92 election.

Still, you could never have done anything even approaching this subject matter anywhere else on network television. So *Star Trek* allowed us a great freedom.

As our second season's shooting was nearing its midpoint, it seemed almost certain that *Star Trek* would be canceled. Our ratings, which had always been rather soft, were now approaching a downright mushy consistency, and NBC had been carefully noncommittal in terms of making future plans for the show. Rumors of our apparently impending demise had begun wafting about the set as early as midseason, and in fact I can clearly recall that throughout the period of time that I was being so heavily made up for an episode we did called "The Deadly Years," the series' demise seemed imminent.

This particular episode centered around a story line wherein Kirk, Scotty and McCoy all begin aging at an incredibly rapid pace, each of them horrified by the ravages of their own physical and mental deterioration. Obviously, in shooting this particular tale extensive makeup jobs would be needed, and that forced Jimmy Doohan, De Kelley and me to spend a great deal of time in Freddie Phillips' makeup area while he buzzed about working his magic and yelling at his assistants. Basically, I

THIS PAGE: ONE OF MY FAVORITE
LUCAS-PRODUCED EPISODES WAS
"THE GAMESTERS OF TRISKELION." IT
WAS EXCITING, ACTION-PACKED AND
FUN TO SHOOT, MOSTLY BECAUSE I
GOT TO RUN AROUND WITH ACTRESS
ANGELIQUE PETTYJOHN ALL WEEK.
(© 1993 PARAMOUNT PICTURES)
OPPOSITE: FROM "PATTERNS OF
FORCE." (© 1993 PARAMOUNT
PICTURES)

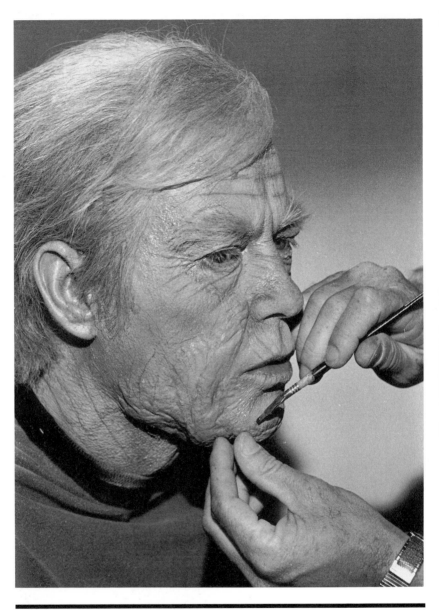

ABOVE AND OPPOSITE PAGE BOTTOM: Two CLOSE-UP LOOKS AT THE MAKEUP JOB
REQUIRED FOR "The Deadly Years" OPPOSITE PAGE TOP: A SNEAK PREVIEW OF
THE MOVIE POSTER FOR "Star Trek XXIV: The Voyage to the Home."
(© 1993 Paramount Pictures)

spent the better part of the week held captive in a reclining chair while big slabs of wrinkly latex were glued to my face. I couldn't go anywhere, couldn't do anything, all I could do was sit perfectly still so as not to ruin my makeup job. At the same time, as makeup artists ran about the room and fellow crewmen and castmates came to visit, I became keenly aware that the prevailing rumors of the day had us canceled within a week. "The Deadly Years," according to this gossip, could very well be our last episode. It was apparently a done deal, and we would be yanked from the schedule as soon as our first-run episodes had finished airing.

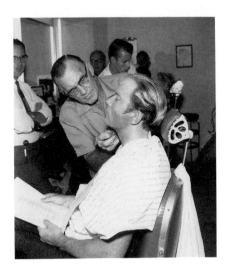

Obviously, the hearsay ultimately proved to be untrue, but for a two-day period we all became convinced that Star Trek was a terminal case.

Strangely enough, these erroneous rumors may have actually sparked the series of events that ultimately saved *Star Trek* from cancellation at the close of our second season. You see, Bjo Trimble, who'd become a close friend of Roddenberry's over the years, and her husband, John, were paying one of their frequent visits to our set as we shot "The Deadly Years." In observing the day's events, they couldn't help but fall prey to this round of cancellation rumors. Bjo recalls:

> The whole cast seemed pretty sure that *Star Trek* was going to get canceled, and that made their performances an amazing thing to watch. I mean everybody looks at actors and thinks, "Oh, I could do that," but this experience proves that theory completely false. I watched the whole cast discussing the rumors, and of course they were extremely unhappy and upset. Then they'd drag their long faces in front of the camera, and in a matter of seconds they'd transform themselves into bright, cheerful, noble *Enterprise* crew members.
>
> I can distinctly remember that Nichelle Nichols was so upset that at one point she was just sitting at her makeup mirror in tears. One of the A.D.s then called her to the set, and she just took a Kleenex, did a little dab under each eye, collected her thoughts for a moment and walked onto the bridge set as Uhura. It was just fascinating to watch this kind of creative talent working so hard in the face of such terrible odds.

The Trimbles left our set that afternoon feeling as if their favorite show was about to die, and believe it or not, this was a good thing. That's because during the couple's long drive home, they simply sat in the car and stewed with anger, frustrated that the network would cancel *Star Trek*, and disgusted with their own inability to correct this obvious programming mistake. At this point, somewhere in a traffic jam just north of L.A., John Trimble looked at his wife and said, "Gee, I hate to see this happen. There must be *something* that we can do."

A light bulb went on over Bjo's head. She smiled, and within hours she'd set into motion the series of events that ultimately saved the show from a premature death and branded her forever as "the fan who saved *Star Trek*."

s we were still driving home, I decided that the best thing we could do would be to contact as many *Star Trek* fans as possible, asking them to write NBC and tell them that you're really annoyed about this. However, I didn't want to open this whole can of worms without Gene's permission, so I phoned him, told him about my idea and he said, "I think that's terrific! Let's do it!"

As it turned out, Gene had also been looking for some way to make some noise about saving the show, so he went out of his way to be helpful. I went right back to Los Angeles, met with Gene in his office and we mapped out a preliminary plan.

Bjo and Gene decided that the logical first step would be to dig up the addresses of as many bona fide *Star Trek* fans as possible and then have Bjo contact them with a printed call to action, urging them to write to NBC expressing their extreme disappointment and dissatisfaction over the network's decision to cancel their favorite show and demanding that *Star Trek* be renewed.

Toward that end, Bjo immediately contacted her friends at the World Science Fiction Convention, asking for their mailing lists, which ultimately supplied them with the names of about four thousand probable fans. Shortly thereafter, an influential bookseller friend who specialized in science fiction supplied Bjo with about a thousand more leads. Last, Gene Roddenberry himself made a raid on the Paramount mailroom and came away lugging several sacks of *Star Trek* fan mail behind him. These provided Bjo with about two thousand additional targets, and marked the one and only time Gene would allow himself to *publicly* get involved in Bjo's plan.

Fearing studio politics and the perception that the resultant letter-writing campaign might just be dismissed as some "Hollywood producer stunt," Gene soon "officially" backed away from the Trimble offensive. In fact, throughout the ensuing weeks of the "Save *Star Trek*" campaign, Gene steadfastly insisted that he knew nothing about any sort of organized coalition of *Star Trek* fans, and took on the bemused posturings of an innocent bystander who was nonetheless overwhelmed by this "completely unsolicited outpouring of affection."

At any rate, once Bjo had attained her solid base of about seven thousand names, all of them likely *Trek* fans, she got down to business and drafted the letter. Once she'd finished, she and John churned out thousands upon thousands of smelly purple dittoed copies, all of which served to urge a good portion of *Star Trek*'s most loyal, supportive and enthusiastic fans into action on behalf of the precariously situated program. Excerpts of the letter follow:

I December, 1967
Oakland, California
TO: STAR TREK fans, fanzine editors, and other interested parties
RE: Keeping STAR TREK on the air.

Hi!

Please relay this info in whatever manner you can ... Action *NOW* is of the essence.

I just got a call from Gene Roddenberry ... [who] says that so far, there has been no word on renewing the show for next season, and in fact, it is highly likely that STAR TREK will die if something isn't done. . . . we don't have much time in which to work.

. . . Morton Werner, head of programming for NBC-TV, Rockefeller Center, New York, is one of the main people who will decide whether or not STAR TREK lives. Letters should be personally addressed to him. . . . We want to combat the good ol' traditional American attitude of "well, *my* one vote won't count much . . . " because your *one* tiny letter just may be THE letter that topples the scales in the right direction. If thousands of fans just sit around moaning about the death of STAR TREK, they will get exactly what they deserve: GOMER PYLE! (Yetch!) But if thousands of fans get off their big fat typers and W*R*I*T*E letters, and do it soon (like, *NOW*), it could happen that the man in charge of this sort of thing will be more impressed with our letters, than with the damned Nielsen ratings. We have to show that there are more people who *want* STAR TREK than who don't really care, one way or another.

So pass the word, and write some letters, people; it's up to us fans to keep STAR TREK on TV. Our own inaction will assure that it never sees a third season!

Bjo Trimble

Bjo's urgent missive was met with overwhelming support among its recipients. All over the country, fan clubs and fanzines pleaded with supporters to write Mort Werner and express their devotion to the show. At the same time, science fiction conventions strongly urged their attendees to do the same. Bjo was overwhelmed with offers of assistance, donations of stamps and envelopes and volunteers willing to donate their time to such a worthwhile cause.

Each of the *Star Trek* fans contacted by mail was urged to in turn contact at least ten fellow Trekkers on behalf of the cause. Bjo even went so far as to supply each recipient of her missive with the names and addresses of their local fellow *Trek* enthusiasts. This created a steadily mushrooming core of letter-writers, and NBC's mail count subsequently exploded. Mailbags began stacking up at the network, ultimately growing to mountainous proportions, and with each new *Star Trek* correspondent recruiting ten more letter-writers, NBC's influx of mail began increasing exponentially. Work those factors through, and you'll realize that Bjo's call to action represents perhaps the most successful chain-letter/pyramid scheme ever.

With Bjo and Roddenberry riding a tidal wave of mail-order adrenaline, they decided that it was time to employ some guerrilla tactics. With that in mind, Gene had several thousand bumper stickers made up, each bearing one of two messages, "I GROK SPOCK" or "STAR TREK LIVES." He had most of them handed out to fans at conventions or at Paramount, but even as these stickers were just beginning to show up on highways all over the United States, Gene had already come to the conclusion that the *best* way to utilize these strategic weapons in the war to save *Star Trek* would be to smuggle them behind enemy lines. Gene ordered a hit on NBC headquarters.

Gene, Majel, Bjo and John then met over drinks, and Gene pitched his idea about actually getting these bumper stickers *inside* NBC's corporate headquarters. The basic idea would be to dig up a handful of local supporters who'd lead the assault on NBC's Burbank offices, and to also find one exceptionally gutsy fan who'd fly to New York and infiltrate the network's Rockefeller Center digs. Once inside, their mission would be to roam the network halls, spreading the word about *Star Trek*'s unwarranted, unwanted demise, then offering bumper stickers and a printed call to action to any employees who seemed the least bit supportive.

Bjo smiled, then got on the telephone and immediately called a group of especially enthusiastic fans over at Cal Tech who'd already offered to storm the halls of NBC. She explained the mission, then had them synchronize their watches and report for duty. Within minutes of the call, a half-dozen Cal Techers were tooling down a freeway toward the evil empire's Burbank offices.

At the same time, a raw but gung-ho recruit named Wanda Kendall was meeting with Roddenberry in preparation for her airlift to New York. She was briefed on how to effectively maneuver behind enemy lines, armed with a handful of bumper stickers, herded over to the airport and shuttled onto an eastbound jet.

Once she'd landed in Manhattan, Wanda made her way inside the lobby of NBC's Rockefeller Center headquarters. However, while she was free to roam the public areas of the building, large, frowning, thoroughly unimpressed security men kept her from getting anywhere near the actual network offices. Dejected, Wanda left, feeling thoroughly defeated.

Then, even before she could hail a cab back to the airport, Wanda was struck by an idea that was brilliant, daring and just a little bit illegal. Having watched several stretch limousines pulling in and out of NBC's highly exclusive "Executive Parking Facilities," and realizing that she was still in possession of several hundred "STAR TREK LIVES" and "I GROK SPOCK" stickers, Wanda theorized that these stickers could best serve the cause by becoming permanently affixed to the automobile bumpers belonging to the very NBC executives who would soon decide the fate of Star Trek.

Now she formulated a plan. Staking out the parking area, Wanda noticed that limousines were routinely making pickups inside the gated facility, and that quite often the cars' drivers would stop just prior to entry for a cigarette break. They'd generally exit their cars, leaving the engine running, and wander over toward the guardhouse, where they'd chat with the security guys while sucking down large quantities of tar and nicotine. With bumper stickers now squeezed tightly in both fists and a grim look of determination upon her face, Wanda realized that it was time for action.

Lying in wait by the side of the facility, Wanda watches for the next limo to approach. Sure enough, the driver pulls up to the gate, exchanges some friendly greetings with the guards and gets out of the car for a quick Camel unfiltered. Immediately Wanda swoops down from her surveillance spot and sneaks into the cavernous back seat of the limousine. The driver has no idea she is there, and within minutes he's unknowingly escorted her into the middle of the lot. The limo driver then enters the building, using the house phone to signal his fare that he's arrived. Wanda takes this opportunity to sneak out the car's back door.

She now takes a moment to paste the back bumper of this particular limo with a green and yellow "I GROK SPOCK," then turns her attention to the sea of Cadillacs, BMWs, Mercedes and Jags that lie in front of her, several rows deep. Silently and with blazing speed, Wanda plasters row after row of gleaming, overpriced executive wheels until the entire parking lot looks like an ad for *Star Trek*. In fact, it's been said that Mort Werner, Grant Tinker and even Johnny Carson went home that night bearing back-bumper praise of our show.

Once Wanda had made it inside the executive parking lot, she had absolutely no problem getting into the building. Whereas the guards in the lobby had barked at her, demanding I.D., the guards at *this* entry, thinking Wanda had *parked* in this lot and was therefore some sort of VIP, simply wished her good morning. She passed their station coursing with adrenaline, thrilled that her break-in was going so smoothly.

Once on the executive floors of NBC, Wanda was able to move about with unrestricted access. With that in mind, she spent the better part of the day papering the place with flyers and handing out bumper stickers to any *Trek* fan she could find. Before she departed, she'd even managed to recruit several NBC employees who agreed to continue her work, spreading the word about *Star Trek* throughout the halls of 30 Rock whenever their bosses weren't looking.

In the days that followed, Roddenberry smirked through several angry phone calls from NBC executives as they complained about a gluey residue that refused to come clean from their bumpers. Suppressing his laughter, Gene pleaded innocence and ignorance of the *Trek* fans' actions. "These people are really devoted to the show," he offered, trying to help his situation. "People LOVE *Star Trek*, who knows HOW far they'll go in trying to save it?"

By now, the "Save *Star Trek*" letters that were raining down on NBC's mailroom, and Mort Werner's desk, had passed the one million mark. The network was simply drowning in mail, without the manpower or the postal budget to even come close to answering it all. Finally, on a late-winter Friday night, in the middle of *Star Trek*'s end credits, the powers-that-were at NBC officially threw in the towel and made the now-famous on-air announcement that *Star Trek* would indeed be renewed for a third season. It went like this:

Ａnd now an announcement of interest to all viewers of *Star Trek*. We are pleased to tell you that *Star Trek* will continue to be seen on NBC television. We know you will be looking forward to seeing the weekly adventure in space on *Star Trek*.

Bjo Trimble's idea had spawned the most massive outpouring of viewer support in the history of television. As a result, *Star Trek* had dodged yet another bullet and would survive to see the 1968–69 fall schedule. NBC, even as they were still shoveling out the mailroom, couldn't help but notice that the show really *did* have a loyal and incredibly devoted following. With that in mind, they spoke publicly about "renewing their dedication to the show's success." They then penciled us into a very desirable Monday night seven-thirty P.M. time slot and urged Gene Roddenberry to once again take over the producing duties. Gene agreed, and *Star Trek* seemed poised to achieve its greatest success ever, both creatively and in terms of ratings.

Sadly, however, this was not to be.

SEASON THREE

or two very big reasons, Star Trek geared up for its third season with renewed vigor and a real sense of enthusiasm. First and foremost, Gene Roddenberry would once again be personally producing all of the season's episodes, and second, the Trimble-inspired postal avalanche that snowed in NBC's mail clerks seemed as if it might have actually slapped some sense into the network. Between seasons, the big technicolor peacock ate crow and publicly acknowledged the "incredible outpouring of faith" demonstrated by Star Trek's fans. Then they announced that Star Trek would soon begin airing in the primo time slot of Monday nights at seven-thirty, a perfect position for our show in that much of our audience was made up of youngsters, students and young adults. Do the math, and you'll realize that most of these people spent their Monday nights at home, bored and staring vacantly at the boob tube. Placing Star Trek, a show they were crazy about, smack in the middle of the Monday-evening blahs would have almost certainly paid off with significantly increased ratings.

With that in mind, the adrenaline once again began coursing through Gene Roddenberry's tired veins, the gleam returned to his baggy eyes, the calluses returned to his carpal tunnel syndromed fingertips and he almost immediately got to work on our third season's scripts. However, within days a major monkey wrench would be tossed into the works, and when the dust cleared, both Gene Roddenberry and our Monday-night time slot would be gone. Majel explains:

s soon as we'd gotten picked up for our third year, Gene and I went down to Palm Springs with eight scripts that he was going to work on down there. And I can still remember him sitting down to start working on these scripts and saying, "I'm going to make this our best season ever. The very best, and we're going to go on forever." Then he started working.

Two days later, Gene gets a telephone call from NBC, and it turns out to be Mort Werner, who says, "Gene Baby!" Gene always said, "I should have known I was in trouble when he called me baby."

Now Werner says, "Gene, Baby, I've got great news for you. We're moving you to a brand-new time slot. You're gonna love it! We're actually letting you have Friday night at ten." Gene knew this was the kiss of death.

The only people who are sitting home watching TV on Friday night at ten is Aunt Maude in Iowa, and the Aunt Maudes of the world wouldn't have watched Star Trek if we were to perform it live in their living room. They said we're giving your old slot to this great show that really needs an earlier time slot. It's called Laugh-In.

We knew it was the kiss of death, so Gene just packed everything up and home we came. He knew it was over.

Laugh-In, which had been airing Monday nights at eight, was one of NBC's most successful programs, but for the 1968–69 season it had been rescheduled to follow Star Trek, starting at eight-thirty. However, when the show's producer, George Schlatter, found out about this, he apparently blew a gasket and absolutely refused to allow this schedule change, demanding that Laugh-In remain a Monday night at eight commodity. The network bean counters then took a look at Laugh-In's ratings, compared them to Star Trek's and made the obvious decision. Rowan and Martin kept their cushy time slot, while Kirk and Spock got banished to the nearest available vacancy . . . which just so happened to be Friday nights at ten.

Fearing the worst, Gene immediately fought one last battle with NBC over the fate of the show. Grasping at straws in a last-ditch effort to change our time slot back to Mondays, Gene informed the network that if the show remained at Friday nights at ten, he would renege on his promise to once again personally produce the series. NBC, smelling a Corbomite Maneuver, called what it thought was Gene's bluff and was ultimately shocked when he stayed true to his word. Gene would remain Star Trek's executive producer, but he would no longer have anything to do with the daily production of the

PAGE 255: **SHOOTING ON THE SET OF "PLATO'S STEPCHILDREN."** (© 1993 PARAMOUNT PICTURES)

show, and for all intents and purposes his working relationship with the series was now finished.

Publicly, Roddenberry would always state that his hands were now tied. There was no way he could back down from his threat to the network, because if he did, from that point on he'd have absolutely no bargaining power against them. Having folded once, he'd never again be able to flex any real muscle, not on Star Trek, and not on subsequent projects.

However, privately Gene would occasionally concede that his departure wasn't solely motivated by the time slot fight, but also by the cumulative effects of four years' worth of network battling. Gene was simply burned out, and no longer able to muster the energy necessary to mount a daily struggle against the neverending onslaught of blue-suited network executives. With that in mind, Gene would sometimes admit that his own numbing fatigue had colored his decision to leave Star Trek, and that if he could do it all over again, he almost certainly would have stayed with the show through our third season. Still, the reality of our situation found Roddenberry gone, Star Trek mired in a lousy time slot and our hopes for the new season dwindling rapidly. Bob Justman explains:

B y the time Gene gave up, the handwriting was on the wall. He knew this was it. We got moved from Thursday night in a good time slot to Monday night in a good time slot to Friday night at ten, which is death for a show like ours. The reason *why* it was death is that our audience was comprised mainly of people between the ages of fourteen and thirty-five, and those people are not home Friday nights at ten.

They're out socializing, doing their thing and trying their best to get into bed with one another. High school kids, college students, young married couples, these people have better things to do than sit around the living room on Friday night. The only fans we had left were the very young ones . . . actually, the only fans we had left were the young ones whose parents would let them stay up late and watch the show. No matter how you looked at it, we were in deep, deep trouble.

With the ship sinking, Captain Roddenberry jumped overboard, taking an office at Metro-Goldwyn-Mayer and beginning work on a film project entitled *Pretty Maids All in a Row*. Produced by Roddenberry, directed by

Roger "*Barbarella*" Vadim and starring Rock Hudson and Angie Dickinson, the film would ultimately turn out to be a major disappointment. However, throughout *Star Trek*'s third season, although Gene retained his executive producer credit, *Pretty Maids* would soak up the lion's share of the Bird's attentions. *Star Trek*, on the other hand, was now being produced by a "new guy." His name was Fred Freiberger.

Hired by Roddenberry, Freiberger had an impressive handful of television credits, working on such programs as *The Wild, Wild West, Slattery's People* and *Ben Casey*, and were it not for a long European vacation, he actually might have produced *Star Trek* from the start. Freiberger explains:

A s Gene Roddenberry was getting ready to shoot the second *Star Trek* pilot, he called me in to be a creative producer. . . . He showed me "The Cage," and I just flipped. I thought it was great.

Then I told him that I'd made plans to go to Europe on a vacation with my wife, and he said, "But we'll need you here. Don't you want this show?" I said, "Yeah, I want it very badly, but I'm not going to disappoint my wife."

So Gene kind of made a face, and I said, "Listen, if the job's still here when I get back and you still want me, I would be delighted to do it." Anyway, by the time I came back, John D. F. Black had come and gone and Gene Coon was just getting started, so I just went off and worked on some other series.

Then, when *Star Trek* was going into its third season, Gene called my agent again and asked if I'd still be interested in producing. So I went down to Gene's office and we talked about the show, and Gene asked me if I'd write a sample episode for him to look at before he made his decision. So I said, "C'mon, Gene, I'm not here as a writer, I'm here as a producer. I don't do auditions, and if that's what you want, I'll have to pass."

At that point, Gene just smiled, let go of the sample script idea and hired his new producer. Freiberger's contract was signed before the week was out, and he quickly realized that in producing *Star Trek*, he was going to face some serious production problems. First, before he'd left, Roddenberry had farmed out the season's first dozen scripts, accepting story ideas designed to fit within the previous season's budgetary guidelines.

However, almost immediately after Roddenberry's departure, the studio drastically reduced *Star Trek*'s budget, assuming that without Gene's guidance, *Star Trek* was doomed to fail.

For that reason, Freiberger immediately found himself in a dilemma, torn between the integrity of his first handful of scripts and the insufficient funds of his studio-slashed budget. Working with new script consultant Arthur Singer (Dorothy Fontana left shortly after Roddenberry), Fred was forced to "revise and compromise" wherever possible, reworking the original dozen scripts until they became shootable within the unfriendly guidelines of his new budget.

As you might expect, this significantly altered many of our third-season stories. "Spectre of the Gun," for example, originally found the *Enterprise* crew beaming into an Old West boom town. However, no longer able to afford location shooting or even the numerous extras we'd have needed to populate the streets of our pseudo–Dodge City, Freiberger and Bob Justman transformed the piece so that it could be played within an extremely surrealistic and minimalist (not to mention cheap) Western set, constructed within the cost-effective confines of our standard studio soundstage.

In the end, "Spectre of the Gun" actually turned out fairly well, but this sort of emergency script surgery wasn't always successful, and our casualties were broadcast across the country. Soon viewers began complaining that the show was going downhill, and fingers began being pointed squarely at Freiberger. Even today, Fred bears the brunt of the negative comments in regard to season three, and that situation is truly unfair. Freiberger simply performed as well as possible, coping with the combined assaults of insufficient budgets, unshootable scripts, and an absentee executive producer. Fred explains:

> Within my first week on the series, Gene Roddenberry called me into a meeting with the network people to introduce me to them and to discuss *Star Trek*'s unsatisfactory ratings and the direction our show should take during the upcoming third season. I was shocked at the obvious contempt with which Gene treated the network, and I sensed that the network had no love for Gene, or *Star Trek*.
>
> A few days later, I got a call from network research, telling me that they'd recently completed an extensive investigation as to

why *Star Trek*'s ratings were below expectations. According to them, women just wouldn't watch a show like *Star Trek* because it terrified them. They said that although there were many women who were loyal fans of *Star Trek*, the great majority of them wouldn't watch the show because it was set in the infinite realm of space. Their research apparently indicated that women needed parameters in which they could feel secure. I asked if they had any suggestions as to how we might ensnare more women viewers. They said no, but the inference was clear: *Star Trek*'s ratings were slipping, and the history of television research indicates that once a series' ratings begin to slip, the slide continues. Obviously, we were in serious trouble, and if our ratings didn't improve quickly, there would be no fourth season.

For all of those reasons, I began to wonder what I'd gotten myself into. I was dealing with a network that hated the series, an absentee executive producer and, of course, an almost impossible production schedule. The one bright spot on the horizon was the fact that Bob Justman was coming aboard as co-producer.

Having read this far, you've got to be wondering why Roddenberry didn't just pass the torch directly to Justman, and I have to admit, that's a question I couldn't quite answer. Freiberger was certainly qualified for the job, but Justman had been with the show literally from day one, and he'd seem, at face value, to have been the most likely candidate to replace Gene Roddenberry. With all that in mind, I asked Bob Justman to explain his initial reactions to the hiring of Freiberger. Bob was hesitant at first, but with a little prodding, he finally opened up.

I felt really bad, but remember, there was a large amount of sour grapes in my reaction, because I really thought I was going to become the sole producer in the third season. Instead, Fred Freiberger was proposed by the studio and approved by Gene. And Freddie's a lovely man, a friend of mine, so I'm a little bit nervous about voicing these ideas.

I was expecting to be rewarded for my two years of deathly hard labor, and when that didn't happen, I wasn't really angry at any particular person, I was more upset by the whole situation. I mean, I could certainly understand the motive. Gene and the studio were determined that whoever was in charge should have a track record as a writer. The studio didn't know I could write, and they didn't know I could be creative. To them I was a line producer, concerned with budgets and schedules, nothing more.

When they decided to give me the title of "co-producer" I'm sure they thought I'd see that as a separate but equal billing. Instead, it was more "separate but unequal." You know, they'd discounted my creative ideas, and that really tapped a button with me. I resented that. My feeling was that I'd given a lot of myself to Star Trek and that I hadn't been properly compensated emotionally.

So I went to the studio head, Doug Cramer, who I was friendly with and who knew I had some creative talent, and I said to him, "I want off the show." He said, "No, we don't want you off the show, we want you to finish it out." I said, "I really don't want to do it anymore."

Then they tried all kinds of things to get me to stay with the show. Offered me perks, and offered to let me produce my choice of any new show that the studio could sell for the following season.

I finally said to the studio, "I'll tell you what, let me off the show, and I promise I won't take another show. I'll wait and come back next spring on anything you want me to do." They said no. They wouldn't agree to that. They wouldn't play ball with me. I mean here I was willing to take five or six months out of my career and not work at all, not earn an income. I really felt like a prisoner.

Adding to Justman's headaches was the fact that several of our early third-season episodes had stumbled through budgetary revisions to become ... well ... pretty bad. In fact, our third-season premiere, "Spock's Brain," is almost universally hailed as the worst of the seventy-nine original Star Treks. This was an episode in which a bunch of scantily clad superbeing Amazon women sweep onto the Enterprise, knock everybody out and steal Spock's large, throbbing brain . . . right out of his head! But surprise, Spock is still alive! He's a zombie, but he's kept animate by this wonderful little metal hat. The rest of this episode finds us scavenger-hunting about the universe in search of the brainless Vulcan's cerebellum. Once we find it and have a nice little chat with the squishy gray matter (it communicates telepathically), there's a race against time to get "Spock's

Brain" back into Spock's head. Bones does the best he can, operating frantically (without cutting or even messing Spock's hair). However, as push comes to shove, it looks like we're gonna lose our pointy-eared pal. But wait, just in the nick of time, Spock wakes up on the operating table and actually gives Bones some quick operating suggestions: "Connect the sensor that works my forefinger, now my wrist," et cetera.

In short order, Spock's himself again, and after a quick closing joke, we all look up at the studio lights and laugh, then the credits roll. It was horrendous, embarrassing, and just shooting this monster filled us with a sense of looming cancellation. In the past, Fred Freiberger has sometimes been pointed out as the cause behind the decline in *Star Trek's* scripts, but when I asked him point-blank about our third-season scripts, his answer surprised me, and illustrated that labeling him as the man behind *Star Trek's* demise is actually a mistake. Fred explains:

> When I came to *Star Trek*, I was quite pleased to find that Roddenberry had already handed out about a dozen script assignments, most to freelance writers, and he'd even agreed to write a couple himself. This seemed like great news.
>
> Later when I'd read the premises of the stories, I was less than enthusiastic about some, and very happy with others. In any case, I

was not arrogant enough to think that I would know better than Roddenberry what stories were "right" for *Star Trek*. So with our production schedule breathing down our necks, Bob Justman and I just told these Roddenberry-assigned writers to get to work, as we were already desperately in need of scripts.

The first three scripts that came in were "Spectre of the Gun," "Spock's Brain" and "Elaan of Troyius." "Spock's Brain" and "Spectre of the Gun" were written by Gene Coon, under the pen name Lee Cronin, and "Elaan of Troyius" was penned by John Meredyth Lucas. Because of that, I felt like I was in clover. These were Roddenberry-approved story lines, written by the writer/producers of the first two seasons. I felt that surely this formidable group knew the show and the characters better than I did. So we moved forward with all three, and obviously "Spectre of the Gun" and "Elaan of Troyius" came out better than "Spock's Brain."

Despite all that, as the season wore on stories like "Spock's Brain" quickly placed a strain on the relationship between Leonard Nimoy and Fred Freiberger, and Leonard, keenly mindful of our production's "family dynamic," truly felt betrayed.

Having worked so hard for so long to make *Star Trek* a success, he had become extremely upset over the recent and undeniable decline in the quality of our show. He was angry that our characters were being compromised and convinced that our show, our stories and our work were no longer being treated with the respect they'd earned. With all of that in mind, Leonard refused to suffer in silence and tried his best to remedy the situation by making his complaints known to Freiberger. Leonard explains:

There was a confrontation that injured my relationship with Freddie Freiberger, and we descended rather quickly from there. I understood that, but I couldn't help it. I did what I had to do, and Freddie took offense at it. I can understand that, and I don't blame him, but it was inevitable.

The tension between the two men began even with our first teleplay of the season, "The Last Gunfight," which would be retitled "Spectre of the Gun" before airing. Leonard wasn't happy with the script, feeling that it was unbelievable, and that the story was full of holes, inconsistent in regard to our characters and needlessly violent. He even went so far as to write a memo regarding his objections and offering possible solutions.

As the third season progressed, our stories regressed, becoming less believable and perceptibly more farfetched. I watched these episodes again for the purposes of researching this book, and whether caused by budgetary constraints or creative changes, it's rather clear that our characters were indeed becoming cartoonish caricatures who contradicted their previously established behavior patterns while populating a series of stories that had grown increasingly implausible. None of us were spared. Kirk's body is entered by a woman (there's a switch). Scotty falls head-over-heels in love with a real live woman and even goes so far as to neglect his first love, the *Enterprise*. Bones discovers he's terminally ill and finds a girlfriend, all in the same episode. Even Chekov, our young, free-thinking ensign, finds himself in an episode where he's suddenly and inexplicably turned into a rigid Rush Limbaugh type. Walter Koenig recalls:

BELOW: **A PAIR OF THE GROOVIEST, NOT TO MENTION GOOFIEST, VISITORS EVER TO BOARD THE *ENTERPRISE*. (© 1993 PARAMOUNT PICTURES)** OPPOSITE: **SPOCK 'N' ROLL. (© 1993 PARAMOUNT PICTURES)**

The lowest point for me came in "The Way to Eden," an episode where I actually had a lot to do. The problem was, as I read the script, I couldn't help but notice that Chekov had suddenly become a really inflexible, Type A, establishment-loving conservative. I mean, this was supposed to be a character that had been conscientiously drawn as a fairly identifiable approximation of the young people of 1969. However, somehow all of that had suddenly gone out the window, and it became rather obvious that somebody somewhere had really stopped caring about these characters, and about this show.

Still, throughout our third season, the character most maligned was easily Mr. Spock. It seemed that this poor beleaguered Vulcan was asked to chip away at his own previously established ethics, beliefs and inner workings in nearly every episode. For example, in "The Cloud Minders," this normally tight-lipped Vulcan actually brags about the sexual habits of his race to a woman he's barely met. He eats meat in "All Our Yesterdays," he brays like a donkey in "Plato's Stepchildren" and worst of all, in "The Way to Eden" he makes like an intergalactic Hendrix, rocking and rolling with a batch of ersatz outer-space hippies.

As you can imagine, none of this went unnoticed by Leonard, and by the time we'd begun shooting our seventy-first episode, "Whom Gods

Destroy," he felt the need to once again put his negative thoughts down on paper. This time, however, he went over Fred Freiberger's head and addressed his comments directly to Gene Roddenberry and studio head Doug Cramer. A portion of the memo follows:

TO: Gene Roddenberry, Doug Cramer
DATE: October 15, 1968
CC: Fred Freiberger
FROM: Leonard Nimoy

GENTLEMEN:

During the first season of "Star Trek," a character named Mr. Spock was introduced into the series. This character has pointed ears, extremely high intelligence, was capable of brilliant leaps of deductive logic, could contact people's minds, could tick off data about earth, space, time, etc. as though he had memorized libraries on the subject, was extremely powerful physically, had a great deal of pride, and a few other things, which in general made him a smart ass.

Now we all know that nobody, but *nobody* likes a smart ass, and above all, a continuing character in a TV series must not only be liked, but well liked! Therefore, I can well understand the efforts this season to change the character's image, so that he will be more acceptable to the American public.

Now we are embarked on re-doing a show that we did during the first season, when it was originally entitled "Dagger of the Mind.". . . Since, evidently, the show was effective the first time around, we have managed to retain much of the storyline for the second shooting.

I note one major difference which is evidently indicative of the change in the "Spock" character. In "Dagger of the Mind," "Spock" picked up some valuable information by mind-melding with a man whose mind was terribly disturbed. "Spock" was able to gather information from him only through the mind-to-mind contact which Vulcans are capable of. In our current episode, "Spock" is confronted with what would seem to be a rather simplistic situa-

tion. He walks into a room, phaser in hand, and is confronted by two "Kirks." One is obviously his real captain, and the other is an imposter.

FROM THE EPISODE IN QUESTION, **"WHOM GODS DESTROY."** (© 1993 PARAMOUNT PICTURES)

Question: Can Spock handle this situation using his deductive logic, the phaser in his hand, his previous experiences with Kirk, his mind-meld, or any of the other imaginative techniques that a smart-ass Vulcan would normally use? The answer is no.

Not only is he unable to cleverly, dramatically, or fascinatingly arrive at a solution, he also proves to be a lousy gun-hand, since he allows the two men to become embroiled in a brawl while he stands there holding a phaser, not sure whether he should shoot one, or both, or maybe just let them fight it out and "hope that the best man wins."

. . . My primary concern in contacting you gentlemen is my concern over my own lack of experience in playing dummies. Perhaps you could arrange for me to get educated in this area. Maybe if I watched some "Blondie" episodes, and studied "Dagwood" as a role model, I could pick up some useful pointers. Or, better yet, I could just get right to the bottom line, by wearing some braids and feathers, and learning to grunt "Ugh, Kimosabee"?

Any suggestions?

Hopefully,

Leonard Nimoy

Wanting to get both sides of the story, I also spoke with Fred Freiberger about all this, and as you might expect, he paints a slightly different picture. Basically, to a producer working amid the absolutely enormous financial and production inadequacies of Star Trek's third season, Leonard's creative complaints were just one of a multitude of serious problems screaming for Fred's attention. Further separating the two men was the fact that with budgetary chaos and a mind-numbing work load hanging over his every exhausted move, Freiberger tried his best to address all of Nimoy's concerns, but ultimately had precious little time to assuage Leonard's fears in regard to the show. Fred continues:

Nimoy sent "The Letter" to Doug Cramer, the head of the studio, and carbon copies to Roddenberry and me. I never heard from Roddenberry about it, but I did get a call from Doug Cramer. He asked what was going on, and I told him there was a person-

Mᴇ ᴀɴᴅ Yᴠᴏɴɴᴇ "Bᴀᴛɢɪʀʟ" Cʀᴀɪɢ, ᴏɴ ᴛʜᴇ sᴇᴛ ᴏғ "Wʜᴏᴍ Gᴏᴅs Dᴇsᴛʀᴏʏ." (© 1993 Pᴀʀᴀᴍᴏᴜɴᴛ Pɪᴄᴛᴜʀᴇs)

ality conflict between Nimoy and me. I said I felt the letter was very unfair, and an obvious attempt to get me fired from the series. I asked Doug what his feeling was, and he replied that as producer of the show, I should handle things as I saw fit. I then sent a memo to Nimoy, stating that I was unhappy that he'd gone over my head, and that I hoped in the future we could make the attempt to settle any differences between us without involving the front office.

With all of that in mind, what we're left with is two seasoned, sophisticated professionals—one consumed with making the best of our budgets and production values and the other constantly monitoring the creative quality of our show. In truth, both Nimoy and Freiberger were working toward a common goal of making every episode of *Star Trek* as good as possible, but they ended up butting heads, as with their own separate agendas they could never quite see eye to eye. Freiberger explains:

Shortly after I came on the series, Leonard Nimoy and I had a meeting during which he told me that he had problems with the way his character had been handled during *Star Trek's* second season. He told me that he and the producer had been far apart in terms of artistic viewpoints, and he cited "Amok Time" as a good example of how his character was being shortchanged. Apparently, the producer claimed that the Spock character had been done full justice in that episode, but Leonard disagreed. I offered to screen the episode, and as I watched it, it seemed to me that Spock, indeed, was heavily involved on many levels. It seemed the kind of role any actor would relish. I think it may have been my relaying this assessment that convinced Nimoy that I had no judgment as a so-called creative producer.

I had numerous meetings with Leonard, and three of them really stand out in my memory. In one he was disturbed because Spock didn't have the final line in a particular episode. We spoke about this, engaging in an academic discussion about the dynamics of the Spock character, the drive of the story line and its climactic scene. According to Nimoy, all signs pointed to Spock delivering the last line, and I simply didn't agree.

The second meeting concerned the relationship between Spock and Zarabeth (as played by Mariette Hartley) in the episode "All

Our Yesterdays." These two characters were supposed to fall in love, until Leonard pointed out to me that Vulcans do not get emotionally involved. Obviously, he was right.

This script was set in the Ice Age, thousands of years ago, and I had been so intrigued by this story, and by the relationship between Spock and Zarabeth, that I obviously had a lapse of memory in regard to the Vulcan psyche. Still, I wanted to preserve this story line and to find some justification for it, and I did come up with a reason. I suggested that since the story was set in the Ice Age, thousands of years before the Vulcans had evolved emotion out of their psyches, Spock *could* fall in love during that time period. That seemed to satisfy Nimoy, and he did an excellent job of acting in that episode.

The third meeting that especially stands out is the one that led to our complete alienation. Leonard and I had become involved in a discussion in which I said something to the effect that Shatner was the star of the series . . . at which point Nimoy insisted that he was a co-star of equal stature. I then realized that this attitude may have been providing the basis for all the misunderstandings between us. Although the Spock character was heavily involved in almost all of our episodes, the "star" of a show *would* have gotten more emphasis.

At the end of that workday, I phoned Gene Roddenberry and told him about my meeting with Nimoy and that I needed official clarification. In our discussions when I first came on the series, we had touched on the relationships between the characters, and it was my understanding that Bones and Spock were very important but that Kirk was the star. If I was in error then I had indeed been doing a disservice to Nimoy. However, Roddenberry assured me that my original understanding was accurate. I then suggested that it might be best for *him* to straighten that out with Leonard, who was not inclined to accept much of what I said. Gene assured me he would.

Freiberger's remembrance of "All Our Yesterdays" stands out as a perfect reminder that when it comes to Star Trek's third season, it's important to look at the bigger picture and note that many of our episodes were *extremely* good. In fact, despite the quarreling and the stifling constraints of our budgets, we did manage to put out some unusual and high-quality shows: "The Enterprise Incident," "Day of the Dove," "Is There in Truth No Beauty?" "The Tholian Web" and "The Paradise Syndrome" (where I got to become Heap Big Medicine Chief Kirok, married to the beautiful Miramanee) all come to mind, as does "And the Children Shall Lead," in which a group of children come under the spell of the "friendly angel" Gorgan, played by world-famous attorney Melvin Belli.

Actually, there's a story regarding Belli's involvement in the show that bears printing. It seems that shortly after this episode aired, Belli and fellow superattorney F. Lee Bailey had gone out to dinner together, and just as their appetizers were hitting the table, they began having a rather silly and good-natured argument over which one of them was the more famous lawyer.

By the time the main course had arrived, their argument had escalated into a bet, and the rather hefty dinner tab was at stake. It seems that they'd decided that whichever one of them got recognized first got his dinner free. Several minutes later, a young couple sheepishly approached the table asking, "Excuse me, sir, but aren't you Melvin Belli?"

FROM "**T**HE **E**NTERPRISE **I**NCIDENT." **K**IRK, HAVING HAD A BROWJOB, GOES UNDERCOVER ON A **R**OMULAN SHIP. (© 1993 **P**ARAMOUNT **P**ICTURES)

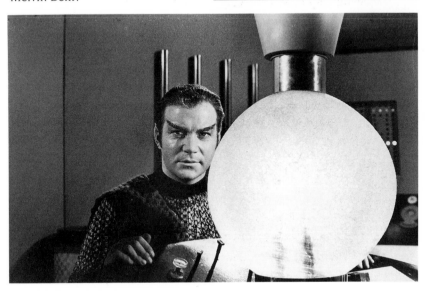

"Why yes I am!" beamed the proud attorney. "Are you law students?"

"Law students . . . uh, no . . . " they replied. "Why do you ask?"

"Well, I am a rather well-known attorney, and I just assumed that . . . "

"You're a lawyer? Wow! We just thought you were that Gorgan guy from *Star Trek*."

Apparently Bailey just stifled a laugh and picked up the tab without a fight, which is probably a good thing, because you can imagine the heated, not to mention long-winded, arguments those two could have concocted over a disputed dinner bill.

I should also take a moment to mention that even though we all felt the show was beginning to suffer creatively and that we probably would not be renewed, the actual work involved in making *Star Trek* was, as always, more than enjoyable. Cast and crew had grown closer than ever, and although our sets had always been filled with competent professionals, these same people now seemed less like co-workers and more like friends, even family.

Last, by now Leonard and I had become quite close, but I must admit, one thing still bugged me. It seemed no matter how well I got to know Leonard, whenever I'd see him on our set, he looked really serious, stand-

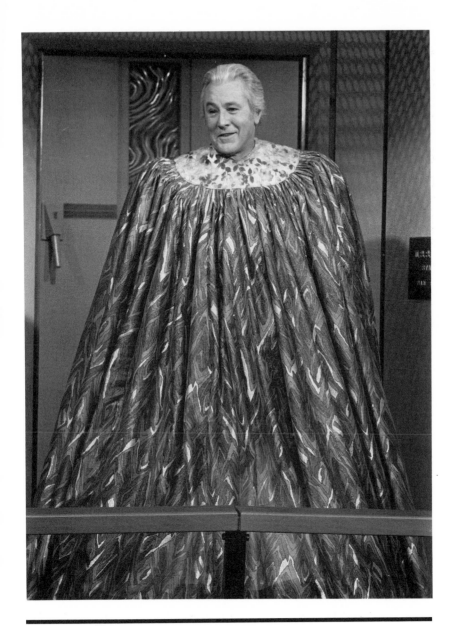

OPPOSITE LEFT: **B**IG **C**HIEF "**K**IROK." (© 1993 PARAMOUNT PICTURES)
OPPOSITE RIGHT: **M**IRAMANEE AND ME. (© 1993 PARAMOUNT PICTURES)
ABOVE: **M**ELVIN **B**ELLI, PROVING THAT AS AN ACTOR HE'S A TERRIFIC LAWYER.
(© 1993 PARAMOUNT PICTURES)

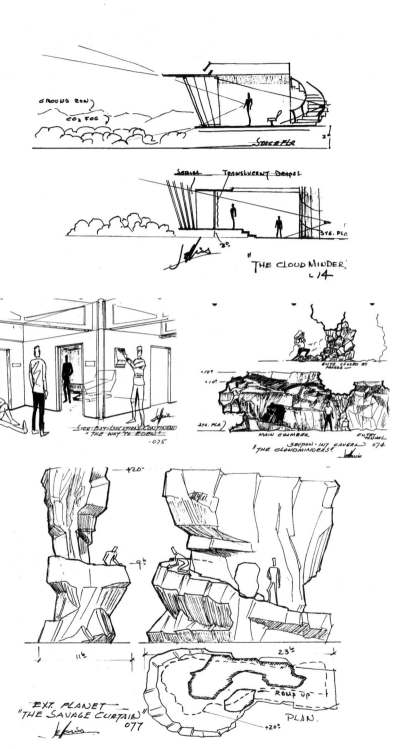

GROUND RUN
CO₂ FOG

STAGE FLR

SCRIM   TRANSLUCENT DRAPES.

STG. PLR.

"THE CLOUD MINDER"
L14

SICK-BAY-ISOLATION CONDITION!
"THE WAY TO EDEN"
.075

ENTR. CLOSED BY
PHASER

+12°
+10°

STG. FLR

MAIN CHAMBER   ENTRY
TUNNEL

SECTION - INT CAVERN 074
"THE CLOUDMINDERS"

+20°

9½

EXT. PLANET
"THE SAVAGE CURTAIN"   077

11½   23½

RAMP UP

+20°   PLAN.

THROUGHOUT OUR THIRD SEASON, MATT JEFFERIES CONTINUED WORKING
CREATIVE AND DOLLAR-STRETCHING MIRACLES, AS EVIDENCED BY HIS SET
SKETCHES FOR "THE CLOUD MINDERS," THE WAY TO EDEN," "THE SAVAGE
CURTAIN" AND "A HANDFUL OF DUST" . . . WHICH WOULD SOON BE RETITLED
"ALL OUR YESTERDAYS." (COURTESY WALTER M. JEFFERIES)

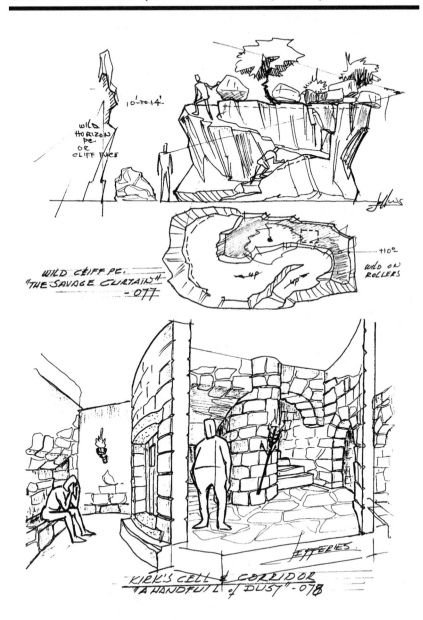

offish, even distant . . . never smiling, never telling a joke and worst of all, never laughing at mine. With that in mind, I asked how playing the Vulcan Mr. Spock affected the very human Mr. Nimoy.

was, in a way, in deep isolation, and having a tough time. The character isolated me, and I think that during the course of a day on the set, I probably projected a certain kind of indifference, intolerance, frigidity, whatever. I remember one day we were sitting around waiting for a set to be lit, and I was sitting there totally stone-faced and out of it. One of our actresses said, "Uh-oh, Leonard's in his Spock bag." I was even told one time that one of our producers said, "Watch out for Nimoy, he's a cold, calculating fucker."

But this was almost to be expected in that nature abhors a vacuum. When a person shows a personality that seems to be devoid of any clear signal of what he or she is thinking, people project into that whatever they perceive. To some people I was probably threatening, remote, cold and distant, all of that, I'm sure.

I actually took great pride in being the only one who was not laughing when a great joke was being told. It just served to confirm that I was successfully staying in character. You know, to make me laugh would have been to suggest that I'm just like everybody else. I'm not like everybody else.

So I prepared to go onstage by getting into character long before it was time to make my entrance. I did not believe it was possible to be "Person A" offstage and "Person B" as soon as you got within the sightlines of a camera. I just didn't believe it was possible. What I *did* believe in was thorough preparation and maintaining the condition of the character during the lighting, during the scene shifting, during the makeup touch-ups and so forth.

And so I probably *was* sending off signals of hostility and of being unfeeling, perhaps superior, but that was my intention. And I did all of that because I thought there was a wonderful springboard here, a great opportunity because Bill, as Kirk, was always so energetic in the work, so forthcoming, so definite, even defiant.

"I'm going to DO THIS! I've made up my mind!" That energy allowed me tremendous opportunities to play reflective. Y'know, McCoy could play the angry quibbling argumentative hand-wringer, "Jim, are you CRAZY?!" and that was great for him. With all that in place, I could play "Hmm, isn't that interesting?" and the relationships worked together wonderfully.

Still, my staying in character was really tough, and I remember that I even had a hard time coming out of it on Saturdays. I was really imbued with this thing, and it was extremely Stanislavskian. It made me distant, even at home. My persona was totally infected by it, and it affected my wife and more so my kids, because they were less equipped to deal with it.

One of Leonard's *most* inflexible beliefs about Spock was that the character should remain almost entirely nonviolent. Instead, Spock would generally rely on his formidable strength in knocking off potential enemies with a minimum of fuss and exertion. As a result, it had become a running joke around our set as to how strong Spock really was. You know, a half-dozen guys would attack the two of us, and Leonard would pinch one, and in the beginning he'd take a halfhearted swing at maybe one more . . . which left me with the other four to deal with. But as the series wore on and he got a little more relaxed, lethargic, cooler, he'd give one guy a little pinch, then stand back and watch. And those stuntmen would beat the hell out of me.

And because I was always in the thick of things with these stuntmen, over the years, in studying them and choreographing scenes with them, I'd come up with some pretty flashy moves of my own. My favorite, head and shoulders above the rest, went like this: The bad guy would be coming at me, and I'd run up, jump into the air and fling toward him with my feet. It was really just like the flying drop kicks pro wrestlers use. I loved that move, I used it all the time and of course every time I used it within a *Star Trek* episode, the bad guy would just sort of flop over unconscious any time I even came close to kicking him. Over the years I'd gotten pretty used to doing this, and I have to admit, I really thought this was cool, this was Kirk's move. You know, I'd throw myself at some guy, looking not unlike Macho Man Randy Savage, and of course, they'd just kinda drop dead every single time.

So on one of my rare days off during this third season, I had taken my kids, my three little daughters, to one of those go-kart places, where the kids can get into the cars and you all race around the track, doing like thirty miles per hour. So now my kids and I are racing around, they're all up ahead of me, and I'm hanging back, acting like Big Daddy and protecting them from the other cars, when all of a sudden this idiot comes racing by and he nearly slams into my daughter Leslie. So, of course, I yell at the jerk. I mean, doesn't he know that my daughters are the most beautiful, intelligent and gifted little girls ever to roam the earth? Doesn't he know that I'm Daddy? Doesn't he know that it's my sworn duty to take care of these children and to smite any man who might dare to injure (or date) them?

Six minutes go by, and our time on the track is up. All the go-karts come in, I screech into a stop, leap from my kart and run up to the idiot's car, yelling, "Wait a minute! What's wrong with you, fella? What the hell did you think you were doing out there?"

The idiot gets out of his kart . . . he's a monster. But I was still running in Daddy overdrive, so I yelled at him some more. "Now LOOK!" I said. "Those are MY KIDS, and it's up to me to PROTECT them from IDIOTS like you, who like to drive around bumping into them on go-kart tracks. Get me?!"

Behind me, my daughters are now smacking their foreheads and rolling their eyes up into their heads. They're mortified.

Now, though, the idiot is joined by three of his friends, seemingly from out of nowhere, each of whom makes him look tiny. "Oh yeah, smartass?" they grunt down at me, scraping their knuckles on the go-kart track as they speak, and drooling all over the pavement. "What are you gonna do about it?"

And now, still riding atop a tidal wave of paternal instinct and adrenaline, I snapped, and for a second there, I swear to you I thought I was Captain Kirk. Because of that, I was just about to launch myself into one of my famous kicks when my brain flashed upon Newton's law, and I realized that if I were to leap into the air at full speed, hit one of these monsters in the chest and kick with all my might . . . I'd probably just end up like those seagulls that fly into 747s. I'd bounce off, fall to the ground and of course at that time these three guys would kick me to death.

So I started talking very quickly, and I managed to escape with my life, although I did have to spend the entire car ride home listening to my daughters' triple-teaming lecture on the immaturity of fistfighting.

Flash forward two days, and we're just beginning to shoot "Plato's Stepchildren," which for all intents and purposes is a rather forgettable, rather dull episode of *Star Trek*. However, it's impossible to dismiss this particular show without taking some time to examine the story behind its most famous element, Kirk and Uhura coupling for television's first inter-racial kiss.

I'd gotten my script, and the producers were almost immediately at my dressing room door, asking, "Would you mind kissing Nichelle?" I said, "Mind? What, are you kidding? You're gonna *pay* me to kiss Nichelle? What a job!" Down the hall, Nichelle had gotten her script, too, and she was also formulating some first impressions.

thought the interracial kiss, in and of itself, was a valid and rather powerful dramatic moment. What really upset me, how-ever, was the bullshit we had to deal with in filming it.

I mean, we get the script, and of course there are these people with telekinetic powers who are going to force us to entertain them. And you have the cap-tain and Uhura, and there's got to be this sensual, sexual aware-ness between them. Although they would never do anything

REHEARSING AND NAPPING ON THE SET OF **"PLATO'S STEPCHILDREN."** (© 1993 PARAMOUNT PICTURES)

about it . . . or would they? It had certainly never been indicated. But in reading the script it became obvious that here were these two beautiful people, professionals, being thrown side by side into a situation that they did not initiate. And it allowed the character of Uhura to rise up and say, "Goddammit, how dare they, how dare anyone force me, Uhura, into a situation against my will."

So we got the script, and I can remember thinking, "Oh, this is beautiful," and it really didn't occur to me that there could be a problem with the kiss, it just did not enter my mind. I mean, the script was clear and strong, and I was able to use all of that, in addition to my own sense of Uhura, her character, her life and where she came from, in preparation for this episode. And all of that came into play so that throughout Uhura's scenes, and in leading up to the moment of the kiss, everything sort of clicked. Everything sort of moved, and everything felt not just motivated, but natural.

So now Nichelle and I walked onto the set, ready to hear "Action," and as she and I prepared and rehearsed the scene, we joked around a little bit, flirted a lot, and I can clearly recall teasing Nichelle by grabbing her into my arms and yelling, "Alright, Uhura, I've finally got you where I want you . . . gimme a big juicy one!" At the same time she was laughing, making jokes and as "Kirk's" trying kiss her, she was saying, "Oh, no, yuck, eeew, anything but that, save me!" But we finally settled down and walked through the scene five or six times, when all of a sudden our director, David Alexander, said, "Okay, take five!" Nichelle recalls what happened next:

Taking an unscheduled break seemed a bit odd, and the next thing I know, I'm called up to the front office where this gaggle of suits sits me down and says, "Now, Nichelle, honey, sweetheart, we've got a problem."

"What problem?" I asked them, and they said, "You know, the kiss, the KISS! You can imagine the problems we'll run into if we shoot this kissing scene, can't you?" And only now is it finally starting to dawn on me. Only now does it hit me . . . WHAM! It's not the fact that Kirk and Uhura are kissing that bothers them, it's the fact that a black woman is kissing a white man. And I have to tell you, until the suits made it crystal clear to me, I had absolutely no idea that this was going to be television's first interracial kiss. And they're telling me that the kiss would make the show impossible to air, that television stations all over the South would simply black out their screens for an hour instead of showing this "highly offensive" programming.

So I argued with them, and I said, "Interracial kiss? So what?! We're supposed to be in the twenty-third century here, and this is Uhura, and we don't have racism where we are." But they weren't buying it, and at one point they actually decided to drop the whole scene.

So now I'm pissed on a whole other level, and to a whole new degree. I mean, for a moment I had to forget about Uhura, and the twenty-third century, and the idiocy of the suits' whole black/white issue, and fight from the position of Nichelle Nichols, an actress who's trying desperately to save her own rare and unusually powerful scene. I mean these guys are about to yank my one really terrific scene without even a defensible reason why. So by now I've gone beyond mad. I'm ready to kill. These guys are dead, DEAD,

PHARMEN'S CHAMBER,
"PLATO'S STEPCHILDREN"
.J67

do you hear me?! I mean, they even went so far as to suggest changing the scene so that Kirk gets paired off with Nurse Chapel and Spock ends up with me. Somehow, I guess, they found it more acceptable for a Vulcan to kiss me, for this alien to kiss this black woman, than for two humans with different coloring to do the same thing. It was ridiculous, absolutely ridiculous.

So we keep arguing back and forth, and by now of course Gene Roddenberry has come to the office. And he's gotten into the act, yelling, "This is ridiculous. This is patently ridiculous." But the network doesn't want to budge. And at this point Bill storms off to his dressing room, very upset and very angry, yelling, "This is absolutely ludicrous. Let's just shoot the whole thing and to HELL with the South."

So now the network suits are really sweating, but even after all of this turmoil and disagreement they still want to cut the scene of the kiss. Finally, Roddenberry stood his ground and said, "No, this has to remain as written, we're not changing it." But at the same time, he came up with his familiar line, "Let's shoot it two ways," and that calmed everybody down, eased the tensions a little bit and allowed us to get on with the business of shooting our show.

Unfortunately, what Gene meant by "Let's shoot it two ways" was that we'd shoot the Kirk/Uhura kiss twice. In the first take, we'd actually kiss on camera, and in the second, Nichelle and I would turn our bodies as we embraced, so that my back was to the camera long before our lips would have ever touched. We'd give the illusion of kissing without ever touching lips. Sadly, when push came to shove, the network got their way and the no-contact kiss made it to the airwaves. For that reason, the widely held assumption that Star Trek features the first interracial kiss in the history of television is absolutely untrue. And if you happen across the episode, look closely and you'll see exactly what I mean.

And even when we shot this compromised version of the scene, I can clearly recall the network suits standing on the set watching us intently, making sure that before the two of us performed our simulated kiss, we fought against it intently, making it absolutely clear that in the case of Kirk and Uhura, this was

ONE OF MATT JEFFERIES' SET DESIGNS FOR "PLATO'S STEPCHILDREN." (COURTESY WALTER M. JEFFERIES)

THE KISS. (© 1993 PARAMOUNT PICTURES)

an "against their will" coupling. Completely devoid of any passion, romance or sexuality. I also swear to you that when we did indeed fake our kiss, me with my back to the camera, they stood there on the sidelines, squinting, intent upon verifying that our lips never actually touched. Nichelle continues:

> It was bullshit! Bullshit! It was simply and clearly racism standing in the door . . . in suits. Strange how a twenty-third-century space opera could be so mired in antiquated hang-ups.

By the time we'd reached this point in the season, morale was beginning to droop. The show was getting sloppy, our scripts were suffering and cancellation seemed a probability. Making matters worse, it had become clear that Gene Roddenberry had drifted away from the show, with no intention of ever getting seriously reinvolved on any creative level. Most disheartening of all, however, were Roddenberry's blatant attempts to milk every possible cent from his dying cash cow known as *Star Trek*, even at the expense of our scripts.

For example, a Roddenberry-approved mail-order house called Lincoln Enterprises (which was actually owned by Gene's lawyer) had recently begun selling a small line of *Star Trek* merchandise. At the same time, we had just begun shooting "Is There in Truth No Beauty?" which would shortly become a battlefield upon which creativity and naked mercenary opportunism would duke it out.

The story starts when an unexpected script revision arrives at Fred Freiberger's office. It's been sent by Gene Roddenberry, who's seemed almost nonexistent of late and who hasn't personally rewritten anything all season. Freiberger's puzzled by this unsolicited rewrite, and even more puzzled when the script change consists of one additional scene that's both pointless in regard to the story and talky as well.

In it, Captain Kirk speaks the praises of a medal of honor known as the "IDIC," which stands for "Infinite Diversity From Infinite Combinations," and he then bestows this "beautiful adornment" upon an absolutely thrilled recipient. Now, what you've got to understand here is that none of this stuff had anything to do with our episode's story line, and with that in mind, Freiberger was stuck in a no-win situation. Fred explains:

> ene Roddenberry had turned his back on the show, and we really hadn't seen or heard much from him all season, so when we got this script change, my story consultant Arthur Singer and I just looked at each other. He asked, "What can we do about this?" and I replied, "Gene Roddenberry created the show, and he's the executive producer. He calls the shots, send it down to the set."

I got my script change, read the new scene and with my jaw still hanging open, I called Fred down to the set, asking him, "What's this 'IDIC' thing all about?" I knew that Lincoln Enterprises would soon be selling these things, and there was no way that I was going to muck up a perfectly good story line just so we could include Gene's rather thinly veiled commercial. With that in mind, I flatly refused to do the scene. Freiberger hemmed and hawed about the difficulties involved in re-revising the script, but as I spoke to him recently for this book, he finally admitted that he was actually relieved that I wouldn't do the scene. It was probably the first time in history that a producer was glad to be dealing with a "difficult" actor.

Freiberger relayed my disdain for the new scene to Roddenberry, and Gene then took my artistic concerns into consideration and threw them out the window when he was unexpectedly presented with a perfect opportunity to simply rewrite the new scene/commercial so that Mr. Spock would have the honor of hosting the IDIC ceremony. Leonard continues:

This was another incident that damaged the relationship between Gene and me. I'm reading my original script, and I notice there's a scene between Diana Muldaur and me which goes on for several pages, which I feel is just deadly dull and almost completely pointless.

I was really agitated about the scene because we were both just babbling at each other, and I complained about it, but once again I couldn't get anywhere with Freddie Freiberger, because the attitude was, "Go away, actor, I'm working on next week's show. This one's okay." At least that was my sense of it. So I called Gene, who had said when he left that even though he was going to MGM and moving off the lot to make this movie with Rock Hudson, he still had a proprietary interest in *Star Trek*, he still had an affection for the show and he still had a strong interest in what was being done.

So I called Gene and explained the problem to him, but I didn't realize how divorced he was from the whole process. I thought, naively, that he was still involved in the creative process behind the show. You know, reading scripts, giving notes and so forth, even though he was across town on another project. But he had really divorced himself from *Star Trek* and was preoccupied with other issues. Anyway, I called him, told him my problem with the script, and he said something to me that was kind of cryptic and I didn't quite understand. He said something like, "You have given me an opening to inject myself into this process. I will look into it."

Now, I read this to mean that it was somehow politically uncomfortable for him to step back into the creativity of the show ... unless asked. And I didn't quite understand this, because as I remember his departure, he told us, "I will still be involved in overseeing and reading scripts and I will be in constant contact with the production." So why, I wondered, does he need this "opening"?

In any case, the scene in question was to be shot the next day, and very early the next morning when I arrived in the makeup department, there were some new script pages. Three pages for a new scene, written by Gene. And I thought "Ah! The old Gene! He must have worked through the night, writing a new script." And usually this process would produce very exciting results. So I thought, "Great! He's written me a new and improved scene!" Then I read it . . . and my heart sank.

Overnight, the irrelevant scene had been replaced with a far MORE irrelevant scene. The dialogue now consisted of Diana Muldaur asking me something like, "What's that medallion you're wearing, Spock?" and I explain that it's an IDIC and then I proceed to spend the next page and a half explaining exactly what this IDIC is and why it's so great. And by now I'm thinking to myself, "This is truly bizarre, I've gone to the devil for help."

Well, I bucked again, and I bucked hard enough that Gene came over to the set from MGM, and from his face I could tell that it was extremely important to him that this IDIC appear in the episode.

By now Leonard and I had both seen through Gene's marketing ploy, and one after another we'd refused to play the scene. Still, when Gene came to the set, he did his very best to push it through. To his credit, Roddenberry was completely honest about the situation and didn't try to mask his free publicity scam behind any half-baked creative half-truths. He simply stated that Lincoln Enterprises would soon be marketing these medallions, and that he'd really appreciate our cooperation in getting the product into this story line.

So I went through a great deal of soul-searching and teeth-grinding over the situation, and finally I just had to say, "Gene, I'm sorry, but I can't do this." Roddenberry accepted my refusal, but kept working on Leonard, who goes on:

Gene and I talked, and I was able to get some modifications to the dialogue, but I lost on the wearing of the thing. I'd also lost in regard to my damaged relationship with Freddie Freiberger, because Freddie, I'm sure, was angry that I'd gone over his head and called "Daddy" in regard to the original scene.

But what bothered me most about all this was my sense of loss in regard to Gene. I mean, if Gene was at his best and on his game, he could help you enormously with a script. Sadly, though, by this time he had refocused his attention and his energies into helping Lincoln Enterprises.

Leonard wasn't alone in his sense of loss, and having suffered through a season of disappointing career developments and compromised creativity, Bob Justman finally got to the point where he simply couldn't tolerate *Star Trek*'s decline any longer, and he quit.

I knew the cards were stacked against us, but I still really cared about the show. That's why the third season was so painful for me. I suffered through the first half-season, but that was it. I was just too upset about what was happening to the show to stick around. I had to walk.

Everybody at the studio knew that the show was not going to be picked up. It became obvious that we were shooting our last season, and when that happened, the studio's penny-pinching got so out of control that it really began hurting the series. During our first season on the air, we had a budget of $193,500 per episode. When the second season arrived, the cast got pay escalations.

Leonard held out and got even more than he was entitled to, but everybody got their raise. I even got a raise, from six hundred dollars per episode, to nine hundred . . . something like that.

Once that was established, the studio adjusted those increases by chopping our budget down to $187,500. They weren't so much robbing Peter to pay Paul as they were robbing *Star Trek* to maximize their own profit potential. Now the season arrives and we're slapped with a lousy time slot, and it becomes fairly obvious that this is going to be our last season. Once that was established, they cut us down to $178,500. It was disgusting.

Adding insult to budgetary injury, the studio also went out of its way to make it clear they thought we were spending too much time shooting each episode of *Star Trek*. Now, what you should know is that by this point, our production crew was so familiar with our rather unique series that we were shooting our episodes in just five days apiece, averaging about thirty different setups (camera moves) each day. We had our routine down pat, and almost never went into overtime. With all that in mind, this studio-issued edict was seen from the start as what it really was, a miserly attempt to squeeze more blood from the stone of *Star Trek*.

Still, despite the transparent falsehood of the studio's accusation, our crew was quite upset. Actually, in less polite but far more accurate terms, these guys were royally pissed! They'd spent the better part of three years working together as one of the finest film crews anywhere in the world, and they fumed over this financially calculated insult. Most angered was of course our most prideful crewman, chief gaffer George Merhoff.

Upon hearing of the studio's concerns, George immediately set out to prove them wrong. Toward this end, he began spending every hour of every day carefully timing and noting every activity on our set. When the crew was relighting, changing microphones or moving the camera, he made note of the situation. When the cast was rehearsing or the director was changing shots, he'd write it down. Finally, after several weeks, he came to his irrefutably documented position that the only people causing any sort of delays on our sets were our directors. He then took his findings to our third-season cinematographer, Al Francis. Al remembers:

SPOCK, LESS THAN PROUDLY WEARING THE **IDIC** MEDALLION. (© 1993 PARAMOUNT PICTURES) aramount bought the Desilu studios between seasons, and as a result, we got moved to their lot, and before we knew it the guys at the top were telling us that we were working too slow. So Merhoff goes out, gets himself this little black book and starts writing. "Episode 65, Scene 20—it takes 20 minutes to light the scene, 10 minutes to rehearse, 15 minutes for the director to work out his shot . . . " Stuff like that.

He literally walked around with a stopwatch, and he did this with every scene of every episode for a month. Then he came up to me one day and said, "Al, I want you to go to the front office and tell them where their money is going. You tell 'em the actors aren't causing any delays, the crew's not causing any delays, but the directors *are* wasting a lot of time."

Merhoff had it down in black and white that the directors were horsing around, or doing five or six extra takes of some scenes, or changing things around at the last minute and causing us to fall behind schedule. Now, all of that was true, but I told him I wouldn't take it up to the front office because he was just asking for trouble. When I turned him down, he took it up there himself.

So now the production manager gets one look at this thing and he takes it up to his immediate superiors, saying, "We've got a spy on our set. He shouldn't be doing this, because it makes us look bad for hiring or at least not firing these slow directors." By now we were shooting our last few episodes, but George Merhoff never worked at Paramount again. In fact, a year later, when I was going to work on *Love American Style*, I specifically asked for George, and I was told, "He's not on the lot anymore, and he'll not set foot on Paramount property again. His notes ruined one of our production managers, and if they'd gotten to the front office, we'd have all been in trouble." So, in reality, though George thought he was doing a favor for his crew, he ended up just shooting himself in the foot. His noble intentions pushed him toward making the biggest mistake he could possibly have made. He ended up not being able to get work as a gaffer anymore and working as a lamp operator wherever he could get hired. He became one of the guys he used to whistle at.

While George Merhoff was being blackballed over his well-intentioned but politically incorrect observations, *Star Trek*'s budgetary problems were rapidly becoming insurmountable. I mean in 1969, a run-of-the-mill hour-long drama cost about two hundred thousand dollars to produce. *Star Trek*, obviously, should have cost significantly more, because we had unparalleled special effects and also because virtually everything we shot had to be constructed especially for the show. We couldn't just raid Paramount for wardrobe, or props, or furniture, or existing sets, we had to design and build everything that we photographed. Bob Justman, who was absolutely disgusted by these events, continues:

Our costs were always high in every department, and when our budget took a bullet going into the third season, it really reduced us to doing radio shows. We couldn't go on location anymore, couldn't afford many guest stars or large casts, we simply had to do cheapo shows. In fact, one out of every four shows had to take place entirely within the *Enterprise*. And I think that really showed.

Gene still had his office, but he wasn't getting involved in making the show what it ought to be. I guess he had just given up. He was worn out by the fight. He fought to save the show, and he ended up getting screwed by the network. It had to have been really painful for him, and I think by this point he was just emotionally burying *Star Trek*, and I just couldn't get him to fight back and do anything about the lack of quality in our product. I yelled and screamed and ranted, but Gene just shrugged his shoulders. He said, "I'm doing all I can do," but really he had just given up. That's what really killed me.

So I didn't like what was happening to the show at all, and I certainly wasn't proud of the shows we were turning out in the third season. The content had basically become a lack of content, the show was being mounted badly and there was nothing I could do about it. The budget cuts were strangling us, we had a different person in charge of the show and the network, it seemed, had just given up on us. So, in the end, I told them to stuff it, and I walked.

With Justman's departure, Eddie Milkis became the senior member of *Star Trek*'s creative staff, but he too had become extremely frustrated over the seemingly irreversible deterioration of the show. In fact, Milkis even went so far as to meet with Gene, cornering him for the sole purpose of venting his anger. Strangely enough, before the meeting was over, Eddie would be treated to a last look at one brilliant aspect of "the old Gene."

During the third season, I got very upset, because it finally dawned on me that Bob was gone and I was left holding the bags. I was the only original left with the show. I was an associate producer, but everybody else had jumped ship. Roddenberry was still executive producer, but he was extremely scarce. I almost never saw him.

So one day, when I knew Gene was actually going to be in his office, I decided I was gonna nail him. I called him, told him I wanted to come speak with him, and then I went down to his office to chew his ass out and to tell him that I thought he was letting everybody down.

I went in there and I said, "Gene, we've got tremendous script problems, and I really think Fred Freiberger could use your help." Now, as I continue talking, out of the back of Gene's office comes Nichelle Nichols, who's wearing one of Gene's long cardigan sweaters, and NOTHING ELSE! No shirt, no pants, nothing.

So now Nichelle says something like, "Oh, I'm . . . uh . . . sorry, Eddie, I didn't know you were here." I immediately go red and I'm completely flustered until I notice that Gene's just kind of sitting at his desk, smiling and enjoying the embarrassed look on my face. At that point I realized that I'd been set up and that Gene had simply arranged for Nichelle to pull this schtick on me. Once I realized that, I just took a beat and kept right on telling Gene about the problems with the show. Nichelle then started laughing like hell, and Gene and I broke up right after. But y'know, that's the kind of stuff Gene loved to play.

That story becomes even more interesting, and your eyebrows will probably rise a notch, when you take into account Nichelle Nichols' surprising admission that she actually had an affair with Roddenberry, even going so far as to describe his "appetite" as "voracious." I've got to admit that Nichelle's story came to me as a real surprise, and that after carefully reviewing the facts . . . I'm kinda jealous. And finally, though she's gone out of her way to state that their romantic relationship came and went quickly, long before *Star Trek* even existed, Nichelle's revelations certainly make

Eddie Milkis' "practical joke" story a bit more . . . thought–provoking.

Back on the set, with the accumulated departures of such key personnel as Roddenberry, Coon, Lucas, Fontana and Justman, as well as terminally poor ratings, we all approached the Christmas season with a decidedly Grinchian outlook. Sadly, Star Trek would receive no last-minute Christmas miracle, and no amount of viewer mail could save us this time. Finally, on January 9, 1969, Star Trek ceased to exist. In fact, I can still clearly recall

SWEATING THROUGH **"T**URNABOUT **I**NTRUDER.**" (©** 1993 **P**ARAMOUNT **P**ICTURES**)**

shooting the final scene of "Turnabout Intruder," our seventy-ninth and final episode, in which Kirk "exchanges minds" with his old flame Dr. Janice Lester. I can also recall the raging nausea that began churning in my stomach upon the realization that this scene was indeed "it." Further, I actually filmed most of this episode while also suffering the effects of a raging fever, which in retrospect I suspect was probably just a psychosomatic incarnation of my own fears in regard to the uncertainty of the future. For me, Star Trek went out not with a bang but with a whimper, a cold sweat and a stomach ache.

On the other hand, not everyone was quite so sad to see the series end. Leonard, for example, disgruntled over the lack of quality now present in the series and struggling to retain his own identity away from the rubbery prosthetics and stilted mannerisms of Spock, had this to say:

> really felt we kind of stumbled to a close at the end of the third season, so I had very mixed feelings about the cancellation. I thought, "I'm sorry to see this go, but on the other hand, I'm glad to see it going away before we have a chance to find ourselves totally in the toilet." I felt we were really on a downhill slide throughout the third year, and when we weren't renewed, I have to say I felt a sense of relief, in that we wouldn't have to worry about the fourth season being even worse than the third.

As for our producer, the cancellation of Star Trek signaled the beginning of "Fred-Freiberger-Season" in which he would become indelibly, inappropriately and incorrectly labeled as the man responsible for Star Trek's demise. Freiberger explains:

When we got word that the series would not be picked up, Art Singer asked me about the future. I said I'd had my fill of producing for a while. It was back to writing for me. He said that he intended to return to New York and the theater scene. His parting words to me were "prepare for the onslaught," and of course I knew what he meant. In too many cases when a series fails, the fragile egos race about covering their own asses. When that happens, the producer is an open target. I assured Art that I could handle it . . . that it would be unpleasant for a time, and then everybody would just put it behind them.

How wrong I was. I've been the target of vicious and unfair attacks even to this day. The fact that at the end of the second season, Star Trek's ratings had slipped, it was losing adult fans and was in disarray carries no weight with the attackers. The dumping was all done on me and the third season. It seemed it was now Star Trek law to lay everything on Freiberger . . . every disgruntled actor, writer and director also found an easy dumping ground on which to blame their own shortcomings. Whenever one of my episodes was mentioned favorably, Gene Roddenberry's name was attached to it. When one of my episodes was attacked, Roddenberry's name mysteriously disappeared, and only then did the name Freiberger surface. As an example, I read an article, which I think was in the L.A. Times, praising "Plato's Stepchildren" as the first television show to allow an interracial kiss. A breakthrough. Roddenberry was lauded for this, when in fact Roddenberry wasn't within a hundred miles of that episode.

I have no quarrel to make with the right of critics, self-styled or otherwise, to dislike my episodes and to state that dislike. What angers me is when they choose to attack my character, sometimes labeling me as indifferent or uncaring. None of that could be further from the truth, and I'm thankful that on occasion people like Bob Justman have gone out of their way to publicly and vociferously stand up for me.

I have read that the fans didn't like any of my episodes. If true that hurts me, but there is another truth. In my travels throughout the United States, Canada and Europe, I have run into many *Star Trek* fans, and not one of them has ever treated me with anything less than courtesy and respect. For that I thank them.

Still, when "Turnabout Intruder" had completed filming, we all struggled to smile, making the best of this sad situation. With that in mind, we closed up shop for the last time, put our best faces forward and later that evening we all reconvened for one last wrap party. We ate, we drank, we joked about old times, made plans to stay in touch, but the thing we all seemed to do most was hug.

Saying good-bye to a room full of family members entails a lot of kissing, a lot of embraces and sadly, some unavoidable tears. We'd been together for a long, long time, and saying good-bye to these people was truly painful, especially poignant since this time *Star Trek* was irrevocably over, done with and out of our lives forever.

Sure it was.

Within months, three separate miracles had occurred. Man had walked on the moon, the Amazin' Mets had won a World Series and *Star Trek* had become enormously popular in syndication. *Trek* fan clubs, fanzines and newsletters were rapidly becoming big business, and Lincoln Enterprises had begun selling huge quantities of such merchandise as original *Star Trek* photos, scripts, artwork and of course IDICs. Shortly thereafter, *Star Trek* conventions began springing up like weeds all over the country, and the first wishful rumors of the series' resurrection began circulating among our most die-hard fans. Strangely enough, at the same time, Gene Roddenberry was finding that NBC's own research indicated that pulling *Star Trek*'s plug may have been a big mistake. Majel Barrett explains:

We found out that the people who were actually watching us during the third season were the young marrieds, the intellectuals, scientists, astronauts, these kinds of people. So, while we never had huge ratings, we had absolutely incredible demographics: eighteen to forty, with above-average intellect.

But we were ahead of our time in that respect. Demographics weren't seriously utilized by the networks until the following year.

However, we found that the people who track these things brought their information to NBC just after we'd been shut down, and they stated that NBC had really killed the golden goose when they canceled us.

Star Trek, it seemed, might have been pronounced dead a bit prematurely. Almost three decades later, continuing syndication success, as well as enormously successful cartoons, merchandising, spin-offs and films, would serve to prove Majel's point beyond a shadow of a doubt, and it's funny how over time the original cancellation of Star Trek has transformed itself from the unhappy ending of a story into the opening chapter of a far bigger tale, an astounding tale that's unsurpassed in the history of entertainment . . .

But that's a whole other story. Maybe six . . . maybe seven.

CAPTAIN'S
EPILOGUE

othing would make me happier than to close out this book with the simple phrase "And the cast, crew and creatives of Star Trek lived happily ever after." However, since we all have to live in the real world, without scripts and outside of the protective confines of the U.S.S. Enterprise, things don't always turn out as planned. None of us are perfect, personal relationships aren't always free of turbulence and happy endings are never guaranteed. This has been proven to me time and again in the quarter-century since Star Trek's premature demise, and it was made unflinchingly clear to me in researching this book.

On February 10, 1993, I spent the morning and a good chunk of the afternoon interviewing Nichelle Nichols, who as always was bright, beautiful, extremely funny, easy to talk to and hard to keep quiet. This woman can talk! We sat together reliving old times, laughing, flirting and catching up with each other. Then, as the afternoon shadows began growing long, I thanked Nichelle for all her help, closed up my tape recorder and started packing my notes. "Wait a minute," she told me, "I'm not finished yet. I have to tell you why I despise you." My gut response was to laugh, but the look on Nichelle's face proved she wasn't kidding. I quickly wiped the grin off my face, and now a bit dumbfounded, I clumsily pulled the shrink-wrap off another cassette, popped it into the machine and hit "RECORD."

She began with, "Okay, now I'm going to tell you about all the times you made me angry at you and pissed me off." My eyebrows went up, I swallowed hard and I choked out a reply of, "I want to hear about that . . . I do . . . really."

"Whenever I'm in public," she continued, "I put on a facade of 'Hello, everything is wonderful!'. . . My attitude has always been, 'I may call him a son of a bitch, but don't YOU dare'. . . But I've got to tell you, you can be very difficult to work with, and really inconsiderate of other actors who need to be considered! . . . You may not realize it, but there are times when you get totally involved in yourself, and unkind." Genuinely surprised and a bit intrigued by all of this, I asked Nichelle to elaborate, and to give me specific examples of her accusation.

This went on, on the set, from day one to this day. It really hasn't affected me as much as some of the others, because any time that you caused me pain, I always let you know about it immediately.... For example, I can remember we were rehearsing a scene on the bridge one time, and you were talking to the director about this scene, saying, "Look, Uhura doesn't NEED to say that! It's extraneous." You didn't realize it, but you had just said something very, very painful to me. You were putting me down. You said to the director, "Nichelle's lines are not important," and of course, without those lines, I'd have NO scene in this show.

So I let you know about it, and I said something like, "Goddamnit, Bill, don't talk about me like that." And you turned around as if you hadn't realized what you'd done, and then you walked over to me, and put your arms around me and said, "I'm sorry, I'd never hurt your feelings. I'd never hurt you."

I'm glad I was capable of that, and I'm also glad that Nichelle felt comfortable enough with me to make me aware of her displeasure. I mean, in truth, in most situations like the one she described, Nichelle's lines probably *were* unnecessary in terms of our story line, and they were most likely tacked onto our script in an effort to get Uhura involved in the episode. However, while they may not have been vital to our plot, they were indeed vitally important to our show in that they showcased a regular cast member, and of course to Nichelle, whose role was at stake. This is a perspective that blindly eluded me on the set, and with that in mind, I must admit that Nichelle's criticism is probably valid. Further, while I've never set out to hurt *anybody*, I may have, at times, been ignorant of my fellow actors' need for screen time, not to mention their feelings. She opened my eyes.

As I listened to Nichelle, I also suspected that she was probably not alone in her indignation, in that over the years a couple of other castmates have publicly been rather cool toward me, especially at conventions. Nichelle strengthened my suspicions when she told me that "Other people aren't like me, and they won't say, 'Goddamnit, Bill, you hurt me, instead they'll go away grumbling, pissed off and building up a resentment.'"

Shortly after I interviewed Nichelle, I found out that she, Walter Koenig, George Takei and Jimmy Doohan had all spoken, conspiring to use the interviews for *Star Trek Memories* as an opportunity to confront me, face-to-face, with their own negative feelings. George Takei was next on my list, and as we met, I braced for the worst. Surprisingly, though, throughout our time together George was upbeat, funny and seemed more than happy to see me. While I was waiting for him to lower the boom, we spoke for hours, and it did indeed strike me as odd that I was really just getting to know this man whom I'd worked with for more than a quarter-century. He told me how as a small child, during World War II, he and his family were interred in a U.S. Army camp, simply because of their Japanese ancestry. He told me of the schoolteacher who routinely referred to him as "the Jap kid," and of the pain she caused him. He told me about his love for his parents and of his political aspirations. I knew NONE of this, and I found myself wishing that I'd taken the time to "meet" George Takei years earlier. He's a fascinating man, and I'm sincerely saddened that we haven't spent the past quarter-century as closer friends.

Still, throughout our conversation, I was on the lookout for the same sort of negative comments I'd heard from Nichelle. They never came. George was wonderful toward me throughout our conversation. I'd find out later that he too had intended to vent his frustrations, and his wholly pleasant demeanor was a result of his own sudden decision not to hurt me, a welcome side effect of our thoroughly enjoyable discussion.

Walter Koenig was next on my list, and while he expressed views similar to Nichelle's, we also talked a lot about *Star Trek*, about Gene Roddenberry, about specific episodes and about our movies. Walter, too, told me of his disappointment in my lack of contact with the group he refers to as "the gang of four," and I had to admit that in talking to my former co-workers I was now at a loss in attempting to understand how more than twenty-five years' worth of shared experiences never quite translated into stronger friendships.

Last, having spoken to Nichelle, George and Walter, all of whom seemed a bit surprised at my willingness to listen to, accept and even agree with some of their criticism, I prepared to meet with my most vocal critic, Jimmy Doohan. A meeting was set up, Jimmy canceled. I left repeated messages trying to reschedule, but Jimmy never returned my calls. I even went so far as to have a mutual friend try to reschedule for me. Finally, months after our original meeting date, I got the official word that Jimmy flatly refused to speak with me, and I was told that he explained his position by saying, "Bill won't use what I have to say, he won't want to hear the negatives, he won't print what I say, and if he does, he'll twist it to his advantage." Though I tried to explain that nothing could be further from the truth, Jimmy still shut me out, and it is truly a shame that he chose to keep his voice from being heard. Certainly this makes me angry, but for the most part it just makes me sad.

Still, a lot of good did come out of my visits with George, Walter and Nichelle. I mean, I always knew they were terrific actors, but now I've been lucky enough to discover that they're pretty nice *people*, too. I hope we'll continue to strengthen our ties in the future . . . and Jimmy, any time you want to sit down, knock back a couple and clear the air, on *or off* the record, all you have to do is call. You've got my number, and you know I'd jump at the chance to see you again. I hope to hear from you.

And last, although it's an uncomfortable topic, I feel like I'd be less than honest if I didn't take a moment to explore my own strained association with the man who started it all, Gene Roddenberry. Sadly, although Gene and I always worked fairly well together, our personal relationship was lousy: rather formal, cool and strained. I never got a chance to settle things with Gene, and he died before I ever *really* got to know him. With that in mind, I tried to sort things through with his widow, Majel, and at one point I even went so far as to ask her point-blank, "Why didn't I get along better with Gene?" Her answer really surprised me.

One thing you might have resented was the fact that as far as Gene was concerned, when it came to *Star Trek* he was God, and you may have been turned off by that impression. It would be a natural reaction. . . . Also, I've always felt that after a while, both you and Leonard started to deny his involvement in your creation. That kept you apart, too.

It's the little kid thing. Actors are nothing more than a bunch of kids. . . . Very seldom, and only with real age, do they ever mellow out. As a kid, you naturally resented your creator. The guy who brought you there. . . .

Let's face it, Gene was the idea man. You could not have created the characters without his creativity. . . . You were one of his
kids, we all were, and at some point, all children will hate their
parents.

I didn't particularly agree with Majel. I won't begin to deny Gene's creativity or the fact that there would be no Captain Kirk without him, but at
the same time, I can honestly say that unlike Leonard, I never saw Gene as
a father figure. I never resented the man, and I never disliked him either.
In fact, I always thought the *opposite* might have been true. I honestly felt
that Gene didn't like *me*. As a result, I withdrew. I brought all of this up in
rebutting Majel's statement, and she seemed a bit surprised, going out of
her way to make sure I knew that "Gene didn't dislike you . . . not ever. I
know that for a fact."

With all that in mind, what I'm left with is lingering confusion, guilt and
an unfinished piece of business. Gene is dead, and I'll probably never get
a chance to really understand our relationship. It saddens me to think that
the two of us, with such strong creative ties, could have remained so far
apart as people.

Even sadder is the fact that the latter part of Gene's life was more often
than not filled with chaos, personal problems, legal hassles and creative
arguments in regard to the direction of *Star Trek*. It's no secret that Gene
had such constant battles with Paramount over every *Star Trek* film that he
eventually became a bit of a persona non grata around the lot. At the
same time, he was also fighting with the studio's marketing types,
demanding that they maintain high standards of product quality and
truthfully report their earnings in regard to *Star Trek*'s merchandising.
Finally, though Gene continued to own *Star Trek* and the characters he'd
created, he ultimately lost the ability to effectively demand changes in our
films. With each new *Star Trek* film, Gene would be hired as a consultant
and asked for his comments, but creative differences between him and
some of our films' producers and directors, coupled with the fact that
Gene was now officially separated from any flexible creative muscle, conspired to ensure that over our decade of moviemaking Gene's suggestions
went from honored to respectfully considered but ultimately disregarded.
In effect, he lost final artistic control of his own creation. This bothered

Gene greatly, and it's no secret that he felt many of the Star Trek films were needlessly violent and far too militaristic.

At the same time, Gene's personal life became troublesome. He was sued by his ex-wife for half of all Star Trek 's series, movies and Next Generation profits, and at home his relationship with Majel was being tested as well. One continuing sore point centered around the fact that though the characters Gene created were always built of unbreakable, even unbendable moral fiber, Gene was fallible, human and could never quite live up to his own scripted ideals. He made a habit out of living life to the fullest, and by the second half of the eighties the cumulative effects of the voracious Roddenberry lifestyle had begun affecting Gene's health.

Causing further problems were the after-effects of a brief misguided sexual relationship Gene had stumbled through with one of his secretaries. Majel had found out about the situation, and of course this caused a great deal of trouble between them. In the end, however, they realized how important they really were to one another, reaffirmed their marital commitment and decided to stay together. In time they overcame their problems and not only did the marriage remain intact but their spirited relationship actually grew stronger.

However, amid the personal and professional problems, Gene's body betrayed him and he became suddenly ill. And while no one knows *exactly* what went wrong, the lingering after-effects of this abrupt illness were undeniable, slowing Gene down and obviously demanding immediate medical and therapeutic attention. Toward that end, Gene spent some time recuperating at the Pritikin Center. Working hard to overcome his physical ailments, Gene ultimately came back stronger than before. His cholesterol and blood pressure levels improved tremendously, and before long he was actually walking better and working harder than he had in quite some time, overseeing the production of Star Trek: The Next Generation with a renewed focus and energy. Unfortunately, Gene's period of revitalization was all too brief, and in July of 1991 he became ill once more.

Gene had been fighting, arguing vehemently with the aforementioned secretary as she drove him home from the office. Apparently, she'd made the wrong turn on the way to the house, he snapped at her and their trivial argument soon escalated into a screaming match. Suddenly, in the midst of the verbal war, Gene got very quiet. There was silence throughout the rest of the ride, and when he got to the house, something definitely seemed wrong. Gene insisted that he was all right and refused to see a doctor, but Majel knew she had to get him to the hospital. Finally, at her insistence, he reluctantly agreed to go.

Gene later underwent an MRI, and the prognosis wasn't good. Doctors had discovered a major blood clot on Gene's brain, and they decided that immediate surgery would be necessary to remove it. At 7:45 the following morning, they operated. The results were mixed.

Gene survived, but he never really came back fully. Physically he lost a lot of weight and lost his strength, and mentally, though he'd have periods where he'd be clear as a bell, he'd fade quickly, weakened by the devastating after-effects of his illness. Sadly, this formerly inexhaustible bear of a man had become a shadow of his former "larger-than-life" persona.

At the same time, he grew closer to Majel than ever before, and she became very much the loving wife/nurse/companion. Though scared, she held out hope for Gene, because he'd recovered so well in the past, and of course, because she loved him.

Two months later, Gene was beginning to make some progress. He was well enough to attend a screening of Star Trek VI, and was even regaining some of his lost mobility, when tragedy struck. Just two days after the movie screening, during an office consultation with a neurological specialist, Gene began having serious trouble breathing. He had suffered an embolism. He lost consciousness and his condition deteriorated rapidly. Paramedics arrived almost immediately and were followed by a half-dozen specialists. Though the doctors worked hard trying to keep him alive, Gene's diminished body would not respond, and he passed away, literally in Majel's arms.

Still, despite the inescapable indignities of a vastly imperfect real world, Gene Roddenberry's name lives on, firmly attached to the far more orderly, far more exciting and perhaps far preferable universe of Star Trek. More than three decades after planting the seeds of his creation, Star Trek continues stronger than ever. The Next Generation is the most successfully syndicated show on television, and Deep Space Nine already seems likely to grow even more popular. Finally, rumors refuse to die in regard to a seventh motion picture, this time perhaps uniting the original and Next Generation casts.

With all of that in mind, nothing is more certain than the fact that Star Trek's wondrous mission has just begun.